A Church Drawir

A CHURCH DRAWING NEAR

Spirituality and Mission in a Post-Christian Culture

by

PAUL AVIS

T & T CLARK INTERNATIONAL
A Continuum imprint
LONDON • NEW YORK

T&T CLARK LTD

A Continuum imprint

The Tower Building
11 York Road
London SE1 7NX, UK

15 East 26th St
New York, NY 10010
USA

www.continuumbooks.com

British Library Cataloguing-in-Publication Data
A catalogue record for this book is available from the British Library

ISBN 0 567 08968 1 (Paperback)
ISBN 0 567 08967 3 (Hardback)

Typeset by Fakenham Photosetting Ltd, Fakenham, Norfolk NR21 8NN
Printed and bound in Great Britain by The Cromwell Press, Trowbridge, Wilts.

Contents

Preface

In this book I set out a model of the Church's mission and ministry for our times. It is designed to make sense in a society that hangs on the cusp of late modernity. In the developed world our culture is marked by individualism, consumerism, instantaneous communication, high mobility and the breakdown of conventional forms of community. These aspects of late modernity (which are not of course the whole picture) go hand in hand with the erosion of traditional patterns of overt, public religious practice, particularly of regular church-going. Conventional religious practice has been giving way to a range of self-selected, privatized and experimental responses to a rather nebulous sense of the sacred. The central question of this book is: How can the time-honoured, God-given tasks of ministry that comprise the core of the Church's mission – the ministry of the word, the administration of the sacraments and the exercise of pastoral care – be effective in the late modern context?

A certain view of the Church's role in the *missio Dei* underlies this book. It is focused on the Great Commission of Matthew 28.16–20 where the risen Christ gives the Apostles – and therefore the Church – a threefold task: to make disciples, to baptize and to teach. Here we see that mission takes the form of a triple ministry. My working assumption in all that follows is that this threefold mandate can never be superseded and that all authentic expressions of mission ultimately return to the word, the sacraments and pastoral responsibility. A proper theological justification for this approach lies beyond the present study, in future work on the theological essentials of mission and ministry.

Nevertheless this book is through and through a work of theology. At virtually every point – cultural analysis, exposition of the 'wholeness paradigm', the treatment of the sense of the sacred and of religious experience, the discussion of the occasional offices and of the Church's role in 'the community' – theological evaluation is attempted. The theological resources for the renewal of pastoral ministry that I am looking for here are drawn from Scripture, the tradition of the Church

vii

and dialogue between theology and other relevant disciplines (reason). So here is an exposition of contextual, practical, pastoral and applied theology. But it stands 'on the threshold' of the Church, so to speak, looking out to those who have not yet entered; and putting itself in their shoes, looking in to what is on offer that might meet their needs.

I put down a major marker about my aims and intentions in the first chapter where I stress the need for the Church to point society as a whole beyond the privatization of faith as one of the ultimate values that people seek to live by. Then I explore the key idea of the healing of human identity and the biblical links between healing, wholeness and salvation. I examine the nature of modernity and of post-modernity and conclude, as others have done, that post-modernity is an intensification of the dynamics of modernity and that the best term for our present cultural situation is 'late modern'. I go on to explore the phenomena of generic spirituality, the vitality of the sense of the sacred, especially in the form of 'common religion'. The term common religion is used here to refer to the sacred values, beliefs and practices of people who are not much involved in the life and worship of the Christian Church, but who nevertheless see themselves as being within the Christian ethos, tradition or community. I attempt to evaluate common religion against the benchmark of the committed discipleship that the Church expects of its fully initiated members. I explore the pastoral methods that can help individuals to move beyond the inadequacies of common religion. I also consider the extraordinary flourishing of religious experience outside of church life and draw some conclusions for mission from that.

Next I focus on the connection that is effected sacramentally by rites of passage (the Church's occasional offices) between Christian meanings and the changes in their inner being that people experience in their life course. After this I examine the relationship, presupposed by this pastoral approach to ministry, between the community of the Church and the wider, diffused community, taking my cue from the sociologist Bryan Wilson's dictum that religion is 'the ideology of community'. In the final chapter, I outline the implications of the pastoral method in mission for the Church's profile in the public forum. I argue for the priority of belonging over believing and for the primacy of pastoral ministry as the leading edge of the threefold mission, the triple ministry of word, sacrament and pastoral care. The sustaining vision of the book is that of a church drawing near to human needs and sensitive to human aspirations. There is the need for forgiveness and life-changing power through the Cross; the need for purpose in our lives as we follow Christ in daily discipleship; the need for authentic community that points to the communion *(koinonia)* that is grounded in the Holy Trinity. In spite of the best efforts of many Christians, not least clergy and bishops, the Church is generally perceived to be remote, aloof, judgemental and out of touch with everyday human concerns. Regrettably, many people are at a loss to see how the Church relates to them or is relevant to their lives. The guiding thread of my argument is that only a renewal of close pastoral involvement – not preachy public statements and not a purist liturgical diet in parish churches – can help to bridge the widening gulf between Church and people.

A major prerequisite for bridging the gap is the building of trust, the creating of rapport. We are told that only about 43 per cent of people trust the Christian Church. Half of all women but only a third of all men trust the institution. Among young people (18–24), less than a third trust it. The Church has about the same rating as the civil service and somewhat less than the educational system. It has almost half the trust rating of the armed services (for analysis of research data on religious belief and practice see Avis, 2003). The loss of people's trust in the Church must surely rank as one of the greatest of all impediments to mission. It would be useful to know why the Church scores so abysmally.

The strategy being advocated in this book pivots on the building of trust between the Church and individuals, households, local communities, the bodies that make up civil society, and the institutions of the state itself. Of course there are ways in which representative persons, particularly bishops and archbishops, can contribute to this through mass communication, when it is used with enormous skill and an awareness of the positive and negative dynamics of projection. But the real work of building trust and establishing rapport – the sine qua non of effective mission and ministry – can only be done piecemeal, 'on the ground', in thousands of particular situations, when commitment is sustained over time. That agenda points to the fact that parochial and chaplaincy ministries remain the front line of mission and that compassionate pastoral involvement is the leading edge. In that connection, I explore the crucial role of sacred places, sacred persons and sacred occasions.

I am not under the illusion that there can be a blanket prescription for a national mission. The essential principles of pastoral ministry are constant, but they are mediated in diverse contexts. Diversity of context sharpens the question of the Church's mission in parish, diocese and nation. Two of the most difficult contexts are the inner urban and the remote rural. In urban high-rise housing developments old patterns of community life have long since been dissolved through slum clearance, but there are now distinctive ethnic, other-faith communities. It was instructive to be living in central south London during the final stage of working on this book. Towards the end of the book I stress the importance of the public visibility (or 'findability') of the Church and its ministry in the community, and I suggest practical ways in which this could be enhanced. But I will say here that in central south London a recognizable parish priest or any other identifiable ordained minister going about his or her work in the community is a very rare sight. Indeed in four years I have not seen one.

Turning to the remoter rural context: in the sparsely populated parishes of East Anglia, for example, only a handful of people seem sufficiently committed to shoulder the responsibility of mission. They find themselves weighed down by the burden of maintaining, in a reasonable state of repair, an enormous church building that stands out against the level skyline – a splendid relic of a wealthier and more populous community half a millennium ago. In such parishes traditional, clergy-dominated patterns of ministry and mission are breaking down. Mere goodwill towards the Church, on the part of parishioners, costs nothing and leads to little. This context is, I imagine, much harder work than the large team ministry in North Devon, centred on the market town of South Molton, where I served as assistant curate for five years in the late Seventies. The semi-rural multi-parish benefice, within the gravitational pull of the cathedral city of Exeter (Stoke Canon, Poltimore with Huxham, and Rewe with Netherexe), where I was vicar for eighteen years until 1998, was different again. There I had the care of five parishes (with three parish churches and two chapels of ease), all situated within a radius of three miles of the vicarage. Committed parishioners, within a total population of 1,400 people, maintained the five church buildings excellently. They also sustained several home groups including an ongoing Alpha course, a Sunday school, a church youth group, a monthly healing service and a Church of England voluntary controlled primary school that was bursting at the seams. Three parochial church councils and two church meetings supported the fairly intensive pastoral activity that these structures reflected.

Paul Avis
Council for Christian Unity
Church House, Westminster
Centre for the Study of the Christian Church
Exeter Cathedral and the Department of Theology,
University of Exeter

Acknowledgements

I am particularly grateful to Dr Grace Davie of the Department of Sociology in the University of Exeter, a colleague of mine in the interdisciplinary Centre for the Study of the Christian Church. She has been unstintingly generous with advice, information and the loan of books and was good enough to read some material in a very inadequate early draft several years ago. It was useful to have the opportunity to try out some of the ideas in this book at two consultations which Dr Davie and I jointly convened at St George's House, Windsor Castle, in the early 1990s.

I am also especially grateful to Dr Anne Richards, Theological Secretary to the Board of Mission of the Church of England and Theological Consultant to the ecumenical Mission Theological Advisory Group (MITAG) for reading and commenting on some earlier draft material.

Some material on secularization is adapted from my chapter, 'Spiritual Authority and Leadership in Society and Church', in the symposium edited by Professor Robert Hannaford, *A Church for the Twenty-First Century* (Gracewing, 1998). Material from Chapter 2, on the wholeness paradigm, was shared with the team of therapists at Holy Rood House, Thirsk, Yorkshire, at a training day and benefited from discussion with skilled practitioners. Some material went into a course of three lectures that I gave in autumn 2002 at the City of London church of St Andrew by the Wardrobe at the invitation of the Rector, the Revd Dr Alan Griffin. Extracts from C. G. Jung, *Letters* (Routledge, 1973), vol. 2, and M. Polanyi, *Personal Knowledge* (Routledge, 1958) are used by kind permission of the publisher.

Biblical quotations are from the New Revised Standard Version unless otherwise indicated as REB (Revised English Bible) or AV (Authorized (King James) Version).

The – at times rather outspoken – views expressed in this book are entirely my responsibility and are not necessarily those of the Council for Christian Unity or of the General Synod.

1

Beyond The Privatization of Faith

Public faith and the death of Diana

In early September 1997 we, the British people, behaved in what seemed to many people a highly untypical way. We tuned in to a televised church service *en masse*. We entered churches and cathedrals in large numbers to register our feelings of grief and concern. We lit candles by the thousands and created wayside shrines decked with bouquets of flowers. We swelled the ranks of regular worshippers in church. We filled the streets of central London around a church that is a great symbol of historical continuity, religious tradition and the place of the monarchy in national life. Altogether, the overwhelming collective response to the death of Diana Princess of Wales seemed completely out of character for a secularized, individualistic, pluralist, post-Christian, materialistic society! It certainly was if you think that those adjectives accurately or exhaustively describe our culture. However, this book is predicated on the conviction that those events were not atypical, anomalous or inexplicable, but that, on the contrary, they revealed or confirmed what is still the case deep down in the spiritual roots of the majority of people in our society. They were not maverick phenomena, but part of an emerging pattern of spirituality (cf. Drane, in Sugden, 1998, p. 30).

The extraordinary popular response to the death of Diana yields several lessons, and we have not exhausted them yet. It certainly caused some of our religious leaders to think again about the assumptions they had been making about the secularization of society, the decline of religious practice and the decay of the sense of the sacred. It showed that a plural society can still value representative traditions and that those traditions, held in trust by historic institutions, can become a common possession

1

once again. It has been observed that 'the language of national unity suffuses accounts of the Diana phenomenon' (Johnson, in Kear and Steinberg, 1999, p. 33). The death of Diana (reinforced in 2002 by the funeral service for Queen Elizabeth the Queen Mother and the national celebration of Queen Elizabeth II's Golden Jubilee) brought into sharpened focus the role of the churches – particularly the Church of England. That church, which does its work steadily and unobtrusively week by week in all the communities of the land and is often taken for granted, patronized or mocked, came into its own again at that moment. The Church of England (emphatically not only that church, but that church particularly) ministered to large numbers of people who were caught up in a wave of complex emotion: grief, sympathy, anger and bewilderment. It gave those feelings a voice and a name. Through prayer, the ministry of the word, sacred symbol, music and measured liturgy it executed on a grand national scale what it performs on a local, intimate and personal scale every day, everywhere: the pastoral mission of making people whole in the name of Christ.

These events revealed that universal sacred symbols, such as candles, flowers and other offerings, prayers, silence and shrines, can attract and express the inchoate feelings of many people who seem to be outside the normal ambit of such symbols. The flowers, invariably still wrapped in cellophane, were not simply the conventional symbol of beauty threatened by decay, but were above all gifts, sacred offerings – though, unlike sacrifices, they were left outside, not inside, the church – and had to be ritually consumed (cf. Davies, in Walter, 1999, pp. 16, 38). The mourning for Diana used such symbols in a way that seemed spontaneous. It was certainly not institutionalized, though the presence of the historic, public institutions, the churches, facilitated it. But it was actually deeply conditioned by the legacy of Christianity. The elements of pilgrimage, vigil and sacramentality stood out. The national response encouraged many clergy and lay Christians to feel that they were needed at that moment, even though they could not control what was happening and had to allow themselves to become the channels of something much bigger than the churches, bigger even than the Christian religion. (Bunting 1999 warns against assimilating the phenomena to traditional ecclesiastical agendas.)

In these circumstances, churches that are strongly linked into the community, locally and nationally, can play a vital role in first responding sympathetically to the national mood and then shaping public emotion in a clearly Christian direction. The combined funeral and memorial service for Diana in Westminster Abbey showed that this can be done in a way that is not confrontational and does not put people, with a genuine spiritual hunger but only a tentative or wistful rapport with the Christian faith, 'on the spot'. That service did not preach at anyone and no one could have felt 'got at'. There was no sermon. But a careful analysis of the service shows that the Christian hope of eternal life through the grace of Christ was conveyed in numerous ways, directly and indirectly. Some were left with misgivings about the blend and balance of ancient and modern in the funeral service – that obviously had to be negotiated with all those concerned. But it exemplified the pastoral method, advocated by the Dean of Westminster, Wesley Carr, in his writings, and expounded and applied throughout this present book, of seeking to respond to people's spiritual expectations before carefully trying to reshape some of their assumptions.

Public and private

A viable model of the Church's mission or tasks in late modernity needs to weld together the public and the private, the corporate and the personal aspects of Christian mission. Public and private are not, of course, absolute concepts. They are not universally fixed categories but are like 'permeable spheres' of value and activity that overlap in differerent ways at different times (Cochran, 1990, pp. 3, 18). Marx showed that our notions at any one time of what is private and what is public are socially and economically constructed. But the conceptual polarity of public and private is almost indispensable when discussing the relation between the individual and society. Because the private and public dimensions stand in tension, they are often played off against each other. In the working theology of Christians, salvation is seen in either a predomi-nantly private or a predominatly public way. Some Evangelicals channel all their efforts into bringing about the personal conversion of individuals, while some liberal or Catholic Christians lay most stress on engaging with social and ethical issues. Securing a public dimension for Christian witness is problematical in a late modernity that is characterized by multi-culturalism, the privatization of values and the dominance of personal choice. Simone Weil wrote in *The Need for Roots* that 'Religion has been proclaimed a private affair... It means that it is a matter of choice, opinion, taste, almost of caprice', (like choosing a tie). Having become a private concern, it had lost the obligatory character associated with public matters. Weil thought that it was ludicrous for a person's relationship to God to be seen as something irrelevant to the public good – as well she might (Weil, 1952, pp. 125f.).

Privatization represents a major change in the status of religion. It requires considerable mental gymnastics even for Christians today to get to grips with the idea that Christian biblical moral values and standards of behaviour are intended to be universal and should be reflected in the law of a Christian country and indeed of every land. That loss of confidence in the universality – the catholicity – of the Christian revelation is a measure of the weakness of privatized faith. As Berger wrote thirty years ago: 'Private religiosity, however "real" it may be to the individuals who adopt it, cannot any longer fulfil the classical task of religion, that of constructing a common world within which all of social life receives ultimate meaning binding on everybody.' He added: 'The values pertaining to private religiosity are, typically, irrelevant to institutional contexts other than the private sphere' (Berger, 1973, p. 137). Moreover, as Edward Norman points out, modern privatized religion lacks backbone; it often turns out to be 'an affair of sentiment, emotional satisfaction, aesthetic sensation and welfare' (Norman, 2002, p. 46). The assumption that religion should be confined to heart and home is seen in the hostility with which politicians and the press greet the ethical pronouncements of religious leaders. They clamour for them and then find fault with them when their demands are met. This double bind presents a radical challenge to the mission of the Church: to speak or not to speak? For religion is indeed a personal, but not a private matter.

The public dimension of Christian faith concerns its status as public truth that can be corporately owned. Because the

Christian gospel is grounded in the nature of God and in God's revealed purposes for humankind, it is – by definition – universally valid. It is this generic validity that constitutes the catholicity of the Christian faith. The gospel of God's salvation in Jesus Christ is given 'for the healing of the nations' (Revelation 22.2), not merely for private consumption. The public aspect of faith demands a clear public profile for the churches as institutions within civil society and (in the case of established churches) as institutions that have a recognized place and voice constitutionally and in law within the body politic. It requires also an ability to articulate the Christian contribution in ways that are persuasive and gain a hearing in the mass media.

The personal dimension is the more private, intimate and localized approach that characterizes much of the Church's pastoral outreach to the communities that make up the nation. This approach is sensitive to the often unspoken spiritual needs of individuals and families and responds to the opportunities and claims of community life. It nurtures individuals in their faith, however minimal that faith may seem to be to human eyes, and leads them through the various steps of Christian initiation to committed discipleship in the communion of the Church. The pastoral method builds trust and practises confidentiality. It is low-key, long-term, cumulative and specific to locality. It builds slow but it builds strong.

In this book I aim to show that these two dimensions of mission, two mission agendas – the public, cultural and social aspect, on the one hand, and the pastoral, local and personal aspect, on the other – are not alternative strategies, but stand or fall together. They support and lend credibility to each other. Neither is effective without the other. What unites them is the way that both of them tap into generic human meanings and universal human aspirations. It is of the nature of religious faith to form an interface between the private and the public because it plays into the realities of moral character, meaningful narrative and the institutional expression of both. Religion is a standing reminder of the distinction and at the same time the interaction of public and private (Cochran, 1990).

When as pastors we lead people through baptism, confirmation or marriage, or minister to them in circumstances of pain and loss, it is not actually because they have expressed a merely private preference for these ministrations and have joined some sort of a club. Rightly understood, in the light of Christian truth, these occasions are not examples of the privatization of religion. The events of birth, puberty, marriage and death are universal and in the Christian understanding are inherently related to God. The Holy Spirit is active at all times, in all places and in relation to all persons, for all are created in the divine image. When people seek to sacralize their life course sacramentally through liturgy and Christian symbolism, they are not playing with items in a supermarket of cultural artefacts. They are doing what God has provided as the right thing to do for everyone: they are dedicating their lives to God and receiving God's strength to live as he wills.

Public truth?

A little over a decade ago, the late Lesslie Newbigin expressed the view that there is nothing sacred to society today (Newbigin, 1991, p. 19). He pointed out that the Christian religion is not generally regarded as a source of knowledge about reality, but is seen merely as an agency of beneficial values alongside other such agencies. Christian beliefs were no longer part of 'public truth'. Newbigin saw clearly the need for a public framework of meaning and called for a conversion of the minds of policy-makers to Christian convictions so that public doctrine might once again be conformed to Christian truth. To this extent, his point is well taken. However, in making his assessment of Christian influence in society, Newbigin seems to have operated with an inadequate model – a predominantly propositional model – of Christian truth. He did not do full justice to the more subtle and elusive elements in the expression of Christian belief, particularly its narrative and symbolic complexion on which much work has been done in recent years (Avis, 1999). He did not allow for the fact that the distinctive texture of Christian truth facilitates the diffusion of Christian ideas in a plural society. This phenomenon is sometimes referred to as the transposition of moral values from their original Christian sources to new 'secular' contexts. Newbigin's concern at the evident marginalization of explicitly

Christian teaching from the making of public policy led him to the untenable view that the sense of the sacred had perished from the modern/post-modern plural society.

In fact, as we shall see, the sense of the sacred persists strongly, though it tends to bypass both the received propositional forms of Christian doctrine and the institutional forms of Christian community. Of course, that is a serious enough issue and Newbigin is absolutely right to sound the alarm, but it is not the whole picture. The sense of the sacred also comes to focus mainly in family and group activities which rehearse the significant stories that give meaning to human life and it enacts these in significant ceremonial activity. The sense of the sacred that flourishes in the private sphere (though by no means exclusively there) draws on traditional Christian truths and Christian symbols, but adapts them to some extent for its own purposes. While it values the Christian heritage, common religion (as we shall call it in this book) does not accept that the Church has a monopoly of sacred symbols and insights, even though these still permeate the prevailing cultural tradition.

The great milestones of life, those transformations of being that are sanctified and celebrated sacramentally in the occasional offices in their role as rites of passage, are a key manifestation of this sense of the sacred. It is here, in family and community life, where such values as personhood, relation, faithfulness, compassion, chastity and mutual obligation (to which Newbigin rightly wants to recall us as a society) are primarily located. The significance of these personal and familial expressions of the sacred should not be overlooked, however inadequately articulated they may be. Nor should they be regarded as purely private moments. They can be seen as intimations of the sacred. They relate to generic human meanings and so they may be said to have intrinsic public significance. When they are affirmed in the Church's public discourse – in liturgy, in preaching and in teaching – as having universal human significance, they become our allies in promoting a more Christian vision of society. When they reach critical mass, they impact on public doctrine, social mores and the law of the land.

Radical privatization?

A recent book on religious commitment in a secular context (Audi, 2000) has raised the question of the privatization of values in an acute form. The centrepiece of this clear philosophical analysis of the role of religion in liberal democracy is a cool case for the radical separation of Church and State. But as the author drives his argument to its logical conclusion, we find ourselves staring into an abyss: the disastrous combination of publicly sponsored secularism, on the one hand, and the terminal privatization of religion, on the other. Liberal democracy is the supreme value in Audi's pantheon. Perhaps in a purely philosophical work the claims of the Kingdom of God do not impinge. Liberal democracy must be allowed to realize its ideal, perfect expression. This implies several ideological commitments for the author. First, it requires state tolerance of all beliefs that do not restrict the freedom of others. Second, it involves equality of citizens before the law regardless of their beliefs and practices. Third, it imports neutrality on the part of the state towards religions and their communities and even (though this is a rather grey area) towards distinctive moral visions of the common good.

Audi supports the thoroughgoing separation of Church and State in opposition to the varying kinds and degrees of establishment that still pertain in the modern world. The greater the degree of establishment in a society, he argues, the less it counts as a liberal democracy (that disqualifies Norway, Finland and Denmark for a start!). The case of 'Great Britain' (he must mean England and Scotland respectively) shows that a form of establishment is compatible with a high (though not the highest) degree of liberal democracy. But there must be safeguards for liberty and a defensible rationale for establishment to continue. Establishment is under suspicion until it can vindicate itself. Like much that is written about 'establishment', there is little depth to the way the word and the idea are used in Audi's book (cf. Avis, 2001).

What is Audi's ideal expression of liberal democracy and of the role of religion in it? First, it patently privileges the claims of the individual over against the claims of the supposed common good. (Even taxation, it is argued here, cannot be enforced unless it can be shown that individuals would support it if they could understand the reasons for it.) Second, government will be overtly and unashamedly secular, not giving credence to any religious tradition or community. Third, public institutions must show no bias toward any religion or even toward religion and sacred things as such. (This, the author deduces, rules out school carol services even when attendance is optional.) Fourth, churches must not use their influence to press for laws that restrict human conduct – 'coercive laws' (are some laws optional?). Fifth, religious people should hold back from campaigning. They should voluntarily limit their zeal because (this premise seems doubtful) they would wish others to limit theirs. Finally, churches should not take up political stances and even when religious individuals speak for or against policies, they should not deploy religious reasoning or be moved by religious motivation, but should confine themselves to secular arguments and satisfy themselves that these also sufficiently motivate them in making their case.

Condensed like that, the platform of Audi's book seems unreal. But the reader experiences a creeping sense of recognition. These nostrums are not a million miles from the shibboleths of political correctness that rule in our society already. The tolerance that is inhibited from making moral judgements, the pluralism that celebrates diversity as an end in itself, and the individualism that makes self-expression the highest value are already enthroned. 'Mature, rational, religious people' in a liberal democracy, the author intones, 'will seek at least a measure of reflective equilibrium' in their beliefs and attitudes. The reader could be forgiven for feeling that the struggle between good and evil is here being turned into an academic seminar.

The flaw in the argument is that it is conducted precisely on secular, relativist premises. Christian theology hardly influences the discussion but is nevertheless made to take the consequences. The result is a simplistic opposition of sacred and secular, Church and State, private and public, in which Christianity loses out all along the line. There is no theology of the State here and no inkling of the idea that such a theology might be important. The State is seen largely as a pragmatic instrument for promoting individual fulfilment, as individuals struggle against the odds to hold on to moral principles without actually grounding them in either religious belief or social structure. The rhetorical question is posed: How well can one serve God and the State?

The Christian tradition has an answer to that question, one that is not considered by Audi and is now generally forgotten by Christians infected with the pervasive liberal relativism of our age. The Church has taught consistently that the State as an institution (and therefore not to be confused with particular political regimes) is ordained by God for human well-being and that those who serve it serve God. That human well-being includes moral and spiritual needs, and the State is obliged to provide for these to be met. Church and State, as two divinely ordained institutions, must relate to each other. State recognition of religion benefits both Church and State. Church involvement in civil society and public doctrine is imperative. Interaction that respects the nature and limits of each is salutary. That is what 'establishment' actually is. Take that seriously and both politics and religion begin to look rather different than they do today – or in the book under consideration. Audi's work at least serves to show what the privatization of values, taken to its logical conclusion, would look like.

The cultural context

Now that I have burned my ideological boats by repudiating the strongly relativist assumptions that govern much theological discourse today, what I go on to say will be dismissed by some as unreal or oppressive. They will raise the spectre of a persecuting church and of religious conflict. However, I do not hanker for medieval Christendom or for a state sponsored religious monopoly such as continued for three centuries after the Reformation. I know that there are gaping holes in Peter Berger's sacred canopy. I am not motivated merely by nostalgia for a lost Christian society. What I advocate is that the Church should not be so mesmerized by cultural change that it passes up the opportunities that a society that still has one foot in Christendom is still willing to offer it. Christianity should fight its corner in the marketplace of faiths. Bridges can be built from private, domestic and communal expressions of religion to public faith and from public expressions of faith back to private religious practice. The abundant opportunities to do this should not be gratuitously renounced through misplaced humility, fallacious thinking or lack of nerve.

I borrow the term 'public faith' from John Habgood, but give it a slightly different twist. Habgood used it to refer to the raft of implicit assumptions that give coherence to a common cause, that make public discourse, with its social and ethical entailments, possible. I am using the term to refer to the public dimension of Christian truth, the Christian instantiation of public truth, over against the privatization of values (Habgood, 1988, pp. 8, 11; cf. Avis, 2001, pp. 79ff.). My aim is to hold together public faith and the pastoral task. I pursue this by examining critically the tried and tested pastoral approach to ministry – the ministry of word, sacrament and pastoral care that still takes place in the parishes of the land day by day and week by week. I ask how this ministry can be renewed to fit the changing role for the Church in what is fast becoming a marketplace of faiths and values. By the end of the argument, I believe I am able to vindicate the pastoral method. I put it forward as the cutting edge of mission, as giving credibility to the mission of the Church in its broadest sense. Why do I feel confident in making these claims? It is because the pastoral mode of mission is essentially the personal mode. It connects with the personal quest that motivates many reflective people in our culture – a quest for wholeness of body, mind and spirit, for wholeness in relationships and in community, for the integrity of the natural environment and for our harmony with it. We do well to reflect on the upsurge of concern for wholeness, on the interest in the healing arts, both within and beyond the Church. The sacred is widely experienced today in the mode of a quest for meaning, for what makes overall sense of the world and of our place in it. Wholeness and meaning come together in the vision of the healing of personal identity: who I am, where I have meaning, how I should live. But that cannot come about without community, without fellowship.

My approach throughout this book is to ask whether the time-honoured pastoral method can rise to the challenge of late modernity, whether it can resist the gravitational pull of privatization and become the power-base for effective national witness and service. In the face of the threat of global terrorism, following the terrorist attacks on the United States of

America on 11 September 2001, there may be a window of opportunity to begin to move beyond the privatization of values and its corollary the marginalization of faith. When our way of life, our basic security, is threatened, familiar assumptions are called into question. Radical individualism, an atomized society and the dominance of personal consumer preference begin to look rather threadbare. There is a new imperative to stand together, to work in harmony, to find patterns of solidarity in face of threat. And for that solidarity to become a reality common values and common beliefs are needed. John Atherton is absolutely right (and utterly timely) in asserting the need for a public theology for our changing times (Atherton, 2000). If the Church can recover its nerve, it may find that it is pushing at an open door in pressing the claims of public faith.

However, current events place a question mark against Atherton's slightly short-cut assumption that we now live on 'a post-modern, post-imperial, post-industrial, globalized, secularized, marketized planet' (Atherton, 2000, p. ix). The situation seems to me rather less definitive, considerably more chequered and perhaps more volatile than that. Post-modernity has received a major check. Perhaps it was not such a juggernaut after all. The targets of terrorist attack, the Twin Towers and the Pentagon, were monuments of modernity, concentrated centres of financial and military power that could be projected globally. The terrorist attack on them was mounted using post-modern means (global networks of radically alternative values; individuals who slipped through the system; suicidal fanaticism). But these instruments of terror were parasitic on the achievements of modernity (jet travel; global airline schedules; telecommunications). The methods that are now being used to eliminate terrorist organizations are mainly typical of modernity (resurgence of the nation state; international alliances; B52s; aircraft carriers; satellite surveillance). This picture, tentative and incomplete as it is, suggests that the view of modernity and post-modernity that I arrive at later in this book is sound. Post-modernity has not superseded modernity. It stands for the intensification of the more subversive characteristics of the modern age. Our cultural situation is more appropriately termed late modernity.

In this book I consider the effect of late modernity on traditional pastoral practices and the assumptions that lie behind them. I examine the contested theory of secularization and the elusive notion of post-modernity. I recognize the need for adaptability, flexibility and creativity in the deployment of these time-honoured tools of mission, the ministry of the word, the administration of the sacraments and the provision of pastoral care. But I conclude that, at the end of the day, the Church's ministry of word, sacrament and pastoral care has not been either discredited or superseded and cannot be. It is still the vehicle of the mission of God in the power of the Holy Spirit. The old pastoral values are still the best ones. They stand the test of time because they comprise mission in the personal mode. There is no substitute for commending the gospel person to person, face to face. The mission of the Church flourishes where pastoral imperatives are understood and faithfully and imaginatively practised. Enquirers come forward, Christian initiation is in demand, congregations grow, disciples are formed, the Kingdom of God is advanced. It is by following this path that effective evangelization is accomplished.

I am fully aware, however, that the mission of the Christian Church is not confined to the pastoral mode but extends beyond it in several directions. 'The healing of the nations' requires a mission that is carried forward on a broader front. Mission is not a discrete activity of the Church, but the cutting edge of the Church's life. It includes the vital areas of social engagement, compassionate care, prophetic critique, Christian education and intellectual dialogue and apologetic. It involves Christian social ethics, where ecclesiology and ethical reflection are linked and where we may very well draw on the resources of the natural law tradition to establish, as far as possible, publicly viable ethical criteria (Best and Robra, 1997; Mudge, 1998; Fergusson, 1998). It needs a commitment to civil society and a theology of the relation between Church and State. But unless all these vital activities are set within a pastoral framework, they will not carry conviction in the wider world. Since I have written separately about Church and State recently (Avis, 2001), I will simply touch on the areas of the common good and of civil society.

Civil society and the common good

A strategy for mission needs also to consider the role of the churches in civil society, that commonwealth of semi-autonomous institutions that acts as a buffer between the world of the individual and the family, on the one hand, and the collective power of the state, on the other. We need to reflect on the place of the churches as institutions among other institutions, including non-governmental organizations. In the final analysis, of course, the Church of Christ cannot be equated to secular institutions, even though it may bear comparison with them in some respects, sociologically speaking.

Civil society is a key concept in moving beyond the privatization of faith. To the extent that we are part of civil society – and there must be very few who are not involved in a society, association or institution of some sort – we transcend our private concerns to form committed collective relationships. In so doing we accept wider obligations. Institutions exist for the good of their members at the very least and in many cases (hospitals, schools, colleges, charitable bodies of all sorts) for the good of those beyond their boundaries. They are communities that persist through time, bearing certain convictions, values and goals. They are sustained by the virtues of vocation, loyalty and service. Although human motives are always mixed, institutions have a sense, not only of what is good for them, but in many cases of what is good for the wider society: the common good. Institutions are prime examples of moral communities. When institutions work in harmony with one another, or even in friendly competition, they are orientated to the common good.

Not everyone sees the connection between civil society and the common good. Some writers hold that civil society is constituted by individuals acting in a private capacity. They see it as the milieu of private contractual relations (Tester, 1992, p. 8). However, this way of understanding civil society seems to fall into the trap of assuming that whatever is not sponsored by the state falls into the private category. It polarizes the public and the private and leaves little middle ground between them. It lines up unwittingly with Marx for whom civil society was the cockpit of selfish struggle. It was to be superseded by what Marx in the Theses on Feuerbach called 'human society or socialised humanity', embodied in the state (Tester, 1992, p. 20). The whole point of civil society is that it comprises a territory that lies between private life and the sphere of state action. As Gellner points out (Gellner, 1994), it was this vast tract of social interaction and collaboration that was sorely missed in the highly centralised, state-controlled societies of Eastern Europe before 1989. Oppressed peoples under these regimes needed no persuading of the merits of civil society with its plurality of institutions, causes and ideologies.

In the West, wariness with regard to the idea of a common good for civil society is premised on the fear of loss of liberty and on liberal relativism – scepticism about the possibility of ethical agreement.

Orientation to a common good is regarded as incompatible with personal freedom. An idea of a common good that serves as the ultimate touchstone for all groups in society is regarded as oppressive. Those societies that have been emancipated comparatively recently in Eastern Europe know differently. Freedom is not unqualified. It comes when diversity of institutions is held within a shared framework. Diversity in itself is not enough: it can lead to a kind of anarchy. In reality toleration is sustained by the institutions and practices that have been developed in Western societies, particularly in the last three centuries, and that are now taken for granted.

Agreement on the common good is also widely regarded as unattainable on grounds of ethical diversity. As Hollenbach points out, in America the idea of tolerance of diversity, 'non-judgementalism', has effectively taken the place of the idea of the common good (Hollenbach, 2002, p. 24). But, as he goes on to show, this minimalist ethic cannot rise to the challenge of division and conflict either within or between nations. The value of leaving others to their own devices suggests that a maximally tolerant society would contain a minimum of human interaction. Mere tolerance is no answer in face of a threat or challenge. However, even the faith rather pathetically placed in undiscriminating toleration can be seen as a desire for a social good, not merely for individual gratification (pp. 68f.). Fergusson argues that one can work towards common moral ground even in the absence of a common moral theory (Fergusson, 1998). The choice is not between full ethical agreement and no common ground whatsoever. There is a need for strategies that point towards or approximate to a common good. What is needed now is a concept of the common good that is suited to pluralist societies. We are feeling after some such concept as the common good of common goods. We strive according to our lights for what we believe is best for society, but we all believe that the freedom to do this out of conviction is an essential element of the common good. We fight our corner and argue it out passionately with rival contenders. We use all lawful means to carry our cause. We win some and we lose some, but we have cleared our consciences and delivered the mandate given by our faith. Because religious bodies (churches) encourage their members to be committed to public life in the name of their faith and equip them to play a useful part, they contribute to the wealth of talent and energy that is ploughed into public life. When the churches and their active members bring with them a commitment to religious freedom for all, they both strengthen the fabric of the common life and uphold the right to dissent. The common good is not the enemy of liberty but its guarantee (cf. Hollenbach, 2002).

Instead of assimilating civil society to the private realm, as some interpreters do, it is more convincing, in my view, to think of civil society as a synthesis of private and public good and of individual and social interests (Seligman, 1992). Ideals of the common good and of mutuality, cooperation and social cohesion are intrinsic to civil society. Therefore belief in the moral agency and moral responsibility of individuals is crucial to civil society. Exponents of civil society stress that it rests on common values. Seligman points out that the idea that human relationships have a religious origin is indispensable to our attempts to work out the basis of a moral, public realm. Warnke insists that contemporary political, social and moral ideas are not self-standing concepts, floating about in the atmosphere, but are derived from bodies of public conviction – often shaped by religious faith – in which certain notions of virtue, of the good life, reside (Warnke, 1993).

The benefits of civil society are generally taken for granted in the West. The extent to which civil society rests on recognition of a common good is not sufficiently acknowledged. As a result, the churches, though already deeply implicated in civil society, are not as aware as they might be of the virtues and opportunities that civil society presents as a major counter-balance to radical privatization and individualism. Gellner has pointed out that a good deal of social theory takes civil society for granted: 'it simply starts out with the assumption of an unconstrained and secular individual, unhampered by social or theological bonds, freely choosing his aims, and reaching some agreement concerning social order with his fellows'. Civil society is simply presupposed. Gellner regards this as 'a naïve universalisation of one rather fortunate kind of man – the inhabitant of civil society' (Gellner, 1994, p. 13).

The idea of civil society counteracts the radical privatization of values and shows how public forms of association are vital to human flourishing. This should be music to the ears of the churches and should be sufficient to motivate them to become thoroughly and intentionally involved in the realm of civil society and in the debates about the shape of the common good.

A pastoral mission

Altogether, to counteract the privatization of faith (and of spiritual and moral values generally) the churches themselves should pay greater attention to the public, corporate dimension of Christian faith. This agenda will take the churches more deeply into in at least three areas: first, ecclesially grounded social ethics; second, the relation between Church and State; and third, the significance of civil society. Underlying all these concerns is the imperative of making fruitful connections, as far as possible, between the distinctive affirmations of the Christian gospel and the prevailing public discourse. For without a meeting of fundamental human meanings all those grand projects, involving civil society, social ethics and Church and State, are doomed to fall flat. So this book will have served its purpose if it helps clergy and ministers, bishops and lay leaders of the Church, to find ways of bridging the yawning gap between the Christian message and the quest and questions that mark our culture. For in so doing, we begin to draw individuals, households and communities into the life of grace that marks the Church.

In his memorable retiring Presidential Address to the General Synod in November 1990, Archbishop Robert Runcie

reminded the Synod that the Church of England has always
been a church without hard edges:

> Confronted by the wistful, the half-believing and the seeking,
> we know what it is to minister to those who relate to the faith
> of Christ in unexpected ways. We do not write off hesitant
> and inadequate responses to the gospel. Ours is a church of
> the smoking flax, of the mixture of wheat and tares. Critics
> may say that we blunt the edge of the gospel and become
> Laodicean. We reply that we do not despise the hesitant and
> half-believing, because the deeper we look into human lives
> the more often we discern the glowing embers of faith.
> (Runcie, 1990, p. 1042)

That is why, Dr Runcie concluded, it has been the Church of
England's method to 'cast evangelism in the mould of pastoral
care' and to make 'no sharp divide between preaching the
gospel and shepherding souls'.

Archbishop Runcie's successor, Dr George Carey, endorsed a
similar approach. Reflecting on the national response to the
death of Diana Princess of Wales in August 1997, Archbishop
Carey advocated a pastoral method that allows people to
'express their longings, their searchings and supplications on
their own terms and in their own way'. In an unpublished paper
he advocated an approach that would make available the
resources of the Church, particularly the beauty and solemnity
of its buildings and liturgy, in order to 'build bridges between
people's innate spiritual needs and the life of the Church'.

The words of the two successive Archbishops of Canterbury
seem to imply that the mission of the Church is in the first
instance a pastoral one. Relationships are created, service is
offered, trust is fostered and the Church is integrated into the
community by innumerable subtle links. It is in this sense that I
argue for the primacy of the pastoral. There is a pastoral imperative to shape a church that maximizes points of access for
those who are not yet active members of the Church yet who
acknowledge the place of the sacred, the touch of God, in their
lives.

2

For the Healing of the Nations

> On either side of the river is the tree of life . . . and the leaves
> of the tree are for the healing of the nations.
>
> Revelation 22.2

The garden and the city

Why does the Bible, as is often said, begin with a garden and
end with a city? 'Its historical narrative begins with nomadic
pastoralists looking for somewhere to settle, and ends in
imperial Rome, the world's truly great city' (Gorringe, 2002,
p. 119). What is the logic of this sequence? Is there a value
judgement implied here? Is Scripture promoting urban living
over the rural way of life or is it simply reflecting a reality found
in the development of many, if not all, societies? After all,
gardens and cities are not incompatible. The dream of
modernist planners and architects was to combine the best
of both, as in Hampstead Garden Suburb and Welwyn Garden
City. The modest artisans' houses in the former are now worth
a small fortune. You can have the best of both worlds only if you
can afford to live in a privileged urban enclave or to commute
from the country, where you live, to the city, where you work.
The interaction, the dialectic of urban and rural runs through
Scripture, as it does through much modern literature. It figures
later in this book.

The biblical images of the garden and the city are shot
through with ambiguity (cf. Bauckham and Hart, 1999,
pp. 147ff.; Ward, 2000, pp. 1f., 32ff.). Both can evoke harmony,
peace and prosperity. Both can harbour threats of treachery
and sinful pride. The biblical Paradise is the paradigm of
ordered peace and well-being. As Voltaire suggested in *Candide*
(Voltaire, 1947, p. 143), there is something imperative,
something incomparably therapeutic about cultivating the

garden. The city similarly stands for stability and security. As Graham Ward puts it, in a book that with grim irony sports the Twin Towers of New York's World Trade Centre on its cover, 'the city is humankind's most sophisticated image of order'. In Scripture, however, Ward notes, 'the utopian dreams of city-builders wishing to construct paradise within their boundaries, is crossed by a dark sense of judgement by God on "all the lofty towers and all the sheer walls"' (Isaiah 2.15: Ward, 2000, pp. 2, 33).

The Eden of Genesis 1-3 is a garden created by God, not made by human hands (Genesis 2.8). Similarly, the city of God, the New Jerusalem, in Revelation 21, comes down ready made from heaven, a city not made by hands, 'whose architect and builder is God' (Hebrews 11.10) – what Hebrews 11.16 calls 'another city' (*heteropolis*). Yet within the garden lurks the serpent of temptation and the potential for the Fall. The first biblical city was founded by the fratricide Cain (Genesis 4.17) and ever afterwards human-built cities are seen in Scripture as symbols of human pride and defiance of God's rule. (Here there is an instructive difference between the Bible and Aristotle, for whom the city or *polis* is the highest expression of human community or communion (*koinonia*), with the emphasis on the political expression of the ethical life, rather than on the built expression of human *hubris*: Aristotle, 1995; Sagovsky, 2000).

The garden as a place of innocence cannot rise to the full biblical vision of redemption. Salvation is not to be equated with the restoration of innocence. While the Fall results in banishment from the garden as the human pair are driven out, God's provision of atonement through sacrifice results in a great gathering in. There is an eschatological embracing of those who have been scattered abroad on the face of the earth, a scattering that is the symbol of their separation from the face of God, as the story of the Tower of Babel indicates (Genesis 11.1–9; cf. John 11.52; Ephesians 1.10).

Jesus sweats great drops of blood in a garden, but is crucified outside the city. He rises again in a garden but appears to his disciples in the city. The garden is incomplete without the city and the city without the garden. The images become fused. The garden is incorporated into the city and the city is depicted as a glorified garden. The images of Zion and the holy city in the

Old Testament contain paradisal features (Isaiah 2.2ff.; Ezekiel 40.2; 47.1; Zechariah 14.8: cf. Bauckham and Hart, 1999, p. 150). In Hebrews 11-12 the imagery of the city, the homeland, the holy mountain and the kingdom are interchangeable. Both the primal garden and the eschatological city are watered by rivers that run through them and both of them enshrine the Tree of Life.

The Book of Revelation's vision of the heavenly city echoes and elaborates not one but two passages in the Hebrew Bible. The first text is, of course, Genesis 2.9f.: the Tree of Life in the midst of the Garden of Eden and the river that flows through Eden and divides to water the earth. The second passage is Ezekiel's vision (47.1–12) of the river flowing from the threshold of the temple and the trees on either side of the river, whose fruit is for eating and whose leaves are for healing. In John's vision the Tree of Life stands beside the river of the water of life in the New Jerusalem – the perfected community of the redeemed, living in unsullied communion with one another and in the bliss of the vision of God. The eschatological fulfilment of God's loving purpose for the world is described as 'the healing of the nations' (Revelation 22.1–2). This biblical expression brings together two fundamental truths about the mission of God in which the Church is caught up. These truths correspond to the overriding convictions that run through this book.

The first conviction that motivates me in writing this book is that the gospel mission of the Church has the power to heal the wounds of sin, suffering and sorrow and to make human beings whole, sound and complete in the image of Christ. 'The healing of his seamless dress is by our beds of pain; we touch him in life's throng and press and we are whole again' (J.G. Whittier). The gospel brings the promise of the healing of human identity, of our deepest selves. It does this by bringing us, through faith and baptism, to a participation in Christ's saving death and resurrection. But his death and resurrection are not simply incidents in the life history of an individual, but are, as it were, cosmic events that have the effect of changing reality. They are corporate facts into which we, as individuals, may be incorporated by the transforming power of the Holy Spirit. Redemption is a truth about the Body of Christ. Thus salvation through Christ brings us into a living relationship with

God and with each other. Both dimensions of relationship, the vertical and the horizontal, are vital. They are so connected in the divine economy that you cannot have the one without the other. The 'wholeness paradigm' that shapes the Christian theology of salvation unites me as an individual with my family, my community, my country and all humankind. It also evokes my solidarity with the natural world and speaks of God's plan to reconcile all things in Christ (Colossians 1.20; Ephesians 1.10). In fulfilment of God's redemptive purpose, the cosmos will be liberated from futility and decay and share in the glorious freedom of the children of God (Romans 8.18–23). Scripture is not speaking of some private experience that has no consequences beyond the individual subject. It is enunciating public truth with a vengeance.

The second conviction lying behind this book is, therefore, that the power of the gospel in mission reaches not just the individual but the community, not just eclectic groups but public structures, flowing into the given contours of human society. God's gracious salvific plan is for the healing of the *nations*, that is to say, in biblical terms, the peoples (*ethne*) of the world in their ordered societies, their gathered communities, the Gentiles who were for so long outside the covenant of grace. To be effective in making people and communities whole, the Church's mission must have a public dimension; it must be involved in the structures of society and address issues of public concern. In order to do this, the Church itself needs a structure that is commensurate with its mission, one that can relate not only to local and regional expressions of community, but to national and international ones. Parochial, diocesan, national (or provincial), and global structures and networks all have their place in the mission of the Church (see Avis, 2001, ch. 1).

The 'wholeness paradigm' of the salvation that the Church's gospel mission conveys is fitted to the ethos of our age which is unapologetically seeking for wholeness, the healing of body, mind and spirit. The emerging contemporary paradigm of salvation draws on therapeutic, ecological, feminist and liberationist insights, from various sources of holistic thought, that resonate with the aspirations of Western culture at the birth of the third millennium. But let not any self-appointed guardians of orthodoxy condemn the therapeutic approach as pandering to secular fashions, as Edward Norman seems to do when he claims that religion has become 'a species of personal therapy' and is now identified with the individual's experience of emotional satisfaction, the 'sacralising of personal welfare' (Norman, 2002, pp. 22, 32, 91). The wholeness/healing paradigm of salvation is actually profoundly biblical, though this fact is rather obscured in some Bible translations. The scriptural norm for humankind is to enjoy the abundance of God-given life or strength in order to serve God with the whole of one's faculties, physical, mental and spiritual, in accordance with God's revealed nature and purpose.

What does militate against the spirit of the age is my stress on the public, communal application of this paradigm. I stoutly resist the reduction of wholeness, healing and fulfilment to individualistic, self-centred, subjective experience. I insist that God is concerned with communities, as they exist structured in societies. For that reason, the Christian mission is ineradicably ecclesiological, for the Christian Church is itself just such a structured, ordered community or society. It is to that community that the mandate of mission is given.

The biblical wholeness paradigm

Let me now attempt to substantiate my claim that what I have called the wholeness paradigm of salvation, concerned with healing in the broadest sense – physical and spiritual, individual and communal restoration and well-being – is 'profoundly and entirely biblical'. To do this we need to consider two families of concepts in the Old and New Testaments respectively (for a thorough survey of all therapeutic aspects of the biblical literature, see Wilkinson, 1998).

The first family of concepts is the biblical background to the idea of wholeness. The Hebrew greeting *shalom* derives from the verb *shalam*, to be complete, whole, safe, sound; to be completed, finished, fulfilled; to be at peace. The adjective *shalom* means sound, well, safe, secure, healthy. This concept stands essentially for a totality of harmonious well-being. In the Hebrew Bible the emphasis is on material prosperity, based on stable relationships between humankind and the Creator and between human beings themselves. (Significantly, for our modern/post-modern context, this term is not used in the Old Testament of inward peace, of peaceful feelings, though its extrapolation in this direction is not necessarily misplaced.)

In the canonical prophetic books the import of *shalom* shifts decisively from its basis in material prosperity to a stronger emphasis on right relationship. It becomes linked explicitly with the concept of righteousness, or right relationship with God. In Ezekiel 34.25 and 37.26 it is said that the 'covenant of peace' promised by YHWH will effect deliverance from oppression and bring material prosperity. But at its heart and as its fundamental condition is covenantal faithfulness between Israel and YHWH: 'you are my sheep ... and I am your God' (Ezekiel 34.31; cf. 37.27). In Isaiah 54.10 the expression 'my covenant of peace' is paralleled by the phrase 'my steadfast love'. In Psalm 85.8 peace is seen as the gift of YHWH to his people and is virtually synonymous with salvation, steadfast love, righteousness and faithfulness. The ideas of peace and healing are brought together in Jeremiah. The false prophets are condemned for having dressed Judah's wounds of sin super-ficially (or carelessly), 'saying, "Peace, peace," when there is no peace' (Jeremiah 6.14).

In the Greek Bible, the Septuagint (LXX), both *eirene*, peace, and *hugiaino*, to be healthy or sound, were used to translate *shalom*, thus infusing the Greek with the holistic sense of the Hebrew. The relational meaning of *shalom* becomes more pronounced in the inter-testamental and early Christian era rabbinic writings. The Gospel writers are more interested in describing the act of healing than in defining a state of health (Wilkinson, 1998, p. 77). However, the New Testament follows the Old in seeing the divine gift of health or life in terms of wholeness, soundness, well-being or strength, and in stressing that this is made possible through a salvific relationship to God in Christ.

This sense of fundamental right relationship between God and humanity is carried into the New Testament writings. In the Lukan infancy stories peace is equated with salvation: 'To guide our feet into the way of peace' (Luke 1.79; cf. 2.14: the *gloria in excelsis*). When the Seventy go forth, charged by Jesus to preach the gospel and to heal the sick, they impart peace with the authority of Christ to those who receive them. In that action, the Kingdom of God and God's salvation have drawn near (Luke 10.1-9). It is this relational sense of peace that is striking in a key text from Paul's epistles: 'Since we are justified by faith, we have peace with God through our Lord Jesus Christ' (Romans 5.1).

The second family of concepts that contribute to the wholeness paradigm, as I have called it, comprises the biblical background to the idea of salvation understood as healing. In the Hebrew Bible there are two roots to be considered.

The first is *yasha*, to save, to give safety or ease, often in a broad sense, as in Psalm 28.9 which is familiar as a versicle at Morning Prayer in the Book of Common Prayer 1662: 'Save thy people and bless thine heritage.' This verb provides us with the substantive *yeshuah*, salvation, deliverance. It is used both in the political-military sense and in the spiritual-eschatological sense of the ultimate redemption of human destiny that will never have an end (cf. Isaiah 51.1–11). The root meaning here, of broadness or spaciousness, lends itself to a liberationist approach, setting free from oppression and bondage. It is of course from this root that the name Joshua (in Hebrew) and Jesus (in Greek) are derived.

The second Hebrew root is *rapha*, to heal. This has both a physical and a spiritual sense, and often it is not clear which sense is uppermost: 'I kill and I make alive; I wound and I heal' (Deuteronomy 32.39); 'I am the LORD your healer' (Exodus 15.26: Moses sweetening the bitter waters); '... who forgives all your iniquity, who heals all your diseases' (Psalm 103.3); 'He heals the broken hearted and binds up their wounds' (Psalm 147.3). The prophets often speak of YHWH healing the faithlessness or backsliding of Israel as far as her covenant relationship with him is concerned (e.g. Hosea 14.4; Jeremiah 3.22).

The two verbs, to save and to heal, are combined in a powerful parallelism in Jeremiah's cry: 'Heal me, O LORD, and I shall be healed; save me, and I shall be saved' (Jeremiah 17.14). Therapeutic imagery is particularly pronounced in this prophet of sorrows.

In the New Testament there are five verbs used for healing, of which we shall briefly consider the two most significant. The first is *therapeuo*, literally to attend to, hence to heal (the verb most commonly used for healing in the Gospels). In the ministry of Jesus the use of this verb does not of course refer to healing by medical means, but by divine authority, as in the curing of demoniacs (Luke 6.18; 8.2).

The second is *sozo*, to save or heal, from the adjective *sos*, safe. There is a broad meaning of deliverance from external perils, say from death or drowning, and there is a specific meaning of healing of the person. Ambiguity of nuance is unavoidable and it is this that constitutes the theological richness of this term. Where the Authorized Version has 'Thy faith hath saved thee,' the Revised English Bible translates, 'Your faith has healed you' (Luke 18.42: *sesoken se*). In the *Theological Dictionary of the New Testament* W. Foerster points out that in the healings of Jesus, *sozo* never refers to a single member of the body but always to the whole person. 'The choice of the word leaves room for the view that the healing power of Jesus and the saving power of faith go beyond physical life' (Foerster, 1971, p. 990). From *sozo* comes the substantive *soteria*, literally safety or soundness, hence theologically, salvation.

All these themes are gathered up in the powerful words of Jesus that at one and the same time healed, blessed and absolved suffering individuals. Perhaps the best example is Mark 5.34: 'Daughter, your faith has made you well [AV: 'whole']; go in peace [cf. Hebrew *shalom*], and be healed [AV: 'be whole'] of your disease.'

Another telling example of the merging of meanings is found in the extensive reflection of New Testament writers on Isaiah 6.10: 'so that they may not . . . turn and be healed'. Mark makes the spiritual meaning explicit with his phrase 'be forgiven' (Mark 4.12). Matthew reverts to 'heal' (Matthew 13.15). Luke the physician is not keen to spiritualize healing and omits the passage he found in Mark, but at the end of The Acts of the Apostles, where he cites the text from Isaiah, Luke seems to have second thoughts and parallels 'heal them' with 'salvation' (Acts 28.27f.). John has 'heal them' (John 12.40). Taking the biblical witness at this point as a whole, in terms of the canon, the ambiguity is inescapable and surely intended. The biblical import of salvation by the grace of God is a wholeness that is physical and spiritual, individual and communal.

Finally, it is instructive to compare translations of Titus 2.11, which is a close relative of the text that provides the motto for this chapter. While the NRSV has 'For the grace of God has appeared, bringing salvation (*soterios*) to all', the REB follows the AV 'healing': 'For the grace of God has dawned (*epephane*) upon the world with healing for all mankind.' Surely we should detect an echo of Malachi 4.2 here: 'For you who revere my name the sun of righteousness shall rise with healing in its wings.' Charles Wesley saw the universal application that is added in Titus but is elusive in Malachi, when he wove into 'Hark! the herald angels sing' the words: 'Joyful, all ye nations rise, Join the triumph of the skies . . .' Wesley here combines Isaiah (9.6) and Malachi (4.2) with two central images of John's Gospel, light and life (1.4):

> Hail, the heaven-born Prince of Peace!
> Hail, the Sun of righteousness!
> Light and life to all he brings,
> Risen with healing in his wings.

In both the Old Testament and the New salvation is a profoundly therapeutic idea, speaking of the healing, wholeness and entire well-being of persons and communities in fellowship with God. Articulating the Christian understanding of salvation in therapeutic terms not only expresses faithfully some central biblical motifs, but also makes a theological response to some deep-seated concerns of our contemporary culture – particularly those expressed in various forms of spirituality, in philosophy, psychotherapy and the arts. But while there is a particular resonance with the culture of late modernity, the therapeutic values of salvation through Christ transcend any cultural epoch. They are universal and timeless. They translate into any culture and any age. They are intrinsically ordered to universal human needs and aspirations. The gospel of wholeness is public truth and lends itself to inculturation in every context.

> Thou who didst come to bring
> On thy redeeming wing
> Healing and sight,
> Health to the sick in mind,
> Sight to the inly blind,
> Oh! Now to all mankind
> Let there be light.

The healing of human identity

Identity has been called the 'grail symbol' of the modern world. In its fullest sense it is a mystical concept that promises personal redemption at the end of our longest and most demanding journey, our lifelong quest for completion (Klapp, 1969, p. xii). In Tolstoy's *Anna Karenin*, Levin speaks for the way that every reflecting human person feels at certain moments when he bursts out: 'I cannot live without knowing what I am and why I am here' (Tolstoy, 1978, p. 823; cf. p. 827). Identity speaks of the meaning of our lives as persons. The quest for identity continually draws us onwards and proves inexhaustible because it concerns the mystery of personhood. 'We do not know who we are and, when we speak of ourselves as persons, we scarcely know what we are saying' (Crewdson, 1994, p. 301). Identity emerges, unfolds, develops, matures and is never definitive in this life. It is an essentially eschatological concept to which the biblical language of 'already' and 'not yet', 'foretaste' and 'fulfilment' applies.

Only God, as our Creator, can specify who we are as created persons. We *are* only in relation to *the one who is*. We only flourish as we dwell in communion (*koinonia*) with the one divine source of true personhood and with others who are receiving from that source just as we are. Human personhood reflects divine personhood and is received as a gift, both in creation and in redemption. Identity is received as grace because God looks upon us in Christ. Our true identity is not man-made, through human effort and attainment and the recognition, even adulation that this evokes in our ruthless culture of competitive achievement and the appalling cult of the celebrity. 'Human identity is constituted at all times by experience of a saving God' (Crewdson, 1994, p. 337). The question of identity is primarily theological, because it cannot be answered without invoking the name of the triune God of the Bible and the Church, the God who is active in revelation and salvation.

The social scientist Hans Mol sees religion as the sacralization of identity (Mol, 1976, *passim*). Religion is the high point of identity formation. It brings order and purpose into the life of the individual and of the community. The strongest defence against the all-threatening chaos that lurks behind the biblical creation narrative in Genesis 1 is the Creator's act of marking transcendent differences – above all, the difference between darkness and light. The puny human imitation of and response to this divine act is the unceasing activity of 'pouring out meaning into reality' (Berger, 1973, p. 36), constructing individual and social identity. Such identity is ultimately theological in that it is grounded in God and is not created so much as discovered, as the human quest is met with the divine initiative.

I am quite clear, however, that any kind of functional or instrumental approach to identity – identity as a tool or a means – is deeply flawed. Identity in the high sense that I have been evoking cannot be constructed or contrived. It does not lend itself to a ploy, a strategy. A morally indifferent, value-neutral sense of identity, such as that continually manufactured by the mass media for 'celebrities' and 'stars', is profoundly suspect. Identity must be held to be a function of truth. Identity must stem above all from moral commitment. Charles Taylor makes this point robustly in *Sources of the Self*. He develops the notion of 'the self in moral space', relating this to the question of identity. 'To know who I am is a species of knowing where I stand.' And to adopt that stance is to be orientated, by ethical commitment, in moral space. Located as we are in moral space, our horizon is bounded by an ethical framework that enables us to make judgements about what is right and what is wrong, what to endorse and what to oppose. Such a moral orientation is absolutely fundamental to our identity. 'To lose this orientation, or not to have found it, is not to know who one is.' 'The portrait of an agent free from all frameworks ... spells for us a person in the grip of an appalling identity crisis' (Taylor, 1989, pp. 27ff., 31).

We do not start talking about identity until it is threatened. We ought to be able to take it for granted most of the time. To flaunt one's identity is vulgar. To agonize about it is pathetic and reveals deep insecurity. Identity suddenly becomes important when an individual or a group awakens to the fact that something vital about their way of life is being threatened or suppressed. Identity is a form of currency and depends on people's willingness to accept it. To question its fiduciary basis is to undermine good faith and to provoke panic.

Identity is a modern term that is not needed in typical traditional societies. In such communities identity is bestowed at birth, is seldom questioned and is rarely changed. The term identity is not found in all languages. Where the group was the basic unit of identity, people did not need such ideas as one's self, one's self-image, one's personal identity, and so on. But in our modern and post-modern urban existence identity is at a premium. A fragmented, fluid, highly mobile society generates acute problems of personal and collective identity. People struggle to maintain identity, to avoid anonymity, in a situation where such variables as class, status, job, income, and the stages of the life course generally are less certain and predictable than they were and where social mobility has weakened people's roots in a community and a locality. Conditions tending to social atomism render salutary forms of identity highly precarious.

Social commentators speak therefore of a crisis of identity and see this as a particular affliction of Western society since the Second World War. Erikson, who devoted a lifetime to the clinical and theoretical study of personal identity, especially in childhood and adolescence, claimed that the study of identity is 'as strategic in our time as the study of sexuality was in Freud's time' (Erikson, 1977, p. 256). Klapp (1969, pp. xi, 4) pointed out that just as no-one knew that they had a neurosis until Freud came along, so awareness of the identity problem had to wait for the theories of the social self developed by William James and his successors in American social science: Baldwin, Cooley and Mead. Klapp added that it was now (in the 1960s) more fashionable to have an identity problem than a sexual neurosis.

The meanings of 'identity' in psychology and sociology are notoriously legion; behind the psychological and sociological debates lies the difficult philosophical problem of identity. The actual identity of identity itself seems elusive (cf. de Levita, 1965, pp. 1ff.). The term is intrinsically ambiguous. Two meanings stand in tension. Identity involves a dialectical relation between two poles, two sets of ideas: on the one hand, continuity, persistence, sameness; and on the other, difference, individuality, development. The continuity or sameness of individual personal conscious identity was emphasized by such philosophers as Locke, Leibniz and Kant. The theme of developing individuality, however, emerged as a legacy of Romanticism and Idealism, with their emphases in different ways on the shaping power of the mind or feelings. Hegel reacted against the Kantian notion of identity as essential sameness, stressing instead relation and mutuality. Unity for Hegel was not a static 'given', but came about through the emergence of difference and its ultimate reconciliation. 'Human nature', Hegel insisted, 'only really exists in an achieved community of minds' (Reed, 1996, pp. 36ff., 54). Psychologists influenced by philosophical idealism gave this aspect of identity added momentum. Among these Jung is the most influential. His *principium individuationis* (principle of individuation) is an exposition of the process of identity formation within the individual. Individuation, according to Jung, is a process whereby we come to terms with our unconscious selves by appropriating and reconciling opposing elements that lie deep in the psyche. This process of assimilation may occur unconsciously and spontaneously (Jung, 1984, p. 175). But when it meets with conscious recognition and acceptance, the process of individuation is raised to a new plane, becoming a journey of self-realization, the creation of a new indivisible unity or whole (Jung, 1983, p. 212). Jung defines individuation as the realization of our 'true' self, achieved by divesting the self of the mask of outward personality, 'the false wrappings of the persona', on the one hand, and of 'the suggestive power of primordial images', on the other (Jung, 1954–, vol. 7, p. 174). To attain this state of enlightenment is the ultimate goal of our existence. 'In the last analysis every life is the realisation of a whole, that is, of a self.' Every individual 'is charged with an individual destiny and destination, and the realisation of these alone makes sense of life' (Jung, 1985, p. 269). Individuation thus marks a progression from a blind unconscious, uncreative unity, through differentiation, to the creative enrichment of conscious existence (Jung, 1954–, vol. 6, p. 448). The dynamic of individuation brings increasing discrimination out of the undifferentiated unconscious *pleroma* (fullness) in which such distinctions are only latent. However, these emerge into consciousness as opposites, creating disturbances and conflicts that may be controlled and reconciled by means of symbols, particularly centring symbols of integration and wholeness, such as the mandala (that Jung himself found particularly therapeutic during a period of psychic turmoil in his own life). By progressively assimilating the contents of the unconscious (first the personal and then the collective unconscious) the psyche gains in strength, creativity and equilibrium. Then, Jung says, 'the centre of gravity of the total personality shifts its position. It is no longer in the ego, which is merely the centre of consciousness, but in the hypothetical point between consciousness and unconsciousness.' This new centre may be called the self (Jung, 1983, p. 19). The self is the archetype of unity and totality, the deepest source of individual identity and wholeness.

Through the influence of depth psychology we have come to think of personal identity in a dynamic way, as an ongoing process of integration whereby unconscious sources of emotional conflict or resource are unlocked and assimilated beneficially into the self. In its contemporary use, identity is a dominantly dynamic concept that calls for a narrative context, though the static sense must necessarily remain as a foil. The two senses of identity that we have noted are played off against each other in Ricoeur's polarity of 'sameness' (*idem*) and 'selfhood' (*ipse*) (Ricoeur, 1992, pp. 2f. and *passim*).

Our identity tells us who we are, where we fit in and what we are worth. It is the most precious and yet the most vulnerable asset of a person. The most difficult times in life are when the relationships that make up our personal identity are damaged or severed by such traumas as bereavement, divorce, redundancy or clinical depression. Our sure sense of identity is our defence against meaninglessness. Berger calls it 'a shield against terror' – the terror of becoming a non-person, a nonentity (Berger, 1973, p. 31). A person whose identity has been taken away is a person whom nobody needs and everybody ignores, a damned soul. From the beginning, our identity is constituted in relation to others. Hence Ricoeur's teasing title *Oneself as Another* (Ricoeur, 1992).

The making of identity implies a process; it comes about as part of an overall development and falls into a pattern. Under the suggestive heading of 'Redemption as Wholeness', Joan Crewdson writes in her exposition of the thought of Michael Polanyi: 'Redemption is a process by which things that are fragmented come to wholeness.' She adds: 'All life is a process of growth by integration.' Hence the twin divine acts of creation and redemption cannot be sharply distinguished, for they are aspects of 'a single process of coming to be in mature relatedness' (Crewdson, 1994, p. 320).

The notion of process comes down to us from the Pre-Socratic philosophers. But it was eclipsed for many centuries by the uniformitarianism of the medieval Latin Christian worldview – the assumption that not only the natural world, but also human experience and history remained basically the same in all circumstances (cf. Lovejoy, 1953). Uniformitarian assumptions undergirded the idea of the fixity of species and were aided and abetted by a literal interpretation of the biblical creation narrative. In theology uniformitarianism implied a textual understanding of authority in which decisive precepts and precedents were enshrined in authoritative texts that were to be received uncritically by their readers and hearers. A dominant theological expression of uniformitarianism is the celebrated touchstone of St Vincent of Lérins in the first half of the fifth century: *quod semper, quod ubique, quod ab omnibus creditum est* ('what has been believed always, everywhere and by all').

In science, uniformitarianism was overcome in the theory of evolution, as process models superseded static conceptions of the natural order. The idea of process was admitted to theological method in a half-hearted way in Newman's *Essay on the Development of Christian Doctrine* (1845). Bergson and Whitehead were the principal authors of process philosophy and, in dependence on this, there is a flourishing tradition of process theology. Process thought emphasizes the creative nature of development, the dynamic unfolding of the universe of life-forms in the direction of ever-increasing complexity and sophistication. Depth psychology presupposes a process framework. This is the case not so much in the positivistic and rather mechanistic Freudian form of depth psychology, as in the analytical psychology of Jung. Jung's emphasis is on the unending quest of the psyche for individuation, for personal growth and development through the dialectical reconciliation of opposing psychic energies that are expressed in symbols that emerge from the unconscious.

The idea of process informs what I have to say later in this book about the lifelong spiritual journey of all God's children and the stages of our life course on that way that we mark as *rites de passage* and sanctify sacramentally in baptism, confirmation, marriage and burial. But the concept of process requires that we show how the process hangs together, what it is that structures and integrates it. It points to the idea of system.

Our heightened consciousness of system derives from modern systems theory that applies this concept to biological and social organisms. It describes these organisms as integrated self-organizing and self-regulating transactional entities. It sees them as channelling and processing both energy and information in two directions: to internal sub-systems and to the external environment. Individual human beings and defined communities such as churches are both systems in this sense. Systems theory is not applicable to the organization of Christian doctrine – systematic theology – except analogically. Systems are organic, not merely conceptual; they are living structures, not just in the mind. (For an introduction to holistic ideas, including systems theory, see Capra, 1983, chs 9–11, and more fully Laszlo, 1972. Systems theory is applied to religion in Bowker, 1987, appendix.) In systems the whole is incrementally greater than the part and the part is determined, though not absolutely, by the whole. Systems are described as *open* when they make exchanges of energy and information with their environment and so develop to higher forms of complexity and sophistication. They are described as *closed* when they are cut off from their facilitating environment. This closure leads to stagnation ('equilibrium') and the running down of the system ('entropy').

Psychotherapy sees individuals as psychosomatic systems, as mind and body bound together. Neurotic physical symptoms and psychological handicaps arise when transactions of information and of energy are not properly processed, or when the system closes in on itself, retreating from reality, from its objective environment. The aim of psychotherapy is to re-establish contact with internal and external reality in order to get energy and information flowing again. If Freud typically fails to see the socio-economic determinants of neurosis, Jung, with his idea of the collective unconscious, sees the individual as profoundly implicated in the widest conceivable human system. Group therapy explicitly recognizes that individuals are, at least in part, a function of the group to which they belong. It aims to treat the individual's dysfunctions within the group by interpreting the group dynamics. W. R. Bion pioneered this approach in the 1940s and '50s (Bion, 1961), but group analysis has been enriched subsequently by the insights of systems theory.

In this book, the idea of system informs what I have to say about the Church as a community and its relation to its environment in society. I argue for openness to the environing culture and to the structures of society and for a permeable boundary between the two. I stress the need to respond pastorally to people's expectations before attempting, tactfully and gently, to correct assumptions that may be woefully inadequate. I affirm the need for dialogue, interaction and apologetic. However, this is no woolly liberal sell-out – quite the reverse. The gospel, rather than the world, sets the agenda. Openness is an economy for the sake of mission. I do not overlook the need for a strong centre of identity in the Church, for clarity of belief as far as this is possible, for a message with a gospel cutting-edge and for a disciplined approach to the Church's ministry.

The narrative structure of identity

The open-ended journey of discovery that we call identity formation lends itself to being told in narrative form. The concept of narrative links together biblical faith (which is clearly expressed in the narrative of God's gracious dealings with humankind, salvation history), much of general literature (especially the novel, saga and biography) and the philosophical notion of identity. Here I only touch lightly on an extensive theological and philosophical corpus devoted to narrative insofar as it concerns our theme, the healing of identity. MacIntyre states the theme: 'The unity of a human life is the unity of a narrative quest' (MacIntyre, 1985, p. 203). But what sort of unity is the unity of a narrative quest? Clearly it is an incomplete unity, a unity in process of being realized, an unfolding unity – even one that may never be achieved, if the quest is unsuccessful.

Charles Taylor stresses that identity is not merely a matter of what I have become, but crucially of what I am becoming, of where I am going, and insists that this can only be grasped as narrative (Taylor, 1989, pp. 47f.). Ricoeur argues that the question of personal identity 'can be articulated only in the temporal dimension of human existence' and that this requires a narrative framework since 'the self seeks its identity on the scale of an entire life'. Ricoeur elaborates Dilthey's concept of 'the connectedness of life' (Ricoeur, 1992, pp. 114f.). MacIntyre defines identity as 'unity of character within a story' (MacIntyre, 1985, p. 202). And Ricoeur complements this when he defines character as 'the set of distinctive marks which permit the reidentification of a human individual as being the same'. As habitual elements are sedimented in a person's psyche they give 'a history to character'. Since 'a character is the one who performs the action in the narrative', character can be seen to be a narrative category also. The guiding thread of a story is the plot, but without characters there can be no plot; there must be actors if there is to be action. This leads Ricoeur to say, rather inelegantly, that characters are themselves plots. Action and character are both forms of 'emplotment'. Identity is revealed as characters take part continuously in action and this complex is construed as narrative (Ricoeur, 1992, pp. 119, 121, 140–3).

Those who write about narrative as a literary genre are right to remind us that we live in a story-shaped world (Wicker, 1975). They love to quote Barbara Hardy: 'We dream in narrative, daydream in narrative, remember, anticipate, hope, despair, believe, doubt, plan, revise, criticise, construct, gossip, learn, hate and love by narrative' (Wicker, 1975, p. 47; MacIntyre, 1985, p. 197). For Barthes, narrative is synonymous with life itself, it is simply there (Barthes, 1977, p. 79). Ricoeur claims that daily experience is characterized by an 'inchoate narrativity'. We find ourselves compelled to tell stories because 'in the last analysis human lives need and merit being narrated'. The history of suffering in particular calls for narrative as it cries out for vengeance (Ricoeur, 1984, pp. 74f.). A human life is a fabric woven from stories told (Ricoeur, 1988, p. 246). Narrative is the vehicle that carries the meaning of life, a sense of the whole. Narrative can give the sense of the whole because intrinsic to narrative is the familiar framework of a story: the beginning, the middle and the end – or to put it in a slightly more sophisticated way: a setting, a theme, a plot and a resolution. But it is the characters that are the *sine qua non*. Narrative binds these together into a unity.

Narrative involves not only succession but also transformation (or as Ricoeur would say, refiguration): it is not only going somewhere, but also achieving something (Todorov,

1990, ch. 3). It is this drive towards wholeness, towards unity that gives narrative an orientation to the sacred. The quest for identity (including worth, meaning and belonging) is intrinsically religious, for it seeks a transcendent ground for the self (and for the community). Kort concludes from his analysis of biblical narrative that narrative can be seen as 'an articulated belief structure' (Kort, 1988, p. 20). Robert Alter, a leading exponent of biblical narrative, stresses that a narrative enshrines 'a moral vision' and that this is what gives it its importance (Alter, 1981, p. x).

The human longing for meaning cannot be satisfied with a purely objective solution. To point to ultimate meaning 'out there' is not the answer. We have to be part of the meaning and the meaning has to be part of us. The instinctive human craving for meaning is the driving force of the identity quest. Surveys of religion at around the turn of the second millennium showed that large numbers of people construe their spirituality in the quest mode. Christians are those who, by faith, identify their personal narrative quest with the gospel narrative of the life and destiny of Jesus Christ. The liturgical life of the Church effects this identification as we participate in the sacramental enactment, in baptism and the Eucharist, of the life, death and resurrection of Christ. Having regard to the biblical background, we can say that salvation takes the form of the healing of human identity. Modern theologies of liberation, especially liberation theology itself and feminist theology have been strongly imbued with the identity quest.

Psychotherapists themselves have pointed out the connection between the motives that lead individuals to seek analysis and what makes people tick religiously (what follows draws on Avis, 1989, ch. 10 and references there). Fairbairn wrote that what the patient or client was seeking was precisely 'salvation': 'salvation from the past, from bondage to his (internal) bad objects, from the burden of guilt, and from spiritual death'. Fairbairn concluded that the patient's search 'thus corresponds in detail to the religious quest'. There is an acute irony for the Church in the fact that there are about ten times as many therapists in England as there are stipendiary Anglican clergy and that the number of clients 'in therapy' is larger than the normal Sunday attendance at Anglican churches (Bunting, 1999, p. 64).

While for Freud religion was the mass obsessional neurosis of the human race, for Jung the beneficial effects of religion were uppermost. Jung saw Christianity as a great therapeutic system, providing – through its sacred symbols and its pastoral facilities of confession and counselling – the means whereby the innate self-healing properties of the psyche could be activated. For Jung even dogmas are therapeutic. He would have endorsed the wisdom of the Collect for St Luke the 'physician of the soul' in the Book of Common Prayer, 1662: 'that by the wholesome medicines of the doctrine delivered by him all the diseases of our souls may be healed'. The analytical quest is guided by and eventuates in knowledge or insight. It aims to assist the client to effect a closer rapport with reality – both internal and external. The analyst contributes interpretative understanding through empathy, leading (it is hoped) to causal explanation of what has gone wrong in the client's relation to reality, especially the reality of significant other persons. The hermeneutic of analysis seeks not only to decipher a corrupt text but also to rewrite it as it might have been. Symington writes: 'Ultimately the individual is healed by the truth' (Symington, 1986, p. 331; cf. 47f.). There is an obvious rapport here with the Christian faith, for 'there is a sense in which to be unredeemed is to be in a state of fragmentation and to lack transcendent meaning . . . Only when they find their place in God, the source of unalloyed Being, do persons experience *ultimate* meaning and wholeness' (Crewdson, 1994, p. 321).

One aspect of this theme that I will bring out later is the therapeutic significance of the Christ figure. Let me briefly sketch the essentials of this idea here. In Christian discipleship we identify completely with Jesus Christ. Through word and sacrament and through our experience of receiving pastoral care we internalize the character of Christ by projective identification. In the *imitatio christi* that Thomas à Kempis expounded, we respond to the first call of Jesus to the disciples: 'Follow me!' At the outset Thomas sets the quest in the frame of enlightenment, almost of therapy. Quoting Jesus in John 8.12, 'He who follows me shall not walk in darkness,' he comments: 'In these words Christ counsels us to follow his life and way if we desire true enlightenment and freedom from all blindness of heart.' For Thomas, self-knowledge is a prereq-uisite of such inner freedom: 'A man who truly knows himself realizes his own worthlessness, and takes no pleasure in the praises of men ... A humble knowledge of oneself is a surer road to God than a deep searching of the sciences' (à Kempis, 1952, pp. 27–29). Obedience, renunciation and ruthless honesty with oneself are the conditions of spiritual enlightenment in identification with Christ.

If Thomas offers a sort of therapeutic *via negativa*, Jung advocates a *via affirmativa*. Jung believed that the symbols that emerge from the unconscious and that express or represent its primeval collective archetypes contribute to psychological integration. Archetypes govern the form of the symbols but do not prescribe their content. Content is informed by culture. One of the most crucial and powerful of the archetypes, according to Jung, is that of wholeness. This bodies forth the symbols of the self and of God. Importantly, these are indistinguishable in analysis of clinical material such as dreams and free association. In a Christian culture the God/self symbol is christomorphic. Christ is the image of God and the image of the self. Thus it is vital for our wholeness for us to be able to identify in a vital way with Jesus Christ. But this relationship with Christ is only normally possible through his body on earth, the Church. That brings us to the next key concept: relationship or community.

The social matrix of identity

Erikson says that identity is located both 'in the core of the individual' and 'in the core of his communal culture' (Erikson, 1968, p. 22). Identity has two poles, two foci: self and society. A theory of identity must forge a synthesis between what it has to say about the inner self and what it says about the outer context. To understand the concept of identity we need to be able to draw on both psychology and sociology. For the psychologist, identity is located within the individual psyche; it is part of the personality. For the sociologist, on the other hand, identity is a set of roles and statuses. An adequate approach to identity must, therefore, transcend disciplinary boundaries (cf. Baumeister, 1986, pp. 246).

To show that no-one can have identity without relating to others, William James devised the scenario of the person who went completely unnoticed. 'If no-one turned round when we entered, answered when we spoke, or minded what we did, but if every person we met "cut us dead" ... a kind of rage and impotent despair would ere long well up in us, from which the cruellest bodily tortures would be a relief' (James, 1890, vol. 1, pp. 293f.). There can be no identity without relationships, relationships that together comprise some kind of community. Threats to human survival and human dignity in the century that has just passed have compelled us to re-evaluate the imperatives of relationship, cooperation, community and communion. Separateness is sterile. In isolation we soon cease to be meaningfully human. 'We must love one another or die,' as Auden starkly puts it (Skelton, 1964, p. 283: 'September 1, 1939' – not included in Auden's collected poems).

Rich resources for reflection on this theme are provided by the personalist tradition of post-critical philosophy. Zizioulas has developed the argument, from the Orthodox tradition, that 'there is no being without communion' (Zizioulas, 1985, p. 18). Macmurray insisted in *Persons in Relation* that, at bottom, there can be no human being until there are two human beings in communication with one another because 'persons are constituted by their mutual relation to one another' (Macmurray, 1961, pp. 12, 17). Behind recent personalist philosophies and theologies – among which MacFadyen's *The Call to Personhood* (McFadyen, 1990) is outstanding – lies the mystical personalism of Martin Buber's seminal work *I and Thou* (Buber, 1937).

The foundation for Christian reflection on the life of persons in relation must be the revealed knowledge of God as a Trinity of three Persons and of the person of Jesus Christ as divine and human. Jesus, revealed in the Gospels, is the truly related one, the fully integrated one, the paradigm of what it is in the creative purposes of God to be fully human and the source of the healing of our own identity (see here the essays in Schwöbel and Gunton, 1991). Yet he is no autonomous, unscathed, pagan god-like figure. His dependence and his suffering are integral to his perfection. His identity is not *a priori*; it is mediated, accomplished, or rather (to use an archaic but useful word) 'vouchsafed'. As we see in the temptations in the wilderness and in the agony in the Garden of Gethsemane, his identity and integrity are hard-won. Jesus was not self-sufficient: he needed others. As Tillich put it: Jesus could not be the Christ without his people. Above all, he needed the Other who was not 'wholly other' to him, *Abba*, Father.

Our own purely human identity is not an *a priori* 'given', some kind of perduring ontological substratum; it is mediated, gifted and upheld. It remains vulnerable at the best of times. That is why I do not agree with de Levita's definition of identity (in Mol, 1978, p. 131) as 'the most essential nucleus of man which becomes visible only after all his roles have been laid aside'. I regard that notion of identity as seriously infected with hyper-modern individualism and social atomism. Identity is dynamic and relational. It subsists in a network of interdependence, in which social roles are crucial. It comes about through interaction with the other, beginning with the earliest stage of personal existence.

Before a baby has learned to distinguish itself from the mother, that other is the mother's breast. According to Winnicott, there is a primal identity of being between the baby and the mother's breast. 'When the baby finds the breast, it is the self that has been found' (Winnicott, 1971, pp. 82ff.). Lacan sees what he calls the mirror stage as a 'drama' leading to the structured awareness of the self as a physical and psychical whole (Lacan, 1977, pp. 1–7). From the breast, the locus of identity formation moves to the mother's face. What the mother looks like to the baby as she looks at him/her is connected with what she sees there. There is a mutual mirroring in which both mother and baby receive identity in existing for each other. Being seen, being taken notice of, receiving approval enhances our sense of existing in a significant way. The internal mother image becomes a source of confidence, contentment and self-worth (Winnicott, 1971, pp. 111–18; 1965, pp. 29–36).

The image of the mirror remains relevant to later social relationships. C. H. Cooley spoke of 'the looking glass "I"' and 'the reflected self'. He quoted the ditty: 'Each to each a looking glass/ Reflects the other that doth pass' (Cooley, 1983, pp. 183f.). For Cooley, there is no Cartesian ego in splendid isolation, but only a field of mental relations in which others' imaginative ideas of us go to make up our own identity, while our imaginative ideas of them go to make up theirs. The individual and the community in which he or she subsists are abstractions from 'the human whole' which is 'one body' (pp. 35ff.). With his idealist metaphysic, Cooley can claim that 'the personal idea is the real person' and that 'it is in this alone that one man [*sic*] exists for another and acts directly upon his mind' (pp. 118f.).

For the behaviourist school, of which G. H. Mead was a classical exponent, on the other hand, social reality is not located in the mind but in objective social interaction. Yet in his own way Mead makes as much use of the mirror metaphor as does Cooley. All the time, Mead states, 'we are more or less unconsciously seeing ourselves as others see us. We are unconsciously addressing ourselves as others address us' (Mead, 1962, p. 68). For Mead, as for William James, 'the social self' is the only self there is (cf. James, 1890, 1, pp. 293ff.). However, for the behaviourist interpreter of society, the social self is constituted not by the interplay of mental images or ideas, but by absorbing the social roles, the vocal gestures and other significant symbols that are already 'given' in social reality. Thus, for Mead the mind is 'nothing but' 'the individual importation of the social process' (Mead, 1962, pp. 186ff.). He speaks of 'the generalized other' which is a sort of reified abstraction that stands for all the socially available influences, roles and stereotypes that impinge on the formation of an individual's identity. It is through the authority of the generalized other that the process of socialization is carried out and 'the community exercises control over the conduct of its individual members'. In this way 'the social process ... enters as a determining factor into the individual's thinking'. It is this educative, constraining, directing process that creates a coherent social whole because it constitutes 'a universe of discourse', 'a system of common or social meanings' (pp. 155f.).

In *The Call to Personhood*, McFadyen sides with the objective rather than the subjective approach, by implication with Mead against Cooley. McFadyen construes personal identity as the outcome of a process of 'sedimentation' of the individual's significant relationships. Individuality is the concrete form laid down by innumerable interpersonal transactions. Selves are located as centres of communication in the two dimensions, the two worlds of the physical and the social. 'Personhood is a social gift given in processes of social communication in which one is addressed by and responds to others' (McFadyen, 1990, p. 82). McFadyen's systems theory approach leads him to describe personal identity as 'deposited or sedimented at a point around which communication has flowed and at which information has gathered in a unique way' (p. 85). However, this identity is not fixed and static: because a person is a 'location' in a context of communication, personal identity develops as the context changes. Identity is a dynamic, evolving phenomenon.

The point where my approach is somewhat at odds with McFadyen's is where he argues that the internal structure of personhood is primarily public and only secondarily a matter of appropriation by the individual as a personal psychological complex. Concerned as I am to stress that identity can only emerge in community, I nevertheless think that McFadyen has gone slightly too far in the direction of passivity. It is at this point that his (acknowledged) debt to Harré's *Personal Being* becomes salient. Harré argues that a person is 'a cultural artefact' and that 'cognitive activities are primarily public and collective'. He insists that 'personal identity is symbolic of social practices not of empirical experiences' (Harré, 1983, pp. 20f., 212). My own instinct is to resist awarding priority to either the public or the private components in identity formation. I see them as interdependent and reciprocal, as dialectical. On the one hand, we are shaped by social patterns that are greater than the individual. On the other hand, we are actively involved in shaping the social world that we inhabit. The actual dynamic of identity formation resists both the tendency of some thinkers to social determinism and the unreconstructed reified concept of the sovereign ego against which they are properly contending.

Psychotherapy has insights to offer about the nature of salutary relationships. The therapeutic relationship is governed by an attitude of 'unconditional positive regard' (in Carl Rogers' phrase) for the client. As Freud insisted to Jung, psychoanalysis is 'a cure through love'. Others have spoken of the unique New Testament term *agape* as a factor in the therapeutic relationship (Lambert, 1973). The minimum therapeutic relationship is two people. 'There is always an other, even an Other, in the sense of a significant other. This can be the unconscious itself, the analyst, the patient, the [alchemist's] *soror* [*mystica*], the blank page for the writer, his audience for the lecturer, God for the mystic' (Samuels, 1985, pp. 17f.). However, groups can function therapeutically too (see further on this aspect, Avis, 1989). For Jung, the process of individuation cannot occur in isolation (Lambert, 1981, pp. 188ff.). It requires relationships, in which the processes of projection and introjection operate (Jung, 1954–, vol. 6, p. 448). The Jungian M.-L. von Franz speaks of 'reciprocal individuation' taking place within a 'soul family' and insists that every process of individuation presupposes relatedness to one's fellow human beings (von Franz, 1980, p. 177). For Jungians, the individuation of the person is simply a moment in the great saga of the individuation of the human race. At the individual level, the process is reflected in dreams and fantasies, with their personal constellations of symbols. At the collective level, it is reflected in the world's religious systems and their archetypal symbols. For Jung, religion is concerned with the forming of our ultimate human identity, and religious symbols are the means of forming it.

For Christian theology, redemption is not only about the salvation of the individual. It is about the life of communion in the body of Christ, the personal integration that comes from social integration. Feminist theology, especially in the work of Mary Grey, understands salvation in terms of the healing of relationships – a deeply biblical theme, as we have seen (Grey, 1989). In the ecumenical movement, unconditional mutual acceptance is the *sine qua non* of the quest for the unity of the Church. This involves the healing and reconciliation of memories. The vision of full communion or full visible unity is seen as an appropriation of *koinonia*. It is grounded in the common incorporation of Christians into Christ. In ecclesial community we find our full identity in union with Christ.

In this book relationship within community is a major theme. But it is not deployed uncritically or invoked like motherhood and apple pie. As I say later, 'community' is a much abused word, but one that we cannot do without. The communal dimension of the Church's mission, expressed through word, sacrament and pastoral care, is taken on board in a fundamental way when mission is defined as essentially ecclesial. The pastoral method in mission is expounded here as a direct response to the premium that is placed on true community in our fragmented, mobile and selfish society. The Church, in Anglicanism (but not, of course, exclusively there) always stands in relation to its social *milieu*, the structures and institutions of civil society.

Symbol and vulnerability

The idea of symbol is the golden thread that binds all this together. As I have written extensively on literary and mythic symbols in religion and theology (Avis, 1999), I will be brief here. Symbols represent *in nuce* the surpassing reality that is the goal of our quest. They not only stand for that reality, but (as Hooker, Coleridge and Tillich, notably, emphasized) they share in it, as sacraments do in a pre-eminent and unique way. They unite the particular and the universal, the empirical and the transcendent, the finite and the infinite. Symbols are vehicles of psychic and spiritual energy and like turbines (as Jung put it) they convert raw energy to constructive purposes.

Symbols actually integrate our themes. They give continuity to processes and focus systems. Symbols are the currency of identity formation both for the individual and for the community (cf. Mol, 1976). To interpret symbols in, for example, dreams is a crucial skill in depth psychology; it unlocks their integrating, healing power. Symbols embody the transpersonal values that make a community what it is and mediate the tradition, whose dynamic lies behind every community, to the present. The strength of a community's cohesion depends on the vitality of its collective symbols. These need continual maintenance and revitalization by drawing on the sources of communion. Symbol expands into myth, which comprises a constellation of numinous symbols in narrative sequence, and into ritual, which gives dramatic expression to personal and social meanings and so objectifies and reinforces them.

An understanding of the power of sacred symbols permeates the applied pastoral theology of this book: the role of images in post-modernity; the interpretation of generic spirituality; the pastoral importance of *rites de passage*. But I do not want to leave it there. By emphasizing the givenness, the objectivity of the Church's message, its means of grace and its sacred symbols, I am aware that I may be in danger of conveying the impression that the Christian mission can be carried out in a painless way, without being changed ourselves. There is another angle, that of vulnerability, that needs to be recognized at this point.

The open, dynamic and relational approach to mission has its price. The engagement with individuals, communities and nations that is entailed in mission is a recriprocal one. Sometimes they kick back. The vital self-giving of pastoral ministry involves being vulnerable. One cannot be the agent of healing without being wounded in the process. 'To fight and not to heed the wounds, to toil and not to ask for rest,' as the well-known prayer of St Ignatius Loyola puts it. 'I carry the marks of Jesus branded on my body,' claims St Paul (Galatians 6.17). Through the vulnerability and sacrifice of ministering to others at a profound level we are inevitably changed. In being changed there is the possibility of being transformed.

To be the *milieu* and agent of salvation, the Church needs to be a healing community. Clearly, so often it is not. For the sort of rapport between Christianity and therapy that I have envisioned here to become fruitful, the Church has to become even more of a therapeutic community than it already undoubtedly is – infused with the attitude of unconditional mutual positive regard and acceptance. Is this possible to any large extent while the Christian community functions signifi-cantly (as experience suggests it does) as a refuge for damaged egos, for wounded spirits – as a sort of hospital for incurables (as Luther said of marriage)? What would have to change for the Church to become more fully a therapeutic society? Just as a good marriage works over time to enable two people to sustain and cherish each other, healing the wounds of life in the process (cf. Dominian, 1987), so the Church can be a sustaining, cherishing and healing community. But this depends, among other things, on the quality of its pastoring and a grasp of the means of grace that are given to it precisely for this purpose.

When the Church talks about the healing of human identity, it invites the rejoinder *tu quoque* – or in the biblical phrase, 'Physician, heal thyself!' The Church that ministers 'for the healing of the nations' stands radically in need of healing herself. Jeremiah cries, 'I am wounded by my people's wound ... Is there no balm in Gilead, no physician there?' (Jeremiah 8.21f., REB). This is the paradox of the Wounded Healer and it takes us to the heart of Christian ecclesiology: the Church as the body of Christ still marked by his wounds on the cross. As Luther said, though in the eyes of God the Church is a pure, holy, spotless dove, in the eyes of the world (empirically, we might say) 'the Church is like its bridegroom Christ: hacked to pieces, marked with scratches, despised, crucified, mocked' (Luther, 1967, p. 262). Just as we readily affirm the true humanity of Jesus Christ who came in the flesh (1 John 4.2; 2 John 7), so too we should never seek to disguise the human frailty of his Church on earth.

It is an unchallengeable rule of psychotherapy that only those who have themselves undergone (or are undergoing) analysis can conduct analysis. First you must know your own heart. More than this: the therapist does not conduct analysis *de haut en bas*, as one untouched by human frailty, but is him- or herself directly implicated in the psychological dynamics of the therapy through the mechanism of counter-transference. Therapists have to be aware of their own reactions, alert to the emotional ecology. Those who are worth their salt are, above all, conscious of vulnerability: they know they are wounded healers.

The Wounded Healer *par excellence* is Jesus Christ. 'For in that he himself hath suffered being tempted, he is able to succour them that are tempted' (Hebrews 2.18, AV). His self-giving knew no limit. Early Christian symbolism depicts him as the pelican that, so it was believed, tore the flesh from its breast to feed its young. His very life-blood was poured out for others long before he was impaled on the cross. In his High Priestly Prayer (John 17) he speaks again and again of all that the Father had 'given' him and that he had 'given' to his own. St Mark signals this continuum of divine depletion when he says that, at the touch of the woman with a haemorrhage, Jesus was aware that power had gone out of him (Mark 6.30).

In what is intended to be a very practical, 'hands on' account of public pastoral theology in the chapters that follow, I emphasize that the ministry of word, sacrament and pastoral care is a true interpersonal engagement. In it we extend ourselves, sometimes going out on a limb. Pastoral relationships are genuinely interactive and are consequently negotiated. We feel our way in ministering to individuals – and are sometimes rebuffed. We are inevitably exposed to the gaze of the community – and that is hard to bear for some. In fulfilling a national role, we sometimes feel that we are at the mercy of the media – there is little forgiveness for our human frailties and mistakes there. In all these spheres of ministry we have to be able to manage the language of symbolism: representation by image and icon is of the essence. There is a risk we take and a price we pay. But that is no more than to be disciples of the Wounded Healer. T. S. Eliot evoked our theme in the *Four Quartets*:

> The wounded surgeon plies the steel
> That questions the distempered part;
> Beneath the bleeding hands we feel
> The sharp compassion of the healer's art.
> > (Eliot, 1974, p. 201: 'East Coker')

The paradox that is hard to stomach is that the divine touch that makes us well hurts in order to heal. St John of the Cross cries, 'Wound me and make me whole!' (Matthew, 1995, p. 23).

Always windows into reality, symbols at their highest expression may be epiphanies. This possibility leads me, finally, to speak of transformation. Therapy in a clinical, professional context applies to individuals whose personality problems prevent them from living useful or happy lives and from making sustained relationships of love and self-giving. These are the ones among us who may seek specialized counselling help or embark on analysis. However, healing in a broader sense is the ongoing process of being made whole which, we trust, applies to us all, for we all know ourselves to be incomplete. While some Christians undergo analysis or psychotherapy, others may benefit indirectly through the general dissemination of psychological awareness and insight and perhaps by participating in small group experiences. Healing is a lifelong process of personal and spiritual growth which, for Christians, is sustained and shaped by word and sacrament, supported and encouraged by Christian fellowship and pastoral care, and leads to more fruitful service of God and others.

However, the growth and change that we experience on our pilgrimage, as we are sustained by the means of grace (above all, word and sacrament) is incremental and points to real ultimate transformation. 'All of us, with unveiled faces, seeing the glory of the Lord as though reflected in a mirror, are being transformed into the same image from one degree of glory to another' (2 Corinthians 3.18). Transformation is a bold claim for how we are now, *in via*, but makes convincing sense when it refers to our ultimate destiny in Christ. That destiny includes the total healing of the human person in union with God and with Christian sisters and brothers. It entails the redemption of what drives and motivates us every day (and night) of our lives, the life force or desire (libido). William Temple wrote: 'Christian hope is the consecration of desire, and desire is the hardest thing of all to consecrate. That will only happen as you begin to think how lovely the life according to Christ is' (Temple, 1963, p. 44). Dante's experience at the consummation of his vision cannot be quoted too often: it refers precisely to the transformation, the rebirth of what is deepest, most obscure and most intractable within us.

At this point high imagination failed;

> But already my desire and my will
> Were being turned like a wheel, all at one speed,
> By the love which moves the sun and the other stars.
>   (Dante, 1981, p. 499: *Paradiso* XXXIII)

As Thomas Aquinas spoke of the *visio dei*: 'By a single, uninterrupted and continuous act, our minds will be united with God' (Aquinas, n.d., p. 65: *Summa Theologiae* 1a 2ae, 3.2 ad 4). Such transformation of human being in the presence of God, when we shall see face to face and know as we are known, when we shall be like him because we shall see him as he is (1 Corinthians 13.12; 1 John 3.2), is the ultimate, eschatological goal of Christian discipleship. But from time to time a foretaste, a first instalment, a guarantee, a pledge is granted to us now through the witness of the Holy Spirit in our hearts (2 Corinthians 1.22; 5.5; Ephesians 1.14).

3

Modernity and Secularization

Changing context: unchanging task

The essential tasks of the Church's mission are God-given. They are grounded in the Church's apostolic mandate and are, therefore, unchanging. At every point in history and in every kind of culture the Church carries out, more or less faithfully, more or less effectively, the Great Commission. It proclaims the word of God through preaching and teaching. It administers the sacraments of baptism and the Eucharist, together with other means of grace of a broadly sacramental nature, especially confirmation and the other occasional offices. And it provides pastoral care and oversight for all those who are willing to receive it. The core tasks of mission are not dependent on social variables.

However, Christian mission always takes place within a specific context – the social, economic, political and cultural reality that prevails at a given time and place. This reality constitutes the milieu or environment within which, and in relation to which, mission occurs. The specific social and cultural reality that defines the context of mission needs to be interpreted if mission is to be effective. The Church's mission (which is, of course, primarily the mission of God) is not like firing a long-range missile into enemy territory. It involves a close engagement with the texture of human life lived by individuals in particular kinds of communities and under particular social, economic, political and cultural conditions. That social reality is continuously undergoing change and development. Clearly, the Britain of the Celtic missionary-saints, the Britain of the medieval wandering Friars or the Britain of John Wesley are not the Britain of the twenty-first century. Modern Britain is frequently said to be a secular society, in the sense that faith is diminishing, the influence of the churches is declining, and religious practice is on the wane. This familiar comment is extremely simplistic.

Clarifying 'secularization'

The issue of secularization is a minefield, not only for theologians, who are not on their home ground when they try to grapple with it, but even for sociologists of religion, who are far from agreed about the meaning of the term or the helpfulness of the theory. The glib assumption is frequently made in the media that western society has become secular (in a way that is not clearly defined, but often approximates to non-religious, unconcerned with spiritual matters, this-worldly and materialistic) and is becoming more so and that this process is inevitable. There is much careless talk, about the supposedly 'secular society' in which we live in the West. This language is often adopted uncritically by religious pundits, such as bishops and other church leaders. Sometimes they are simply taking their cue from theologians. The American theologian Harvey Cox revelled in the jargon of secularization with uncritical abandon in *The Secular City*. 'Secularization is the liberation of man from religious and metaphysical tutelage,' he trumpeted. Secularization, claimed Cox, implied a historical process that was 'almost certainly irreversible' (Cox, 1968, pp. 31, 34). Now the pendulum has swung and some theologically aware social analysts point to the re-sacralization of life, the persistence of religion and the resurgence of theological issues in public debate (see Casanova, 1994; Berger, 1999).

Talk about secularization would benefit from a shot of semantic precision. This chapter attempts to clarify the meaning of secularization before asking what the implications are for the Church's role in society. But before we go any further, it is worth noting an important distinction: 'secularization' is a completely different kettle of fish to 'secularism'. Secularization is a descriptive, sociological term, while secularism stands for a militant godless ideology. Secularism was propounded by the great reductionist thinkers of the nineteenth and twentieth centuries, notably Feuerbach, Marx, Nietzsche and Freud (for a critical account of these and other

figures see Avis, 1995). Secularization can be discussed by
scholars who are Christians, such as David Martin, Grace Davie,
Robin Gill, Peter Berger and Andrew Greeley, to name but a
few.

Having distinguished secularization from secularism, we now
have to note several senses of the term 'secularization'. We can
begin with a general definition and then narrow it down a bit.
Secularization in the broadest sense is concerned with the interaction between Christianity and modernity. It can be defined
neutrally as the process of mutual adjustment between the
Christian tradition and its institutions on the one hand, and
the social forces of modernity on the other. It is important to
say that it is a process of *mutual* adjustment because the
adjustment is not merely one-sided. It is certainly not simply a
matter of Christianity being passively changed by powerful
social and intellectual forces over which it has no control.
Christianity is deeply diffused through the structures and values
of western society – its ideas, beliefs and values are sometimes
so deeply transposed into western culture that their origin is far
from obvious – and makes its own proactive contribution to
cultural change. For example, it is something of a common-
place that, through its doctrine of creation and its insight into
the human stewardship of the natural order, Christian theology
provided the ideological basis – a framework of value, meaning
and purpose – for the rise of modern science and technology,
which is, of course, a vital aspect of modernity.

Moving from this broad-brush definition of secularization, we
can now make it more precise. The term 'secularization' is
correctly used when it refers to the diminished social significance of religion, its reduced effect on public policy and social
mores, the decline in its influence and impact on our common
life. In this sense it does not imply the demise of religion, which
evidently continues to flourish, though often in the private
sphere, in voluntary groups, in the home and in the heart,
rather than as a plank of public policy and as the cement of
social cohesion (cf. Bruce, 1992).

However, the classical secularization thesis went well beyond
this more restricted usage (Wilson, 1969). It had overtones of
the eclipse of faith, the passing away of religion and the
inevitable and terminal decline of the churches. The fate of
religious practice – a sense of the transcendent, holding

religious beliefs, saying one's prayers, living in the light of God's presence – was not distinguished from the fate of historic religious institutions, the mainstream churches. (Of course, to distinguish these for the sake of clarity is not to imply that they are not connected in vital ways: one of the aims of this book is to explore these connections.) Recent re-statements of the secularization thesis (Bruce, 1992) are considerably more cautious and incline to the more modest, somewhat chastened version of secularization as the decline in the public impact of organized religion. Discussion of secularization tends to be bedevilled by a confusion between the ideological and the descriptive senses of the term.

Sacred and secular

The sacred is necessarily defined over against the secular. Sacred and secular constitute a polarity: they are inter-dependent concepts – not opposites, not contradictory, but existing in a tension. Both sacred and secular are constellations of meaning denoting significance for human life in society. They are value judgements made in relation to human well-being. In his long-forgotten *magnum opus* entitled *The Natural and the Supernatural* (1931), the distinguished Reformed theologian John Oman clarified the nature of the sacred in a way that is still helpful today. Oman showed that we know our total environment – not just the material environment, but the spiritual, moral and aesthetic environment – as *meaning*. Within the world of meaning that we inhabit, we are aware of transcendent or ultimate meaning. Oman usefully distinguished between four aspects:

- The unique *character* of the experience or feeling that ultimate meaning, discerned in our total environment, creates. He called this character the *holy*.
- The unique and unsurpassable *value* that ultimate meaning, discerned in our total environment, has for us. He termed this value the *sacred*.
- The conviction of the objective *reality* of a special kind that the ultimate meaning discerned in our total environment enjoys. He called this reality the *supernatural*.
- The need for a special intellectual *discipline* in which we

attempt to think of this ultimate meaning discerned in our total environment in a coherent way in relation to the rest of our experience. Oman identified this intellectual discipline as *theology*. (Oman, 1931, pp. 58ff.)

Oman recognized Rudolf Otto's contribution to the under-standing of the holy in Otto's classic work *Das Heilige* (ET *The Idea of the Holy*: Otto, 1959), where Otto coined the term 'the numinous'. But Oman disagreed with Otto's interpretation of the numinous. It was true that, as Otto had pointed out, the oldest strata of the Old Testament understood the holy in terms of a mysterious dread, a non-ethical awe, rather than in moral or ethical terms of goodness or righteousness. However, Oman believed that Otto's celebrated definition of the numinous as *mysterium tremendum et fascinans* was a restricted notion of the holy because it was by definition divorced from the ethical realm of human life. Oman insisted that humanity transcends primitive irrational and non-moral awe in moments of reverence, when we acknowledge the sacred. The valuation springing from awe is not the only valuation we place on ultimate reality and ultimate meaning, Oman insists. There is also the valuation springing from reverence and this designates the sacred.

> If it is a feeling which is wholly directed towards our own advantage, it is not the sense of the holy: if it has to do with incomparable value, to which desires, convenience and profit must be subordinate, in the presence of a reality before which one may not seek his own pleasure or walk after the imagination of his own heart, it is. (Oman, 1931, p. 62)

The sacred, asserts Oman, means 'absoluteness of value, that which is of incomparable worth . . . not merely super-excellent, but that which may not be brought down and compared with other goods' (p. 65). The relation between the holy and the sacred was not linear and could travel both ways: the sacred valuation could follow or precede the experience of the holy. 'We value things because they appeal to our feelings, but we also feel about them largely as we value them.' However, Oman is inclined to hold to the general primacy of the sacred: 'More frequently perhaps than any other feeling, the sense of the holy follows and depends on its value' (p. 66).

Though, for Oman, the sacred is certainly not the whole of religion (there is the experience of the holy, the conviction of the supernatural and the theological evaluation of this), he affirms the interpenetration of religion and the sacred: 'Everything that is sacred is in the sphere of religion, and everything in the sphere of religion is sacred' (p. 69). This insight is suggestive for our project in this book. Today the sense of the sacred remains significant, while the public profile of institutional religion has declined. Where the sense of the sacred persists, religion survives, albeit in less public and structural forms.

'Secular' literally means 'of this age [*saecularum*]'. To that extent, to say that society is secular is a truism. What else could it be? It cannot belong to any age but its own. But in common parlance secular means something more. The sense has been extended from 'of this age' to 'of the world, wordly, natural' as opposed to 'of another world, spiritual, supernatural'. From the Christian point of view, there is nothing intrinsically objectionable about this. Christianity affirms the value and integrity of the natural sphere as God's good gift of creation and sees it as the presupposition of the working of divine grace. In this sense secular and sacred belong together, like nature and grace, reason and revelation, immanence and transcendence. Sacred and secular are not inherently opposed but go hand in hand. As David Martin has said, 'There is almost nothing regarded as religious which cannot also be secular, and almost no characteristics appearing in secular contexts which do not also appear in religious ones' (Martin, 1969, p. 3; see his analysis of the range of meanings of secularization in ch. 4). We need another word for what is opposed to the sacred. It is not so much the secular that is opposed to the sacred, as the *profane* – literally, what is outside, excluded from, the temple.

Secularization was not originally a value-judgement term. In medieval times it had a political meaning and referred to the export of aspects of social life from the control of the Church. It stood for the loosening of the ties that bound human life in all its activities to the supervision of the clergy. Later, under the impact of the industrial revolution and the capitalist economy, that process intensified through the process of the differentiation of various spheres of society (see below). The absence of coercive clerical control is intrinsically bound up with secularization but that certainly does not make it equivalent to the profane. Clerical direction of life, backed by sanctions, has virtually disappeared in the West. In a plural society, lay people ultimately decide for themselves whether they will accept clerical teaching and direction (that does not mean that there are not religious traditions and mores that still exert a significant influence). But the sense of the sacred remains strong. So what is secular, in the sense of being beyond the immediate reach of church authority, can become consecrated to a holy purpose by the free choice of individuals and groups, since all human activities can be devoted to the glory of God. The Chief Rabbi, Jonathan Sacks, quotes with approval the rabbinical saying, 'The secular is what is not yet holy' (Sacks, 1991, p. 98). The whole created, natural order has the potential to be brought into the service of the kingdom of God and made subject to God's final (eschatological) purpose.

Historical roots of secularization

How did this promising non-dualist evaluation of the secular as the 'potentially sacred' emerge in the theological tradition? To answer this question, we need to go back to St Augustine of Hippo and other western Fathers. One aspect of Latin patristic theology's legacy to the Middle Ages was a dualism of earthly and heavenly, natural and spiritual, the earthly city and the city of God (an idea reflected in the title of Augustine's *De Civitas Dei*). Humanity's God-given destiny was to be redeemed from the earthly city and brought into membership of the city of God. But, unlike the early sectarian, millennarian movements such as Montanism and Donatism, Augustine had not at all condemned the earthly, natural sphere in which the elect were called to live out their temporal existence. He had, in fact, rather neutralized it and left it ready for development, for occupation, we might say. During the early Middle Ages, the earthly, natural realm provided the location for prophetic hopes for a universal Christian regime (*imperium*). It was thus strengthened and freed from dependence on the spiritual realm. To this development some have traced the origins of secularization (Pocock, 1975, pp. 42ff.; Markus, 1970).

One aspect of this secularization process (in the sense of affirmation of this world and of the natural side of life) consisted of a reaction against the inordinate claims of the sacred as it was institutionalized in the Catholic Church. For example, the 'Carolingian renaissance' of the late eighth and early ninth centuries in Charlemagne's empire can be seen as an attempt to achieve a baptismal regeneration of the whole of medieval society, to create an ecclesiological empire. Where ecclesiastical dominance had been strongest, in the areas of government and administration, a reaction began that derived its inspiration, not from the Bible or from canon law, but from models of classical antiquity and Roman law. It was a movement to recognize the validity of a purely human 'unregenerate' society, freed from ecclesiastical constraints. Gaining confidence from the study of classical literature, it began to fill the vacuum created by the theological dualism of earthly and heavenly.

It is at this point that historians detect the beginnings of civic humanism, a movement that was not in essence anti-Christian but certainly anti-scholastic and fundamentally opposed to the hierarchical character of medieval sacral society. Against the absolutist theological worldview that orientated the whole of human existence in this world to one transcendent focus, located in the world to come, and consequently devalued the natural life of human beings (recreation, sexuality, marriage, family life, daily work, artistic creativity), civic humanism affirmed the validity and intrinsic worth of the natural (*naturalia*), the human (*humana*) and the this-worldly (*mundana*). This assertion of the autonomy of the natural order is regarded by distinguished interpreters as of the essence of medieval humanism (Southern, 1970, p. 57).

It is significant, however, that it was still within the Christian worldview that the thinkers of the central Middle Ages made a space for these natural, human and worldly things. They implicitly reasserted the immanence of God in the world and redressed the balance between nature and grace. St Thomas Aquinas articulated this reassessment of the natural theologically, following on from the interest that his teacher Albert the Great had shown in natural phenomena, in physiology and psychology. 'Precisely because Thomas rehabilitated natural man, his doctrines can be said without fear of gainsaying to constitute the opening bars of renaissance humanism' (Ullmann, 1977, p. 100). The case of Aquinas serves to remind us that a positive attitude towards civic life and the affairs of this world was not the sole prerogative of the humanists: scholastic philosophers and theologians also contributed to the growth of a civic mentality (Seigel, 1968, p. 241).

The inspiration that stemmed from classical antiquity was focused in the figures of Aristotle and Cicero. The rediscovery of Aristotle's political thought in the first half of the thirteenth century provided a complete secular theory, a legitimization of humanism with its twin pillars of the natural ends of human life and the non-religious foundations of society. Together with Aristotle, Cicero was the greatest influence on civic thought: he not only provided a theoretical expression of the humanist ideal in his writings, but also embodied in himself what it meant to live the unadulterated life of the natural man in his *vita activa* as citizen.

In this development of medieval thought, a space was made for the secular as referring to the natural realm in its integrity. But when you make room for the natural or secular alongside the sacred you thereby alter the character of the sacred. It is no longer all-encompassing; it does not absorb into itself such areas as scientific knowledge and natural causation. It becomes chastened and purified and learns to acknowledge limits. It becomes disentangled from magic which is the mixture of the sacred and the scientific.

Desacralization?

In *The Decline of the Sacred in Industrial Society* Acquaviva usefully distinguishes between 'secularization' and 'desacralization'. Secularization, on this account, is 'the rejection of the magical use of the sacred', while desacralization is the loss of the capacity for experiencing the transcendent, the 'Wholly Other' (Acquaviva, 1979, p. 35). This suggests the interesting possibility of seeing secularization as a salutary reform of an abuse of the sacred – bringing our use of the sacred into line with our scientific knowledge of the natural world. For some, it will imply an unpalatable curtailing of the supernatural, but most will probably agree that magic – the manipulation of sacred power for partial or selfish purposes – is no true part of the sacred. Desacralization, in Acquaviva's sense, is another matter. He identifies not merely a rationalization of the magical use of the sacred – secularization – but also a decline in the human capacity to experience the sacred at all. He detects a fading away of the perceived presence of the Wholly Other and seems personally to regret this:

> From the religious point of view humanity has entered a long night that will become darker and darker with the passing of the generations, and of which no end can yet be seen. It is a night in which there seems to be no place for a concept of God, or for a sense of the sacred, and ancient ways of giving significance to our existence, of confronting life and death, are becoming increasingly untenable. (pp. 201f.)

This gloomy prognostication seems to blur Acquaviva's own distinction between the decline of religious practice and the loss of the sense of the sacred. The fact that there has been a significant reduction in overt, Christian religious activity in the West is unchallengeable. As Acquaviva himself puts it: 'Everywhere and in all departments, the dynamic of religious practice reveals a weakening of ecclesial religiosity and, within certain limits, of every type of religious belief, including belief in God' (p. 83). But it is a fallacy to deduce from the decline of formal religious practice and orthodox Christian belief in Western Europe that, even there, modern people have lost their sense of the sacred.

Religious awareness flourishes in many forms, especially in the private and personal sphere. In the 1960s Luckmann claimed in *The Invisible Religion* that this was already true in the United States. 'The effective social basis of the modern sacred cosmos', Luckmann claimed, 'is to be found in neither the churches nor the state nor the economic system... [It] is characterized by the direct accessibility of an assortment of religious representatives to potential consumers' (Luckmann, 1967, p. 103). That may have been true of the United States then (though it was somehow largely contained within the churches) but it is becoming increasingly the case in more conservative societies such as that of Britain. The decline of ecclesiastical dominance of the sacred – the clerical policing of the transcendent – has been matched by a flowering of unofficial expressions of religiosity. Beckford points out that, while the public bases of religion have been eroded in advanced industrial societies since the 1960s, religion and spirituality 'have survived as relatively autonomous resources'. They still retain the ability to symbolize 'ultimate meaning, infinite power, supreme indignation and sublime compassion' (Beckford, in Wilson, 1992, pp. 22f.). Beckford suggests, therefore, that religion has been evolving into a 'cultural resource' instead of a social institution and comments that 'the deregulation of religion is one of the hidden ironies of so-called secularization' (p. 23; cf. Cox, 1982, p. 266).

Is secularization inevitable?

Some proponents of the secularization thesis seem to assume that the process of secularization (in the broad sense of the weakening of Christianity in the face of modernity) will continue remorselessly. Callum Brown, though a critic of classical theories of secularization, predicts the complete demise of Christianity in Britain. He achieves this conclusion by extrapolating the drastic indicators of decline since the early 1960s (Brown, 2001). In fact, there is no steamroller inevitability about the secularization process, in Britain or elsewhere. The theory that assumes this inevitability is prescriptive and ideological. The extrapolation of past or even current trends is fraught with peril. Sociologists are not prophets. The facts of religious history will not fit this Procrustean bed (Turner, 1993, pp. 3f.). The picture is much more complex, a shifting pattern of light and shade, secularization and sacralization (Woodhead and Heelas, 2000). Mundane, demographic factors, as well as cultural, ideological factors, can be decisive in religious decline (Gill, 1989, pp. 61ff.). Several topical examples substantiate this point:

In the United States 95 per cent of the population believes in God and 98 per cent says its prayers; about 40 per cent of the population attends church on Sundays and 60 to 70 per cent claims a religious affiliation. Moreover, indicators of religious belief and practice have changed minimally over the past half-century (Greeley, 1989) This example alone shows decisively that science, technology, urbanization and modernization do not necessarily lead to the decline of religious practice. It may well be, as Casanova and others have suggested, that the absence of a state-sponsored monopoly religion in American history is significant for the vitality of religion in that country. For, as Casanova argues, 'It was the caesaropapist embrace of throne and altar under absolutism that perhaps more than anything else determined the decline' of institutionalized Christian religion in Europe (Casanova, 1994, p. 29).

The power of the Roman Catholic Church in the heavily industrialized areas of Poland where Solidarity operated, and the influence of the Orthodox Church in other communist countries, during the collapse of the Soviet empire, show that religious vitality that is latent at the margins of society under a hostile ideology can kindle into action and assume centre stage at crucial times of transition. Then religious communities reveal themselves as custodians of continuity with a nation's past and bearers of hope for the future. Sacred symbols become the vehicles of a sense of common purpose infused with value (Martin, 1996).

The resurgence of religion at the turn of the twentieth century, in the forms of international militant Islam and American Protestant 'Moral Majority' fundamentalism, to become major political factors, both nationally and internationally, calls into question the assumption that modernization leads inevitably to the privatization and marginalization of religion (cf. Casanova, 1994). While this fact does not invalidate all aspects of the secularization theory with regard to Western Europe, it does call in question the inevitability and universality of secularization. Islamic and Protestant forms of fundamentalism do not evince this emancipation of public doctrine and social patterns from the tutelage of the clergy and religious norms, and the relegation of sacred values to the private worlds of individuals, families and voluntary organizations. In militant Islam the mullahs are the agents of theocratic rule, and in Protestant fundamentalist churches the ministers maintain a tight curb on morals.

Globalization and re-sacralization

The relationship between globalization and secularization and the possibility that globalization may actually counter the effects of secularization, generating a phenomenon that has been dubbed re-sacralization, needs to be considered here. The portmanteau word 'globalization' essentially denotes the heightened political, economic and cultural interaction between societies (see further on globalization Giddens, 1998; Baylis and Smith, 1997; Sedgwick, 1999, ch. 4; Raiser, 2002). Such intensified interaction means that boundaries – not just frontiers, but boundaries of time and space – are weakened through the effect of instant communication and rapid travel. Globalization refers to 'processes whereby social relations acquire relatively distanceless and borderless qualities' (Scholte, in Baylis and Smith, 1997, p. 14). The interaction of societies affects their sovereignty and autonomy: sub-state and supra-state structures of governance mediate and disperse the authority vested in the sovereign state. The result is that political and economic policies become common to many states in a similar stage of economic and social development. The economic consequences of these aggregated policies are like juggernauts sweeping poor, vulnerable, underdeveloped economies and political units before them (for a collection of Christian responses see Reed, 2001).

But the impact of globalization should not be exaggerated. It has not abolished time and space. Jet-lag is still an uncomfortable reality! The negotiating and sharing of sovereignty is no new thing: treaties, alliances, tutelage and satellite status are as old as history. The dynamics of nationalism are at least as powerful today as they ever were, and states still guard their sovereign rights and cede sovereignty reluctantly and in small doses where it is in their interests to do so. Globalization is offset by trends to 'localization' and regionalization (sub-state and supra-state politico-economic arrangements). The identity of late-modern humans may be shaped by consumerism as a global phenomenon (see Sedgwick, 1999), but small-scale forms of identity will not be crushed and will re-emerge in other channels – religious, cultural or national. Globalization should not be identified in an ideological way with an irresistible process of universal homogenization. Paradoxically, global economic forces can provide an opportunity for the assertion of local distinctions. Cultural difference can be marketed as a commodity (Harvey, 2000, p. 66). Globalization does not imply the end of the nation state. Although the authority of the nation state becomes modulated by global factors, there is a sense in which its role becomes more crucial than before (cf. Avis, 2001, pp. 88f.). As David Harvey has recently argued, the liberal, consumerist society can only work if the state penetrates more deeply and in a more interventionist way than under classical capitalism, into parts of national economic life (Harvey, 2000, p. 65). For example, the state is required to adopt a proactive role in relation to immigration issues, in defence of the environment and against the threat of global terror.

Globalization is more complex and paradoxical than some journalistic treatments allow. Western liberal-democratic values, tied to a free-market economy, are not solely responsible for common economic patterns the world over. The so-called tiger economies of the Far East, linked in some cases to non-democratic or inadequately democratic regimes, torpedo this glib assumption. Electronic communication can link you up across the globe, but it only touches a minute proportion of the world's population. Globalization can even be debunked as the latest phase of western imperialism (cultural and economic). While the economic realities are real enough, especially to nations caught up in a spiral of debt, the ideological and rhetorical connotations of this inflated term should not be overlooked.

Having said that – having, as it were, put globalization in perspective – it remains true that efficient, cheap and instantaneous forms of communication, with their economic, political and cultural consequences, may actually serve to activate trends which revitalize religious identities and the values that sustain them and that they sustain. Beyer has argued that 'the global system corrodes inherited or constructed cultural and personal identities; yet also encourages the creation and revitalisation of particular identities as a way of gaining control over systemic power' (Beyer, 1994, p. 3). The resurgence of religion can be a way of asserting the identity of a faith community, which in turn is a way of competing for a place in a global system. The phenomenon of globalization is significant for religion, for religion is generally acknowledged to have a special affinity with particular local identities, and traditional religions are intimately linked to defined cultures: they are bearers of the sense of wholeness of a community. As those cultures are relativized within a global context, religious traditions fight back to maintain their influence and claims (Beyer, 1994, pp. 3–9; cf. Robertson, in Beckford and Luckmann, 1989, ch. 1).

These considerations do not dispose of all the issues raised by the secularization thesis, but they do undermine any assumption of the inevitability – what some writers have called the 'myth' – of secularization. In 'Secularization: A Contemporary Myth' (1969), Luckmann argued that the term secularization 'encapsulates a historical narrative which contains a number of fictitious elements... based on tacit assumptions about the course of history that predispose us to look at contemporary society and culture in a highly selective and perhaps distorting manner'. Luckmann designated the theory of secularization as an element in 'the mythology of modern society'. It was 'largely fictitious' and in effect 'camouflages the nature of religion in the contemporary world' (Luckmann, 1983, pp. 125f.). Basically, Luckmann argues that the two historical narratives associated with the theory of secularization – that of a golden age of religion in the past and that of a progressive liberation of humanity from the shackles of priestcraft and superstition – are both mythical. As for the first, there never was a golden age: the 'primitive fusion' of religion and social structure is a postulate of the pre-modern world. As for the second, although social structures no longer reinforce religious belief and practice, these are still sustained in the private sphere of the individual and group. As Luckmann puts it, 'the individual is not secularized' (p. 132). Luckmann could not have anticipated the post-modern twist to these modern developments. But, as we shall see in the next chapter, the breakdown of the social and cultural structures of modernity in post-modernity has created a new space for the re-emergence of the sacred.

The sources of secularization

So we should resist any global, unnuanced judgement, such as we hear so often, that we live in a secular society or that the process of secularization is continuing with steamroller inevitability. While religious practice, according to various traditions, is still significant, and a majority of the population accepts the core beliefs of Christianity and many others hold dear certain 'sacred' values (all points to be substantiated in the following chapters), we cannot be said to live in a fully secular society. It is true, however, that there are strong forces of secularization at work in our midst. The term 'a secular society' refers to a state that we have not yet reached and may never reach, but the concept of 'secularization' refers to a process that has made powerful inroads into our culture.

What factors lie behind this development? There is no simple answer to that question. 'Since there is no unitary process of secularization one cannot talk in a unitary way about the causes of secularization' (Martin, 1969, p. 16). However, it would be widely agreed that, to the extent that it has shaped today's world, secularization is a consequence of modernity. It eventuates from a cluster of socio-economic factors in developed societies (Chadwick, 1975; Bruce, 1992, pp. 8ff.; Beckford, 1989). What then, within modernity, are the deep socio-economic sources of secularization as we have defined it: the reduced public impact of institutional religion?

The differentiation of society

The differentiation of society refers to the long-term process of the diversification and specialization of the various institutions that service and regulate our lives. To use the language of systems theory, this process can be seen as a function of the progressive complexification of society as a system. The separating out of institutions, as they increasingly specialize in a particular area of social life, means that society can handle the destabilizing effects of change brought about by the influence of the environment. Systems theory suggests that complex systems need time to process information and come up with appropriate responses. Not all subsystems can be embroiled in change at once. The differentiation of institutions within a society can be seen as replicating internally, many times over, the difference between a system and its environment, resulting in numerous subsystems each with their own environment, constituted by other subsystems, each interacting with the other but preserving its own sphere. This process of progressive differentiation and complexification militates against shared beliefs and common assumptions, reducing them to highly generalized symbolic 'meanings' or reducing them to a cognitive framework that is local, ephemeral and private (Luhmann, 1982, pp. 230, 248).

How does this process of institutional differentiation affect the Church? Institutional religion shares the same fate as other institutions in a society characterized by a high degree of structural complexity: it too becomes differentiated out and institutionally specialized (Luckmann, 1983, p. 130). In the past, the Christian Church was responsible for forms of community service and social control – such as education, medicine, poor relief, moral discipline and leadership in the community. These functions have since become distributed through various social institutions, leaving the Church largely to its more immediately spiritual functions. That is not to suggest that the churches have withdrawn from community service, ministry to the poor and those on the margins of society, but only that statutory provision – inadequate though it may often be – is the ordinary means by which society administers such areas, the churches operating as the junior partner in the form of voluntary effort.

This relativization of the Church's social role offers the temptation to retreat to a purely 'spiritual' message and to collude with the marginalization of Christian witness. But that is not the only possible response. In an institutionally differentiated society the churches as institutions must fight their corner. They must play a full part in civil society. Where they are established (that is to say where they are recognized in some sense by the state and have corresponding pastoral obligations and opportunities) they need to hold the state to its part of the bargain (without overplaying their hand) and be proactive in the partnership, demonstrating in a public way that they have much to offer to the well-being of society.

The dispersed organization of social life

In the not too distant past, people's lives were organized, to all major intents and purposes, at the local rather than at the regional or national level. Local units, based on the parish, had the Church at their centre. For historical reasons, the Church instinctively understands locality and relates to people as individuals, families, congregations or parishes. Education, health care, work and leisure were locally circumscribed. Now they are structured nationally and regionally. Here the Church is not as strong or as well organized as it is at the local level, and consequently it finds it difficult to make its influence felt on policy. Many people are employed by national or international corporations and the decisions that affect their well-being are made at a distance. Vast numbers of commuters travel far from their homes to work. These factors take people out of the immediate sphere of the Church's influence for some of the most crucial aspects of their lives. How can the Church make contact with them outside of home and community? This question points to the importance of a national profile and corresponding national resources for the churches, so that it is able to engage with major social, political, moral or educational issues. It also underlines the crucial role of sector ministers and chaplains as the authorized representatives of the Church (see Legood, 1999).

Impersonal technology and communications

An industrial society, one that is typical of high modernity, subsumes the individual into the requirements of its macro-structures. He or she becomes merely a cog in a complex machine of production, distribution and exchange. This depersonalization can become intensified by 'post-modern' systems of communication. Our present increasingly post-industrial society – which seemed to hold the key to greater freedom and scope for the individual – may prove to be equally hostile to the well-being of individuals. Where information is mainly transmitted electronically, the personal factor in communication is once again at a premium. Both modernity and post-modernity, then, militate against the interdependent nature of traditional, pre-industrial patterns of work and sociality centred on the local community.

However, it is characteristic of the Church that it addresses people as persons at the deepest level of their being. Its ministry is conducted in the dimensions of truth, beauty and goodness: the truth of divine revelation and adequate human interpretation; the beauty of liturgy, music, vestments and architecture; the goodness of moral discipleship in the Christian community (see on this theme, Avis, 1999). Clearly, Christianity stands for an attractive alternative to the impersonal forces that are now dominant. In this context the Church needs to put its best foot forward. That means developing activity that builds trust, forges relationships and contributes to real experiences of community. It means getting out, being visible, occupying public space and engaging in matters that concern and motivate people.

These three areas of socio-economic development have brought about a changed situation for the churches in society. The three factors are continuing to contribute to the fragmentation of human life and the loss of integration and well-being. They play their part in the break-up of moral communities with their traditions of belief and practice, and in the consequent privatization of values, including religious values. The first casualty of these processes is the reality of community; the second is religion in its public manifestation, its institutional form. Religious and ethical values depend on moral communities that generate, legitimate and sustain those values (MacIntyre, 1985; Gill, 1992). When communities lose their cohesion and break down, due to economic and social pressures, corporate life, infused by shared values, suffers accordingly until new forms of community are generated to fill the vacuum.

Aspects of modernity

The three major sources of secularization that we have identified – differentiation of institutions, the society-wide organization of services, the increasingly impersonal nature of our human relations – manifest themselves in a number of ways that are typical of modernity. The distinction between sources of secularization and aspects of modernity is not watertight, but is adopted here for greater clarity. So let us now look briefly at six aspects of modernity: toleration, urbanization, privatization, geographical mobility, individualism, and competition in worldviews.

Toleration and relativism

The privatization of moral values and religious beliefs in modern society could be regarded as the culmination of the gradual process of extending toleration that began in the seventeenth century and continued until the late nineteenth century with the admission of atheists to Parliament (see further Avis, 2001, pp. 63–7). Given the reservations of some Christians about tolerance considered as a virtue, we should note straight away that toleration is simply a necessary political strategy. It is not actually a viable cognitive stance. An attitude of tolerance on the part of an individual does not imply acceptance of all beliefs (which is manifestly impossible), nor even necessarily a relativistic scepticism about the attainability of truth. On the part of a state, toleration is a strategy for maintaining unity, the opposite of the oppression or persecution of minorities. Of course, there are ideological overtones. The emergence, in the wake of the religious wars of the seventeenth century, of laws providing toleration for dissenting religious or political groups has led to toleration for individuals whatever their private convictions and however antisocial these might be if put into practice (e.g. anarchists). As Chadwick puts it, 'From the moment that European opinion decided for toleration, it decided for an eventual free market in opinion' (Chadwick, 1975, p. 21).

We need not concern ourselves here with the various causes of toleration – weariness with religious conflict, concern for the cohesion of the realm, the desire to trade freely, the need to make common cause against an external threat. But we should note that the principle of toleration received a Christian justification from the sanctity ascribed to conscience and the value accorded to every person created in the image of God. Therefore, as Chadwick points out, Christian conscience was the force that began to make Europe secular (Chadwick, 1975,

p. 23). The plural state is the non-confessional state: it gives scope under the law for all sorts of belief systems to flourish. Even if, as in the United Kingdom, the state has a Christian foundation in the established churches and the relation of the monarchy to these, it sees this not as a reason for discriminating against other peaceful religious groups, but precisely as the ground for sheltering them.

Urbanization and faith in the city

'The rise of urban civilisation and the collapse of traditional religion,' claimed Harvey Cox in his celebration of secularization and urbanization, *The Secular City* (first published in 1965), 'are the two main hallmarks of our era and are closely related movements' (Cox, 1968, p. 15). The alienation of working-class urban dwellers from the Christian Church is now massive, but is not altogether a new phenomenon. It was first identified statistically in the 1851 national census. The interpretation of this and other statistics has recently been challenged by Callum Brown (Brown, 2001). His point that different variables must be distinguished within the same set of findings is well taken. Social, economic and gender variables tend to be conflated when speaking of the urban masses. But Brown's case, that the bulk of church membership was composed of working-class people, does not substantially affect the point that the vast majority of the working class was unchurched. Because urban working people comprised the largest section of the population, the phenomenon of a largely unchurched population inevitably centred on them. The testimony is cumulative and convincing.

In 1865 William Booth, troubled by the fact that the urban masses not only did not attend the parish church but did not darken the doors of Methodist chapels either, had launched the 'Christian Mission to the Heathen of Our Own Country' in a tent at Whitechapel. When, at the end of the First World War, the Enabling Act of 1919 established representative government for the Church of England, Bishop Hensley Henson deplored the dearth of active participation that the Church Electoral Rolls revealed: an electorate of one-tenth of a population of about 35 million and a communicant constituency of even less – 2.5 million (Henson, 1929, pp. 9–11). After the Second World War, when church attendance was actually buoyant, the Archbishops' report *Towards the Conversion of England* (1945) lamented 'the drift from religion' and the fact that 'only a small percentage of the nation today joins regularly in public worship of any kind' (presumably the latter phrase is meant to include non-Anglicans) (Church Assembly, 1945, pp. 2f.). In the early 1980s, David Sheppard, Bishop of Liverpool, warned: 'It is impossible to exaggerate the gap between very large numbers of urban working class people and the organised Church' (Sheppard, 1983, p. 218).

The linkage identified by Cox and many others between urbanization and religious decline cannot easily be denied; yet it is not causal. Callum Brown and others are right to challenge any determinative link between urbanization and secularization. Secularization is not an inevitable consequence of urban living, as we see in Islamic cities such as Tehran or Islamabad, to look no further. In the USA, where up to 70 per cent of the population claims a religious affiliation, actively religious people are clearly not confined to rural areas. The Methodist report *The Cities* points out that urban Methodists seemed to have no difficulty in identifying themselves as simultaneously Christians and city people. 'While the apparent conflict between the spiritual and secular nature of the city is a major preoccupation of academic theologians,' the report continued, 'it is an issue which most Methodists in [British] cities today seem to have resolved for themselves in living their daily lives' (Methodist Church, 1997, p. 54). In the English inner cities, while the historic denominations may be struggling, the Black-led churches are filling the vacuum. Their members are evidently not ashamed to speak of their faith in daily life or to read their Bibles on buses or sitting on park benches. The fact is that all public institutions, not just the historic churches, are ignored in working-class areas (Sheppard, 1974, p. 314). Black communities may have more durable social networks simply because, as an ethnic minority, Black people have been compelled to preserve their identity.

Already slightly more than half of the world's population lives in cities (for an introduction to urban growth, urbanization and urbanism, with material on the global city, see Clark, 1996; on the global city, see Sassen, 1991). While exponents of urbanism predict an urban future for the vast majority of humankind by the middle of the twenty-first century, politicians and planners in Britain are becoming concerned by urban haemorrhage, the flight to the countryside, and plans for urban regeneration are being drawn up. The picture is not all one-sided and both the causes and the consequences of urbanisation are complex.

The fact remains, however, that urban living tends to dissolve the structures – both social and cognitive structures – that support Christian existence. When pluralism is combined with the concentration of population in urbanization it produces what Berger calls 'cognitive contamination'. As long as individuals are faced with one prevailing set of beliefs and values (cultural norms), these take on the quality of inevitability, a worldview that is taken for granted. The cultural interaction of the urban environment undermines this certainty (Berger, 1992, p. 68). Urban life is also subversive of traditional, stable, defined communities, where physical boundaries such as rivers, roads and hills are still significant for identity and there is continuity from one generation to another. In cities, where there is little sense of given, fixed boundaries, but life is fluid and mobile and anonymity prevails, parish boundaries are fragile, congregations are partly or largely eclectic and therefore the traditional social parameters of the mission of a particular congregation are weak.

The former Archbishop of Canterbury, Dr George Carey, tells of a missionary to an Islamic country, who when asked whether he was yet reaping a harvest of souls, replied that he was not reaping a harvest, neither was he yet even sowing the seed; he was still picking the stones out of the ground! Though churches may have to work very much harder in urban areas to create the groundwork of Christian community, there is no inevitability about religious decline in cities, as Cox seems to assume. There are many beacons of hope, flourishing inner-city churches, and radical forms of mission that are effective. These have seized the opportunities of social renewal, community action and the healing of broken lives as the basis of urban mission. The alienation of urban, working-class people from the Church can be overcome in many cases by steadfast, unconditional love and pastoral care. We should ask ourselves why Jesus' ministry was so largely to the poor, the alienated, the outcast, the mentally scarred and spiritually afflicted, those cut off from the community of the people of God (Israel) and suffering the consequences, but who found a new home and family in the community of Jesus' disciples. There is a living experience of redemption and a vibrant Christian spirituality in the city. (See 'Church and Community' in Chapter 7, below, and cf. Northcott, 1998; Morisy, 1997; Bradbury, 1989; Beesley, 1997; Marchant, 1999; Rowland and Vincent, 1995, 1997, 1999; Duffield, 1997. For American examples see Carle and Decaro, 1997).

The privatization of faith

The pluralism promoted by toleration had the effect of relativizing religious belief in the urban marketplace, that is to say, of undermining the credibility of exclusive claims to salvation. The increasing privatization of sacred values represents a further step from relativization to fragmentation. Privatization of religion means that 'religious language, religiously based assumptions about the world and religiously legitimated moral principles have become the preserve of committed minorities, rather than being part of the taken-for-granted assumptions of society as such' (MacLeod, in Young, 1995, p. 4).

Pannenberg has commented (1989, pp. 29ff.) on the way that the pluralization of social institutions has contributed to the privatization of values. The function of integrating the diverse aspects of the world we experience (embodied in the plurality of institutions), which used to be performed by religion, can no longer be accomplished in the public world (or worlds) of secularized culture. Instead, Pannenberg suggests, integration depends on the individual in the private sphere, mainly the family. But, he goes on, family life cannot stand the strain of being the centring, integrating factor in life. Longevity also puts strain on marriage, as marriage now lasts (potentially) longer than ever before in human history and the partners pass through many changes of scene and inner development. The pressures of urban living have fragmented the private sphere also. Broken marriages and disrupted families are casualties of advanced industrial practices. What continues to elude us in both the public and private spheres is a coherent world of meaning and value, worthy of our ultimate commitment and which can sustain us through the vicissitudes of modern living. Hopelessness and alienation mark many lives, especially among the young (cf. Barton, 1996). A word of qualification is in order here. Privatization is not necessarily equivalent to atomic individualism. We have not yet reached the point where every individual legislates values for him- or herself (though one could be forgiven for jumping to that conclusion). That would be privatization taken to its logical conclusion. Privatization may refer to the appropriation and domestication of values by groups within society. The extreme form of privatization of values in America has been typified by Bellah *et al.*, in *Habits of the Heart*, thus: '"Values" turn out to be the incomprehensible thing that the individual chooses when he or she has thrown off the last vestige of external influence and reached pure, contentless freedom' (Bellah *et al.*, 1986, pp. 79ff.). Bryan Wilson characterizes privatization as 'a manifestly libertarian phase in the development of religion... shorn of social control, divested of its cultural connotations, released from its institutional contexts, and liberated from its erstwhile social functions' (Wilson, in Repstad, 1996, p. 33). Elsewhere Wilson has claimed that the continuing role of religion in the public domain is merely 'a lingering rhetorical invocation in support of conventional morality and human decency and dignity – a cry of despair in the face of moral panic' (Wilson, in Hammond, 1985, p. 19).

However, privatization is far from complete even in Britain and is certainly not the only fate of religion in the modern world. Religion is a political player on the world stage in the form of militant Islam, the nation of Israel (though Israel is not a confessional state), the tensions of the South Asian sub-continent, the global political influence of Pope John Paul II, and so on (cf. Casanova, 1994; Beyer, 1994). But privatization is certainly a crucial facet of religion in Western Europe, America and the developed world generally. Its dominance is almost unassailable. It is grounded in Enlightenment assumptions, 'mandated ideologically by liberal categories of thought which permeate not only political ideologies and constitutional theories but the entire structure of modern Western thought' (Casanova, 1994, p. 215).

Upwardly and outwardly mobile

More than thirty years ago the sociologist of secularization Bryan Wilson referred to the churches' 'mobile clientele' and pointed out that the churches, like local authorities, operated on the unreal assumption that people live in identifiable, stable communities (Wilson, 1969, pp. 55f.). I do not think that the churches need to make that assumption – they would be burying their heads in the sand if they did. But it is another matter to claim, as I do in this book, that the churches have an interest (for heaven's sake, human beings have an interest!) in communities with roots, communities that have continuity and communities where mutual support is provided. The economic and social advantages of mobility must be balanced against the blessings of genuine community. Social and geographical mobility, for economic and recreational reasons, has increased apace since Wilson's comments and is subversive of traditional communities – as dwindling Sunday schools on pleasant summer Sundays testify. But there are contrary trends making for greater comparative stability: general economic uncertainty; dual-income families, where one job move means two; shortage of property in prosperous south-east England and the potential negative equity trap for some homeowners.

Research indicates conflicting effects of social mobility on behaviour and attitudes. On the one hand, mobility favours innovation, cosmopolitanism and the exchange of ideas and experiences. On the other hand, it diminishes human intimacy, weakens the hold of traditional moral values and promotes individualism. Both social mobility (being 'upwardly mobile') and geographical, 'outward' mobility (moving house, changing jobs, recreational use of the car) weaken the ties between the individual and community and leave him or her on the periphery. For some this produces withdrawal and isolation; for others it is a spur to get involved. A feeling of rootlessness can lead to compensatory participation in religious organizations. Berger and Luckmann use the rather alarmist language of a 'precarious private universe' in 'a world of radical subjectivism' (see Hornsby-Smith, 1987, pp. 68–88, citing Sorokin, Tumin and Berger and Luckmann).

Harvey Cox made a bold bid to reclaim mobility as a biblical ethos. Pointing out that 'people on the move spatially are usually on the move intellectually, financially or psychologically,' Cox recognized that mobility plays havoc with traditional patterns of religion. 'It separates people from the holy places. It mixes them with neighbours whose gods have different names and who worship them in different ways.' But the Bible tells of a nomadic, homeless people, whose God went with them and is active not in place and space but in time and history. Therefore, 'the Bible does not call man to renounce mobility, but to "go to a place that I will show you"' (Cox, 1968, pp. 66–71). Notwithstanding what I will have to say later about the merits of genuine community: where mobility is an inescapable fact, patterns of mission and of pastoral care can adapt and sector ministries become all the more vital.

Individualism and atomization

The decline of institutional religion and of the impact of religion on the public structures of society is related to the process of the privatization of values – that is to say, to moral and religious individualism (which is not necessarily completely atomic but includes the clustering of individuals in small groups of like-minded people). Bruce, like Wilson an advocate of the secularization theory, claims: 'If we have to pick one single element of modernization that is central to understanding the nature of modern religion, it would be that which explains the rise of the sect, the tolerance at the heart of the denomination, and the amorphous nature of the cult: individualism' (Bruce, 1995, p. 134). Though many people still have religious convictions at this strange cultural juncture of ours, they tend to regard them as their personal and private concern. They generally underestimate the extent to which their beliefs are communicated to them by a tradition and sustained by the socialization provided by a coherent community. They often assume that one's religion is purely a matter of personal choice.

In his comprehensive study of the New Age movement, Heelas identifies the sacredness or divinity of the self as the central tenet and links it with 'unmediated individualism' and the commanding authority of direct individual experience (Heelas, 1996, pp. 2f., 21; see also Bellah *et al.*, 1986, ch. 6, on radical individualism in America). (The absolute value of the self, combined with atomistic individualism, is fertile soil for the reappearance of belief in reincarnation – a tenet that is called into question by the Christian belief in the communion of the saints and the resurrection of the body.)

The trend to individualism has deep historical roots. It is short-sighted to think of the Renaissance as the first great flourishing of individualism and of the Romantic movement as the second. In respect of the value placed on the individual the fifteenth century was anticipated by the twelfth. And even the twelfth century was the beneficiary of early medieval feudalism which, on account of its system of reciprocal rights and obligations, provided a seedbed for the idea of individual citizenship (Ullmann, 1967, ch. 2). In the high Middle Ages, however, it was the challenge of social change that precipitated an upsurge of individual awareness (Morris, 1972). In a Christian society, that new awareness inevitably found expression in a concern for right motivation (the notion of intention) and led to a stronger emphasis on the practice of sacramental confession (penance). Autobiographical writings began to appear in the twelfth century. In the wake of the intense subjectivity of St Augustine's *Confessions* (Augustine, 1961), more than half a millennium earlier, some of those caught up in the movement of monastic renewal expressed their strong sense of vocation in accounts of their inner struggles. We find a widespread tendency among the intelligentsia to examine and publish personal experiences – the story of Peter Abelard's disastrous romance with Heloise, his *Historia Calamitatem*, being perhaps the best-known (Abelard, 1974). In biography the eleventh and twelfth centuries saw a move away from the stylized portraits of the saints, which were largely exercises in typology, to a greater recognition of the variety and individuality of human nature. The unique characteristics of, say, Dante or Petrarch were also treasured. However, the modern concepts of unique individuality or selfhood are anachronistic when applied to the Middle Ages. Individuals were not separated from their group or community and the development of the person is always seen in relation to God and in connection with models or traditions of spirituality (Bynum, 1982, pp. 82–109). It seems worth taking to heart that the Enlightenment and Romanticism – so often pilloried for all the ills of modernity – are not solely responsible for the radical individualism of western culture.

In fact it was counter-Enlightenment political thinkers who attacked rampant individualism (for the citations that follow, see Lukes, 1973, pp. 3ff., 13ff.). Well before the French Revolution of 1789, Edmund Burke pronounced: 'Individuals pass like shadows; but the commonwealth is fixed and stable' (1780). Saint-Simon and his followers used the term *individualisme* to refer to what they regarded as the pernicious, corrosive and subversive ideas of the revolutionary age and accused the thinkers of the Enlightenment of 'preaching egoism'. In 1834 the reactionary publicist Louis Veuillot stated: 'All for each, each for all, that is society; each for himself, thus each against all, that is individualism.' In *Democracy in America*, de Tocqueville developed the connection between individualism and democracy. He warned of the danger of individuals withdrawing into private life, among family and friends, and abandoning public concerns and responsibilities. The logical outcome of this retreat from the public sphere to a private enclave, de Tocqueville asserted, was sheer egoism. What was needed to prevent this was a strong texture of civil society, made up of all the institutions that mediate between the isolated individual and the naked power of the state.

It is widely recognized that the idea of the supreme intrinsic value of every human person derives from the Christian faith, from the New Testament and particularly from the Gospels. The concentrated attention – a combination of compassion and affirmation – that Jesus bestowed on such individuals as Jairus, Zacchaeus, the woman with the issue of blood, the woman at the well, Mary and Martha, the man born blind, the beloved disciple, and many others, has burned into human consciousness. But the Bible also speaks, in its concepts of *ekklesia* and of *koinonia*, of the supreme value of true community. As we shall note in Chaper 7, Scripture does not separate the person from the personal relations that bind him or her into a community, and it sees that community as destined to reflect the fullness of the life of God. The blame for runaway individualism should not be laid at the door of Christianity. There is no divorce of private and public in biblical faith. Christianity certainly treasures the uniqueness of every individual, but its message is 'for the healing of the nations' and the regeneration of the cosmos.

However, the prevalence of individualism, both as an ideology and as a social reality, needs to be qualified. Even in the modern rationalized society (which is now undergoing change), presupposed by sociologists in the Weberian tradition, such as Bruce himself, individualism is not untrammelled and free-floating – contrary to the prevalent myth of the free, unattached and uncommitted self. It is actually heavily institutionalized by the constraints of the social life-course. This runs from early socialization, through education and the gaining of qualifications, through a career or careers, to a predictable retirement and pension for those whose services are no longer required as producers by the economy. This life-course is mapped out by society, and all its members, to one degree or another, have to conform to it. The constraints of the life-course are weakening in late modernity and Giddens suggests that life-course is being replaced by the individualistic notion of 'lifespan' (Giddens, 1991). But the authors of *Habits of the Heart* have a point when they insist that even today's individualistic life-course is still constrained by 'a larger generational, historical, and, probably, religious context' (Bellah *et al.*, 1986, pp. 81ff.).

In a pastoral context, typical English reticence on matters of deep personal feeling compound the general trend towards individualism in western society, as far as this country is concerned. Visiting clergy cannot count even on parishioners whom they know well, being willing to air serious matters of faith. As Helen Oppenheimer has put it (with a nice mixture of anatomical metaphors), English people 'know in their bones that it is not a good thing to wear their hearts on their sleeves' (Oppenheimer, 1986, p. 53). The general privatization of human values that has accompanied the loosening of social bonds, the mobility of families and fragmentation of traditional social groupings has been keenly felt in religion. You can only invite and encourage; arm-twisting is counterproductive.

The marketplace of faiths

The historic, mainstream churches have undergone overall decline for nearly a century, but personal religious belief and commitment to transcendent values persist outside the ambit of the churches. This paradox reflects the current erosion of commitment to all public institutions and voluntary organizations. Active participation in the life of the Church is a function of community participation as such. The degree of stability and permanence in community structures and of the traditions that undergird them is perhaps the most decisive variable factor affecting the fortunes of religion in its public practice. Bryan Wilson calls religion an 'ideology of community'. All voluntary organizations, whether political parties, trades unions or football clubs, have suffered from reducing support in recent decades. Where awareness of community is strongest – in the villages and market towns – commitment to the Church is strongest. Where community spirit is weakest – in the inner cities – commitment to the Church is weakest. Neighbourliness may continue to flourish, but community identity and its structures are in decline, taking the churches with them.

Twentieth-century developments in patterns of recreation, the institution of the 'weekend' and the leisure culture have transformed the role of the churches in society from a constitutive one to a peripheral one. A constitutive institution is one which is organic and fundamental to society, helping to determine the very nature and structure of the community in which it is placed. A peripheral institution, on the other hand, is one which is not determinative of the community in which it is placed, but merely serves a community which exists independently of it. To survive, it must find ways to serve its clientele. Participation is optional; competition with other agencies, also seeking custom, is intense (cf. Gilbert, 1980, p. 92). A peripheral, serving institution must be able to offer a desirable, marketable commodity or disappear. As Berger says: 'The key characteristic of all pluralistic situations... is that the religious ex-monopolies can no longer take for granted the allegiance of their client populations... As a result, the religious tradition, which previously could be authoritatively imposed, now has to be *marketed*. It must be "sold" to a clientele that is no longer constrained to "buy"' (Berger, 1973, p. 142). Now Christians believe, naturally, that the gospel is a highly attractive 'product' for which there will always be a demand. But the voluntaristic character of religious affiliation today implies that the product must be energetically promoted, attractively presented and reliably serviced.

This line of argument leaves Christians uneasy. The suggestion that salvation is a product to be marketed rightly encounters resistance from believers who hold that the Christian message carries the authority of divine revelation and demands to be accepted in the obedience of faith. Marketing the gospel is a metaphor that has its uses but can be taken too far. Regrettably, perhaps, the Christian faith is sometimes seen by those outside the Church as a commodity, competing for custom. It therefore has to make its way in a competitive situation. In the post-modern dissolution of metanarratives (to be discussed in the next chapter), one master-narrative survives: that of the commodification of the human life-world. Commodification forces everything into the perspective of the market. It reduces everything to the same level, that of a saleable item whose value depends on whether it is chosen or not. It is not so much the product that is important on its merits but the purchasing process. This now begins to acquire a religious charge: with the advent of shopping as a Sunday activity for families, shopping malls are sometimes plausibly compared to religious temples: blessings are desired, rituals are performed, sacrifice is offered, absolution is received (Boeve, 1999; Sedgwick, 1999). Let not revulsion at this travesty of worship blind us to the reality that the Christian Church faces stiff competition in the marketplace of faiths and must be presented as persuasively as possible.

4

Post-modernity and Fragmentation

Encountering post-modernity

A few years ago I attended a retreat for clergy at Abbey House, Glastonbury. Between services, addresses, reading and silent meals, I wandered through the town and surrounding countryside – the fabled Isle of Avalon. Like St Paul in Athens (Acts 17.16ff.), I marvelled at the 'shrines' of various faiths, both old and new. The town of Glastonbury brings together in vivid contrast the ancient, pre-Reformation tradition of the Christian Church in England and the latest expressions of New Age 'spirituality'. The visitor can wander through the impressive ruins of the Benedictine Abbey, which held out against Henry VIII's and Thomas Cromwell's dissolution until 1539 when the last abbot, Richard Whiting, was hung, drawn and quartered (for treason) at St Michael's church, now a ruin, on the Tor overlooking the town and abbey. Glastonbury is still a place of pilgrimage for those Anglicans who particularly treasure the pre-Reformation heritage of the Church of England – a church that Anglicans once fondly traced back to St Joseph of Arimathaea.

At the same time, because of its supposed connection with King Arthur and the twilight Celtic world of pre-Christian myth, Glastonbury is a Mecca for New Age devotees who make their own kind of backpacking pilgrimage in ones and twos, together with those who gather here *en masse* for the annual pop music festival. The spiritual requirements of New-Agers are catered for by several shops providing New Age artefacts, souvenirs and aids to reflection. One that made me smile was styled something like 'The Archangel Gabriel Emporium for Personal Interplanetary Ascension'. It displayed in its window gruesome little models of wizards – those primeval gurus – that lit up when plugged into that quintessentially modern facility, electricity. With St Paul, I was 'distressed to see that the city was full of idols', even though some of them had surely been placed there tongue-in-cheek. It was a relief to come to a shop called 'The Orthodox Way'. Alas, the Orthodox priest was obviously struggling to make it a going concern and had supplemented the revenue obtained from books and candles, and so on, with some rather inferior mass-produced icons, not qualitatively superior to the New Age wares down the road.

In desperation, I turned to the parish church. It seemed immaculately cared for and I looked forward to seeing what ministry and literature it offered to tourists and New Age pilgrims who might well turn in to a sacred place. I was baffled to find the gates in the churchyard railings securely locked, so that one could not even reach the church. It turned out, on enquiry, that this was intended to prevent such pagan practices as making love on the tombstones in broad daylight! Whatever the reason for making church and churchyard inaccessible in such a place of pilgrimage, it raised acutely for me the question, where is the mission of the Church in this stark juxtaposition of old and new, Christian and pagan? The melting-pot of cultures, the dissolving of paradigms, the melting away of frameworks and the substitution of personal choice and individual preference is of the essence of post-modernity.

Identifying post-modernity

'Post-modernity' is a word much bandied about but less frequently defined. It is an elusive concept that slips through one's fingers. Part of the slipperiness lies in the fact that the meaning of post-modernity depends largely on the prior definition of modernity. But there is more to the problem than that. Post-modernity is *inherently* difficult to define because the cultural epoch that it represents is intrinsically unconducive to stable definitions and clear distinctions. Difference, yes, but distinctions, no. Differences are dynamic, shifting, kaleido-scopic. In difference, images are constantly juxtaposed and continually moving away. Differences fragment but distinctions cohere. Samuel Taylor Coleridge spoke of the ability of a subtle mind to distinguish without dividing. Distinctions imply a stable benchmark against which meanings can be tested. But it is in the nature of post-modernity that such benchmarks are not thought to be available. Nevertheless certain persisting features of post-modernity can be identified amid the flux.

Suspicion of worldviews

Post-modernity is corrosive of the great overarching themes ('metanarratives') sustained by religions, philosophies or worldviews that provide a sense of purpose and meaning for the self and for society as a whole. For Christianity these architec-tonic themes include: the biblical salvation history as an unfolding drama; the ideas of divine providence and theodicy (the vindication of God's just purpose in the face of evil); the kingdom of God, both already present and still to be fulfilled; and the mission of the Church as a continuous event stretching from Pentecost to the Parousia. Post-modernity tends to demolish, to deconstruct modern notions of time, space, substance and identity that structure such frameworks of meaning. The spatial order predominates over the temporal and absorbs it into itself ('spatialization' – a major theme in Pickstock, 1998) thus putting linear, purposeful, teleological notions of human and social existence at a premium.

This suggests, incidentally, that a striking phenomenon that is often thought to belong to post-modernity, the cluster of beliefs, attitudes, values and group practices dubbed the New Age, is not truly post-modern. In the New Age movement there is an overarching communal (rather than cultural) metanar-rative that is experiential and everywhere exhibits the attributes of inwardness and timeless wisdom. New Age is therefore better seen as an intensification of modern expressivism, going back to the Romantic movement's reaction against Enlightenment analytical and cerebral thinking (cf. Heelas, in Flanagan and Jupp, 1996, p. 70).

It is actually less than accurate to typify post-modernity (if that is where we are) as resistant to all metanarratives. It has its own metanarratives, as it and every epoch must have. For example, as Terry Eagleton has commented: 'Post-modernism tends to be dogmatically monist about pluralism' (Eagleton, 1996, p. 127). Post-modernity's glib dismissal of metanarratives itself deserves to be suspiciously scrutinized. As Eagleton astutely asks: 'Which parts of modernity has post-modernity left behind? All of it? The notion of human equality along with the idea of historical progress? The emancipation of women as well as of the working class? The belief in individual freedom as well as in the sovereignty of Reason?' (Eagleton, 1996, p. 43).

Post-modernity's selective suspicion of metanarratives and the 'big picture' is immediately threatening to Christianity because the Christian faith works with metanarratives (a coherent theology) and finds its identity in an overarching story (the biblical drama of salvation history). This suggests that though post-modernity creates a space for the re-emergence or even resurgence of the sacred (see below), the Church in its gospel mission cannot collude with all the conditions that post-modernity lays down. But, we may well ask, is the Church in a position to bargain and temporize with post-modernity? Is not post-modernity the inescapable condition for the mission of the Church today? The answer to that extremely pertinent question is to be found in the relation of post-modernity to modernity, that we shall turn to in a moment, and in the very substantial carry-over from modernity that constitutes post-modernity. It is highly questionable whether Christians can welcome post-modernity with open arms. Christianity cannot renounce its metanarratives. What it can and should do, however, is first to acknowledge the element of cultural contingency in all the diverse expressions of Christian meaning and secondly to go on to explore ways in which the Christian message can be accommodated (to use a patristic and Reformed expression) to the diverse and fragmentary cultural contexts in which it finds itself so that it can speak to them and to those who inhabit them.

Choice and consumerism

A major legacy of modernity is the dominance of global capitalist economies which both create and service global consumer markets. Post-modernity represents an intensification of the capitalist consumer economy in the direction of insatiable demand for choice upon choice. The end of free choice is not goods themselves, but choice for its own sake. The desire that is thus gratified is itself culturally created. The goods craved by avid consumers are themselves designed to stimulate further consumer desires. In the process, the idea of choice and the act of choosing are debased. As Rowan Williams points out, choice makes us what we are, it limits and defines us. Choice shapes identity. It involves loss as well as gain. Every act of choice shapes the direction of future choices (cf. Williams, 2000, pp. 22ff.).

Under the reign of consumerism, the economy is no longer seen as serving such erstwhile great and worthy (though at the same time ideologically suspect) modern causes as material progress, the subjugation of nature, even the dream of eliminating poverty and ignorance. Instead, it is governed by the imperative of instant consumer gratification, where choice has become an end in itself and is delivered through the proliferation of shopping complexes and malls, superstores and online shopping. The toxic combination of consumer gratification and experiential immediacy is generated by the mass media that are geared to deliver both.

Although some clergy have attempted to respond to the demand for immediacy – notoriously in the total sensory experience of the Sheffield Nine O'Clock Service – the wisdom of the Church is suspicious of the craving for immediacy of experience and the instant gratification of our desires. It knows with Newman that the great acts of God take time to unfold and that the mills of God grind slow, though they grind exceeding small. Selfhood and identity cannot emerge without the passing of time. Rowan Williams posits the grim prospect of 'a world of timeless consuming egos, adopting and discarding styles of self-presentation and self-assertion' as the logical outcome of post-modern consumerist culture (Williams, 2000, pp. 49f.). The clock ticks slow in God's workshop, but it never misses a beat.

My own pastoral experience (confirmed by Finney, 1992) suggests that individuals and families journey to faith over an extended, sometimes a protracted period and that the faith whose foundations have been laid down over time is the most enduring, the least likely to fall by the wayside. The blessings of the Christian life cannot be grabbed from the shelves. They are reserved for those who have been faithful in discipleship: they are the ones who will enter into the joy of their Lord. But that is a tough and unfashionable proposition to put to enquirers and seekers. There is a huge deviant evangelistic industry that denies that truth and offers instead a gospel of prosperity, of material reward and social success as the result of faith – a capitulation to the consumerist ethic if ever there was one.

Self-authenticating experience

Post-modernity is characterized by a loss of faith in what Karl Popper called 'objective knowledge', including knowledge in science, ethics and theology. The Enlightenment's faith in public, universal criteria of rationality – a faith that motivated and sustained the achievements of modernity – has crumbled. It looks rather more attractive now that we have lost it. Post-modernity assumes the self-authenticating validity of individual and small-group subjective experience. Doctrines that are believed to be objectively true do not really belong to the post-modern experience of the sacred. It does not occur to the seekers of these experiences that they might be subject to any public canons of rationality.

In post-modernity, sacred 'commodities' (clusters of symbols from various traditions, different paths of spirituality) can be sampled without being believed in. The integrated, systematic nature of received religious beliefs, with their base in a specific moral community, resists this superficial approach. Pop culture reflects an inane, uncritical subjectivization of truth along the lines of: You tell me your truth and I'll tell you mine (I paraphrase only slightly).

The mission of the Church, however, rests on a conviction of the givenness and abiding validity of the Christian gospel, grounded in the biblical witness to divine revelation. It requires a confidence in the abiding truth of Christian faith. This is compatible, I believe, with a recognition of the huge diversity or plurality of creative expressions of Christian belief and a full awareness of the disagreements and conflicts that are evident between Christian churches and individuals. It is the task of Christian theology to reflect on what is fundamental, of the essence, at the centre and of enduring validity in Christian belief – 'the faith of the Church'.

Juxtaposition of cultural forms

In post-modernity, images, styles, artefacts, from past cultural periods and from completely other cultures, are juxtaposed. Thus cultural juxtapositions are both diachronic (across time) and synchronic (contemporaneous). In architecture, art, literature and music cultural forms are eclectic and free-ranging. Post-modern culture in its extreme form is like a museum in which the departments – Egyptology and the Second Empire, medieval European and *art nouveau*, Victoriana and aboriginal culture – are jumbled up. The selection of items is not according to recognized 'objective' cultural canons but according to individual predilection, 'whatever turns you on'. 'For the modernist, all has to be new and different from what went before. By contrast, postmodernism is the appropriation of, and impulse shopping from, the entire supermarket of western civilisation' (M. York, in Flanagan and Jupp, 1996, p. 50). Together with the cultural *mélange* goes an emphasis on rhetoric, rather than reasoning, the manipulation of ideas and images rather than logical argument. Even allowing for the limitations of analytical, discursive reason, as we have appropriated it in the post-Enlightenment western tradition, is this arbitrary juxtaposition of cultural furniture compatible with a commitment to truth, to intellectual integrity?

Imagination in knowing

Post-modernity espouses an alternative rationality. It is disillusioned with the epistemological legacy of the Enlightenment, its privileging of analytical, positivistic, instrumental modes of knowing (which, though they certainly do not exhaust Enlightenment epistemology, have won out over Kantian and Romantic alternatives). Post-modernity, assisted by the quintessentially modern critical theory of Horkheimer and Adorno which turned analytical reason back on itself reflexively, to undermine itself (Horkheimer and Adorno, 1973), believes that this legacy has led to a profound alienation from the world and from the self. As a result, reason is thwarted in attaining its most obvious goal and, furthermore, cannot deliver that playful pleasure in the creativity of form, movement, colour and life that is one of the hallmarks of post-modernity. Instead, post-modernity has rediscovered the possibilities offered by visual images and by myth and fantasy. Its world is made up of signs that are valued for themselves. Post-modernity loves to give free reign to this creative play in all sorts of combinations and juxta-positions. It revels in the *frisson* generated by bizarre or ironical combinations.

The other side of the coin, however, is that post-modernity (or at least postmodernism) has little interest in attempting to evaluate the truth-bearing potential of these figurative genres. It has little patience with attempts to construct a realist (albeit *symbolic* realist) epistemology, one that makes connections or builds bridges between statements and reality. For post-modernity the world of signs is sufficient unto itself. It is not inclined to ask – it lacks the metaphysical confidence to ask – what is that ultimate but elusive reality which may be inadequately signified and pointed to in metaphor, image and myth.

Christian theology has also been captivated by Enlightenment rationalism. It is equally evident in the dominantly analytical and logical approach to Christian beliefs of Evangelical fundamen-talists and conservative Catholics, on the one hand, and in the sceptical reductionism of liberal modernists, on the other. The post-modern return to creative imagination and to the power of the image, for all its nihilistic lack of discipline, presents an opportunity for the Christian artistic imagination, coupled with rigorous theological evaluation and defence of Christian truth claims, to present the Christian *mythos* – the constellation of revealed symbols in narrative sequence – in a fresh and attractive way (for a full account of the points in this section see Avis, 1999; cf. Blond, 1998).

Loss of hope

Post-modernity evinces a loss of hope and a sense of helplessness and apathy about the future. It lacks confidence, optimism, verve with regard to planning for a better world. The centre of gravity is spatial rather than temporal, static not linear. The metanarratives of modernity that inspired hope and gave a purpose to human endeavour are discounted, leaving a sense of helplessness to control human destiny, the future of humankind (see Bauckham and Hart, 1999). With its loss of teleological perspective, post-modernity lives for the moment, revelling in immediate sensory experience and (among the more sophisticated) intellectual *jouissance.*

Into this vacuum of hope, the Church's mission pours the gospel that brings renewal and transformation and the building of a more whole human experience in community (*koinonia*). But the post-modern malaise has infected the churches too and they desperately need a renewed vision of God's purposes for the world, centred in Jesus Christ, a vision grounded in a rediscovery of the resources of Scripture and of the power of the gospel. The original eschatological framework of the Gospels and the ministry of Jesus should not be deleted, so that the Christian message becomes a timeless philosophy of life without a direction. Though biblical eschatology needs careful interpretation and its imagery should certainly not be taken with crude literalness, it should be re-appropriated in such a way as to retain the dynamic and momentum that is grounded in the biblical revelation of the faithfulness of God to God's own just and good purposes. This alone gives hope.

Threat to Christian faith

There is a distinction to be drawn between the challenge of modernity and the challenge of post-modernity to Christianity (see Thiselton, 1995). Modernity's reductionist critique of Christianity (in Feuerbach, Marx, Nietzsche and Freud) postulated that faith in God was an illusion and called into question the basic truth of Christianity. For these seminal modern thinkers the affirmations of Christian theology were grotesque distortions of desires and longings of which we are not fully aware. Christian beliefs were a projection onto a spuriously objective screen of unresolved conflicts within the individual psyche (Freudian neuroses) or within the social structure (Marxian ideology) (for a critical exposition of the reductionist challenge, see Avis, 1995).

Post-modernity's challenge to Christianity is even more lethal, if that were possible. According to Christian belief, the self or soul is created in the image of God and redeemed for eternal communion with God. But the extreme form of post-modern culture – postmodern*ism* as a self-conscious practice, with its antecedents in Nietzsche and its most subversive expression in Derrida – regards the self as an illusion (on Nietzsche, see Avis, 1995, ch. 4: 'The Implausible Antichrist'). It challenges the very meaning of the Christian faith as salvation history (a metanarrative if ever there was one). It erodes the notion of truth itself, so undermining the possibility of divine revelation and the doctrinal exposition of revelation.

Room for the sacred

Paradoxically, the threat to Christian faith is not post-modernity's last word. For whatever else it may entail, post-modern at least means post-secular. As we have seen in the previous chapter, the phenomenon of secularization is the specific form in which modernity impacts on Christianity. The eclipse of the Enlightenment's faith in the autonomy of human reason seems to leave a space for the emergence of the sacred (cf. Berry and Wernick, 1992). With this recognition of the space claimed by the sacred, we see that with regard to post-modernity, we are not talking about the same world as described by secularization theorists. Post-modernity may be seen as a movement that goes beyond the modern in a way that retrieves possibilities from the pre-modern (traditional) world that lingers on here and there, in fact much more extensively than we often suppose. Of course this can always be dismissed as a case of 'the return of the repressed' and not all manifestations of the sacred are necessarily salutary (Lyotard, 1984; Ward, 1997, p. xxv). However, a greater openness to the sacred, a recognition of the claim that the sacred dimension makes on us, provides the Church with opportunities for evangelism which we can begin to explore in a moment.

Post-modernity and modernity

It would be useful now to establish some clarity about the relation between modernity and post-modernity. Each of these is elusive in itself and the connection between them is slippery also. The clarification of the distinction between modernity and post-modernity is complicated by the tendency of the discussion to shift from descriptive statements about cultures to prescriptive statements about values. There is a difference between modernity and modernism, and between post-modernity and postmodernism. Post-modernity is a period concept; postmodernism is a philosophical position (Ward, 1997, p. xxiv).

Modernism as a programme and an ethic is an embracing of the possibilities opened up by modernity and its economic expression, capitalism. Modernism is motivated by the positive pole within the creative–destructive polarity of capitalism (see below for this idea). Postmodernism as a programme and an ethic is an embracing of the possibilities opened up by post-modernity. Postmodernism is motivated by the negative pole within the creative–destructive polarity of capitalism. Modernism is an ideological orientation to making, building and unifying and to the primacy of structure and form. Postmodernism is an ideological orientation to dissolving, fragmenting, multiplying and the primacy of spirit and the components that are the playthings of spirit. As Ecclesiastes reminds us, there is 'a time to break down and a time to build up ... a time to cast away stones and a time to gather stones together ... a time to get and a time to lose' (Ecclesiastes 3.1-8). Robin Gill brings out the distinction between modernism and postmodernism as cultural dynamics:

> Modernism homogenises; postmodernism fragments. Modernism promotes a functional, bureaucratic and uniform society; postmodernism fosters a pluralistic and diverse society. Modernism attempts to reduce all to rational and centralised control; postmodernism abandons control and promotes eclectic variety, even anarchy. (Gill, 1992, p. 57)

Our concern in this book is not, as far as we can help it, with postmodern*ism* as an ideology, a stylistic preference or set of (ironically be it said) 'values' that may be espoused, but with post-modernity as a cultural epoch within which the Church's mission is now pursued.

The defining characteristic of modernity, its uniqueness, lies in confidence in the human power to change and control the social, economic and political order – and to do so precisely in the light of universal criteria of rationality. Rex Ambler usefully defines modernity as 'the historic attempt to gain freedom and autonomy for man by gaining control over nature and society, first by understanding them analytically, then by manipulating them technologically and organizationally' (Ambler, in Flanagan and Jupp, 1996, p. 142). Modernity therefore fosters the great and powerful religious organizations, the denominations, which both support and control their members, but at the expense of stifling spontaneity and authenticity through homogenization and regimentation. The powerful forces at work in modernity produce alienation for individuals because human beings cannot be treated indefinitely as though they were not part of nature and society but automata, cogs in a machine. Society is not a machine but a living organism made up of individuals, families, communities, and these by nature resist stereotyping and regimentation.

The various aspects of modernity that we identified in the previous chapter are intensified in post-modernity.

- *Toleration* of different belief systems within a common political framework for the sake of peace and harmony in modernity becomes ideological relativism in post-modernity. This categorical relativism has lost the belief in the possibility of belief and in the possibility of systematizing belief. 'Postmodernism presupposes a super-liberalism, more pluralistic, more tolerant, more open to the right of difference and otherness' than modernity (Benhabib, 1992, p. 16).
- *Urbanization* in modernity, with its loss of communal roots and therefore of traditions, is intensified in post-modernity into cultural homelessness and anonymity. Cultural homelessness is exacerbated by the decline of civil society, of medium-scale structures that sustain identity, the erosion of institutions with their traditions and authority (in the jargon of the sociologists: detraditionalization and de-institutionalization).
- *Privatization* of values in modernity – their export from the public, societal level of legitimization to the private, domestic and recreational level of validation – is taken to its logical conclusion in post-modernity. It then becomes

mere ethical solipsism in which there is no reference point of moral value beyond the desires and demands of the individual and the individual's chosen peer group.

- The geographical, demographic *mobility* in modernity that enabled people to 'better themselves', to fulfil their legitimate aspirations and to promote their careers mutates in post-modernity into sheer rootlessness and loss of identity as social classes are levelled and career structures crumble.

- *Individualism*, which made the self with its demands and rights central to modernity, becomes a sad sort of solipsism in post-modernity. Individuals, who should be affirmed and set free to contribute to the common good, are denied meaning and value and become uncentred sites for a series of fleeting sensations.

- *Competition* between churches as they vie for custom in the conditions of modernity has been overtaken by the commodification of the sacred in post-modernity. This retails the sacred in a 'deregulated' way bypassing the approved channels of ecclesiastical structures in a religious bazaar, a 'free for all'.

The mission of the Christian Church cannot collude with the acids of post-modernity. We used to use the expression 'the acids of modernity', but modernity now looks comparatively benign. Christian theology can recognize common ground and common interests with modernity, even in the absence of a common framework of beliefs and values (cf. Fergusson, 1998). Above all, Christianity cannot baptize the post-modernistic dissolution of the self, of community and of reason. While, as Pohier has suggested, following Kierkegaard, God can be found and encountered 'in fragments' (Pohier, 1985), the purpose of the gospel is to recreate a whole person in a whole community. In the ecumenical theology of *koinonia* we speak of 'bonds of communion'. These are the beliefs, narratives, rituals, and disciplines (seen theologically as means of grace) that bind us together in a living community where we are accountable to one another. Post-modernity knows no accountability. Individual or group self-expression is self-authenticating. The rainbow of spiritualities invites no boundaries or bonds. But these constraints are indispensable, nevertheless. As a perceptive person put it in response to a presentation of mine on this theme, in Joseph's amazing technicolour dream coat, the button-holes were still essential!

Thus it becomes more and more apparent that post-modernity is simply a dynamic within modernity, an intensification of modernity. This is presumably why David Lyon uses the terms 'high modern', 'hyper-modern' and 'metamodern' rather than the term 'post-modern' (Lyon, 1998, p. 282). Vattimo follows Nietzsche and Heidegger in asserting that post-modernity cannot escape from modernity because it cannot overcome modernity with its own weapons. All it can do is to dwell uneasily and subversively within modernity, twisting modernity's grand conceptualities against each other. Moreover, trapped within modernity as we are, there can be no systematic analysis and description of post-modernity, since that would be to reinforce the systematic reason typical of modernity and so counteract the solvent acids of post-modernity (Vattimo, 1991)!

As Giddens has argued, we are moving into a period in which 'the consequences of modernity are becoming more radicalized and universalized than before'. According to Giddens, so-called post-modernity is actually a radicalization of modernity. Through the process of self-clarification of modern thought, modernity is enabled to reflect upon itself critically and so to engage in a continuous process of revision. This reflexivity is the key to modernity for Giddens: all forms of cultural expression are inherently subject to self-criticism, feedback, analysis and revision (Giddens, 1990, pp. 3, 36, 39). This is akin to the assimilation to information technology pointed out by Lyotard, who agrees that the post-modern is 'undoubtedly a part of the modern'. What then is its salient characteristic? 'All that has been received, if only yesterday... must be suspected' (Lyotard, 1984, p. 79). The hermeneutic of suspicion, of reductionist critique, employed by Feuerbach, Freud and Marx against particular identified targets (philosophical and religious in the case of Feuerbach, psychological and religious in the case of Freud, and socio-economic and religious in the case of Marx: see Avis, 1995) has mutated into the Nietzschean hermeneutic of *baseless* suspicion – suspicion without a cause – that is all-consuming.

Giddens has claimed that what is characteristic of modernity (and I am including the post-modern in this as an intensification of the modern) is not the embracing of the new for its own sake, but the presumption of wholesale reflexivity, including reflection on the nature of reflection itself (Giddens, 1990, p. 39). Giddens's insight leads us to ask whether this inescapable, all-devouring reflexivity is not a function of economics, of the conditions of production in capitalism. Some modernists clearly revel in the industrial and artistic creativity that, like God, has the power to 'make all things new' (Revelation 21.5), even when they find that these things are as ephemeral as the traditions that they supplanted. Marshall Berman writes of modernists that they can, in a striking phrase of Hegel's, 'look the negative in the face and live with it'. The fact that 'all that is solid melts into air' is a source of strength and affirmation, not of despair. If everything must go, then let it go: modern people have the power to create a better world than the world they have lost (Berman, 1992, pp. 33, 35).

The echo of Marxist tradition ('all that is solid melts into air') in this quotation from Berman offers a useful clue to the nature of modernity and its radicalization in post-modernity. The context in *The Communist Manifesto* is, naturally, concerned with the dynamics of capitalism as in constant economic, social and political ferment. Marx and Engels argued that the bourgeoisie could not exist without constantly revolutionizing the instruments of production, and thereby revolutionizing the whole system of relations in society. 'Constant revolutionizing of production, uninterrupted disturbance of all social conditions, everlasting uncertainty and agitation distinguish the bourgeois epoch from all earlier ones' (Marx and Engels, 1967, p. 83).

The creative destruction (if I can get away with this oxymoron) of all social artefacts, including (we might point out) forms of cultural expression such as images and narratives, is the result of the process in which capitalism continually devours its products in order to reproduce itself in new modes of infinite variety:

> All fixed, fast-frozen relations, with their train of ancient and venerable prejudices and opinions are swept away, all new-formed ones become antiquated before they can ossify. All that is solid melts into air, all that is holy is profaned, and man is at last compelled to face with sober senses his real conditions of life and his relations with his kind. (Marx and Engels, 1967, p. 83)

It is as though capitalism has two magnetic poles of equal strength, the positive, creative, productive pole and the negative, destructive, consuming pole. Culture – the arts and media – is caught up into this continual process of industrial regeneration. Jameson claimed that post-modernity is basically the cultural logic of late capitalism, in which the production of culture has become incorporated into general commodity production. On this basis, Harvey suggests that, in order to sustain its markets, capitalism has been compelled to produce desires and to titillate the sensibilities of individuals so as to create a new (post-modern) aesthetic for mass consumption. Harvey points to Marx's catalogue of the consequences of capitalist production, all of which are usually associated with the post-modern condition: individualism, alienation, fragmentation, ephemerality, innovation, creative destruction, speculative development, unpredictable shifts in methods of production and consumption, a shifting experience of space and time and 'a crisis-ridden dynamic of social change' (Harvey, 1989, p. 111). The difference of emphasis between modernity and post-modernity, according to Harvey, lies not in the presence or absence of the social conditions of flux and instability created by all-devouring, all-creating capitalism, but in the recent incorporation of cultural production – including the production of images and narratives – into the processes of industrial production.

Bauman supports the interpretation that post-modernity is not the antithesis of modernity but its logical outcome, but he suggests that this outcome is unintended and inadvertent. Post-modernity may be interpreted as 'fully developed modernity'; as modernity that acknowledges the effects it produces, yet produces inadvertently, by default rather than design, as unanticipated consequences, as by-products often perceived as waste (Bauman, 1992b, p. 149).

Thus while modernity aimed at universality, homogeneity, monotony and clarity (as Bauman puts it), it actually generated pluralism, variety, contingency and ambivalence. Post-modernity represents the conscious acknowledgement or 'owning' of these attributes, the emancipation of modernity from 'false consciousness' in which they were denied and repressed. But it also represents the overt institutionalization of the attributes that modernity aimed to eliminate or conceal (Bauman, 1992b, pp. 149f.). It gives them legitimacy, credibility and standing.

Post-modernity and the death of Diana

The funeral of Diana Princess of Wales in September 1997 could be said to have been the first post-modern national event. It was certainly the first post-modern state funeral (though it was not in the strict sense a state funeral, but a public or national funeral, a 'people's funeral' that combined royal pageantry with a supposedly democratized informality). It was 'post-modern' in two ways. First, in the extent to which *choice* – the choices of members of Diana's family, the choices that individuals made about how they would participate, even the choices exercised by those who devised the service in Westminster Abbey – influenced and shaped the event. Her brother Earl Spencer certainly did things his own way in using the sermon, not simply for a eulogy, but for an implied criticism of the Royal Family. The symbolism of mourning Diana was markedly post-modern: a collage of elements from different, even antipathetic cultural sources (Greenhalgh, in Kear and Steinberg, 1999, p. 43).

Second, it was post-modern in being profoundly – possibly essentially – mediated by the image. The mediated world that Diana inhabited, and of which she was a past master, is characterized by the elision of image and reality. Which of her many-faceted public identities was the real one, if any? Her image was over-determined, multivalent and held sway largely without the aid of words from her, allowing for broad interpretation and wide identification (Kitzinger, in Walter, 1999, pp. 67f.). Nevertheless, there is no getting away from the fact that (as Douglas Davies says) the death was an injection of brutal reality into a world composed largely of fantasy (Davies, in Walton, 1999, p. 27). (Though for the two and a half billion people worldwide who viewed the funeral on the screen it remained a sequence of mediated, manipulated images – the greatest triumph of her image was in death.) We owe it to her to say that, in spite of everything, 'her life was not a script, her death was not staged; and the public response, though choreographed by the media, sometimes exceeded its mediation' (Kitzinger, in Walter, 1999, p. 75). The arrangements for her burial were also post-modern. While Sir Winston Churchill, following his state funeral in 1965, was buried in the churchyard at Bladon, Diana was buried on an island in a lake in the midst of what was to become virtually a Diana theme park at Althorp. The funeral was also post-modern in the eclectic combination of liturgical and musical styles and genres, with Elton John and John Tavener rather uneasily combined with traditional Anglican funeral liturgy. (That is not to say that it did not work or was not successful.)

Above all, the funeral service of Princess Diana can be described as post-modern because countless individuals joined in through telecommunications on a worldwide scale never before equalled. (That is presumably the reason for the initially baffling claim that this was the biggest event in the history of the world: cf. Kear and Steinberg, 1999, p. 2.) And those who participated outside Westminster Abbey and on the London streets did so on their own terms, expressing their feelings of grief, sorrow, anger and gratitude in spontaneous (though extraordinarily predictable and conformist) ways. That event actually evinced an extraordinary combination of the traditional (pre-modern), the post-traditional (modern) and the post-post-traditional (post-modern).

The sense of the sacred

The analysis of this chapter so far suggests that modernity continues strongly in post-modernity, which is a radical intensification of it. Now one of the features of post-modernity is that it makes a space for the sacred, a space that is not only private and domesticated but is also potentially situated in the market-place, the public square. In what ways then does the sense of the sacred manifest itself in our modern/post-modern society? Let us first try to identify them in summary form. In a culture undergoing secularization and fragmentation we have to confront the paradox of the vitality of the sense of the sacred in a period of the declining influence of institutional religion. The persistence of the sacred is evident in numerous ways.

- There is a strong sense of the sacred to be found in the

widespread phenomenon of 'common religion': the often unarticulated religious beliefs and values of those who do not regularly attend church, so familiar to many parochial clergy, especially in rural and semi-rural areas, though by no means confined to them – particularly in the ministration of 'rites of passage' which provide the Church with irreplaceable pastoral opportunities. Furthermore, these rites of passage today help to bridge the gap between people's everyday, secular lives and the sacred world of Church teaching and worship (see the next chapter).

- The sense of the sacred is finding fresh expression in the welter of expressions of spirituality collectively known as the New Age, with its twin emphases, ecological and therapeutic: concern for the integrity of the environment and for the wholeness of human being. As Heelas has commented, the entire New Age movement is broadly to do with healing: the healing the earth, the healing the diseases of the capitalistic economy, the healing the spirit as well as the body (Heelas, 1996, p. 81). The Church can approach the New Age movement with critical discrimination, approving the resurgence of the sense of the sacred while criticizing some of the ways in which it is manifested. The Christian Church holds out the possibility and promise of a healing and wholeness of personhood, society and creation in Christ.

- The sense of the sacred is still powerful in many expressions of voluntary work, whether organized or informal: concern for the suffering, care of the sick, the infirm and the handicapped; generous giving to charities; neighbourly action and selfless service in innumerable ways. These expressions of concern and compassion would not happen unless people were motivated by the sense that human life – particularly in the very young and those who suffer – is in some sense sacred, so bearing a value that has been placed upon it by a power greater than ourselves.

- The sense of the sacred is testified to by the significant instances of religious experiences that have been researched by the Sir Alister Hardy Institute and others. It enables us to see our supposedly secular society in a new light when we learn that between a quarter and a third of all people claim that they have had an experience of a transcendent reality, often of surpassing value (cf. Hardy, 1997; Hay, 1990 and below). This phenomenon is explored below, under the heading 'Spirituality beyond the Church'.

• The enormous and increasing popularity of cathedrals and parish churches as places of (motorized) pilgrimage testifies to the persistence of the sense of the sacred, identified with holy places, places where prayer has been valid for previous generations and where sacred truths are expressed symbolically in the aesthetic realm, being embodied in soaring architecture and the glorious tradition of Anglican choral music. In 2000, there were about 39 million visits to a Church of England church or chapel.

• Church schools are more popular than ever, with prospective parents being willing to jump through various hoops, including attending church, in order for their children to qualify for admission. With government support, the Church of England is planning to create 100 new church secondary schools, confident of the demand for places. Church schools offer a religious and moral framework for education. Indeed, it could be said that they stand for a deeper understanding of education as such than do schools which, however good they may be academically and even pastorally, lack that religious foundation. I am convinced that this phenomenon testifies to a widespread sense that there is something intrinsically sacred about the developing child, eager and receptive to knowledge, full of unrealized potential, with their life before them. The Christian values affirmed and inculcated in a church school answer to the sacred valuation that we place upon a young life.

• Even the apparently more profane aspects of our culture witness to the inescapable category of the sacred. Media stars – from pop idols and sports personalities to fairy-land princesses and other publicity-conscious royalty or former royalty, and from film stars to extraordinary physicists – are projected as superhuman beings in a way that focuses the aspirations of humanity, especially of the young. Through their exceptional gifts of expression and ability to communicate with their generation, such media stars have the potential to generate the salutary values of compassion for suffering and hope for a better world. (Princess Diana had a uniquely powerful combination of charisma and vulnerability, which was neither flaunted nor concealed, that was Christ-like to that extent.) But, equally, they have the potential to produce the malevolent 'anti-values' of egotism, vulgarity and violence. The sacred is concerned with the source and destination of our being, with the source and destination of the values we aim at, and with the source and destination of the power to fulfil them. This suggests that these charismatic, media-projected figures are the sacred ones of our society – all-too-unworthy saviours in some cases, with feet of clay, offered for our credulity in a world that largely bypasses institutional Christianity and is content with surrogate sacrality instead. The concept of charisma, which derives from the New Testament's vocabulary for gifts of grace, points us to Christology. The Christ or Messiah is the one anointed or endued by God through the Holy Spirit with power and authority to carry out God's salvific mission in the world. One of the greatest challenges facing the churches is how to communicate the messianic character, the *redeeming charisma* of Jesus Christ through symbols that are eloquent in our culture.

We can see then that the persistence of the sense of the sacred (cf. Sacks, 1991) is evidenced in our so-called secular society (which in reality lies somewhere between modernity and postmodernity) in a number of ways: in the tenacity of religious belief even among those who do not regularly participate in the life of the Church and in their desire to receive the rites of the Church at significant turning-points in life; in new forms of ecological and therapeutic concern (for the wholeness of the natural world and of the human person); in the incomparable value generally placed on the human person, human dignity, and new human life; in compassionate action for the suffering; in the extent of private religious experience; in the role of historic places of worship in evoking a sense of the beyond, and in the idealization of representative public figures. We could well ask: Is there anyone for whom nothing is sacred?

These intimations of the sacred tend to find their motive force in the heart of the individual and where two or three are gathered together: in the home, the house group, the congregation or the voluntary society. The element of social givenness is downplayed. The individual aspect is dominant. But the significance of these reachings after the sacred stretches much further than the individual, the home and the eclectic group. They connect with universal meanings and universal values. By their nature they extrapolate from a private base to public consequences. They certainly have their effect on public policy through the weight of opinion on legislators and the executive. But even more importantly, they draw their strength, in ways that are not always recognized, from the vitality of religious and ethical traditions – traditions that are sustained by religious and moral communities.

Spirituality beyond the Church

A sense of the sacred is what constitutes the common ground between explicit Christian faith and generic spirituality. We are engaged here in a critical evaluation of this sense of the sacred and an exploration of how, if at all, the Church's mission can build on it, completing and correcting it in the process. There is a Christian construal of the sacred, a specific Christian shape to the sacred realm, one that is determined by divine revelation and church tradition, with its sacraments and symbols. As far as common religion is concerned, the sacred is dimly apprehended, but it takes explicit form in the sacramental actions of baptism, confirmation, marriage and burial. These sacramental events correspond to those particular stages in the transformation of our existence that most explicitly confront us with the question of the source, value and destiny of our lives. It is this inchoate sense of the sacred that often prompts people to approach the Church. It is directed towards sacred persons (the clergy), sacred places (churches, chapels and cathedrals) and sacred words and actions performed by those particular persons in those particular places, with the competence and authority that belongs to their calling (i.e. liturgically). This is an openness to the sacred that still feels the pull of the institutional Church. But there is also an experience of the sacred that is outside the Church and seems to continue independently of it. Forty per cent of people feel close to God most of the time. Of course this far exceeds the proportion that attends church regularly.

Recent research, carried out notably by the Alister Hardy Centre for the study of religious experience and the University of Nottingham Centre for the Study of Human Relations, provides ample and impressive evidence of an encounter with the sacred that normally never connects with the Church. Hardy himself concludes that the findings indicate that 'a large number of people, even today, possess a deep awareness of a benevolent non-physical power which appears to be partly or wholly beyond, and far greater than, the individual self' (Hardy, 1997, p. 1). It is significant that they do not necessarily identify it as a religious feeling and that it occurs regardless of religious belief, even to atheists and agnostics. In a nutshell, this research suggests that about a third to a quarter of the population of the United Kingdom can testify to a sense of being conscious of or influenced by a power beyond themselves, whether they would call that power 'God' or not (see Hardy, 1997; Hay, 1990). David Hay's and Kate Hunt's recent research (Hay and Hunt, 2000) points to an astonishing figure of three-quarters of all people having had some sort of religious experience.

The first question to ask is, *What forms or modes do such experiences take?* (see further on the philosophical analysis of 'ordinary' religious experience: Davis, 1989, chs 1 and 2; Lewis, 1959; Otto, 1959; Smith, 1968). Out of the first three thousand reports of such experiences, the following salient facts emerge:

- 544 (over one in six) mentioned visions.
- 400 referred to an experience involving light – either being bathed in light or seeing a pattern, such as a cross, of light.
- 431 (about one in seven) heard a voice speaking to them.
- 365 reported a sense of being touched.
- 178 experienced a sense of oneness with their surroundings.
- 179 had out of the body experiences.
- 110 described telepathic experiences.
- 208 reported cases of precognition (foreknowledge).

The second question we will want answered is: *What is the cognitive or affective content of the experiences?* The content includes:

- A sense of comfort, security, protection and peace being given them (a sense of presence was the most common of the experiences reported).
- A sense that prayer had been heard and answered (the second most common).
- Feelings of joy, happiness and exaltation in the presence of a power beyond ourselves.
- An awareness of guidance, vocation and inspiration at a time of uncertainty or challenge (a sense of purpose behind events was strongly attested).
- A gift of certainty, clarity or enlightenment.
- A consciousness of being made whole, integrated with oneself, of being fulfilled.

Third, we want to ask: What sort of occasions triggered these experiences? The triggers included:

- Enjoying natural beauty, such as a landscape or a sunset.
- Praying or meditating in the stillness.
- Enjoying music, literature or drama.
- Times of profound depression or despair.
- Participation in church worship.
- Experiences of sexual union.

These findings are confirmed elsewhere. Research in the United States in 1973 indicated that 35 per cent of American adults testified to a similar religious experience when asked: 'Have you ever felt as though you were very close to a powerful spiritual force that seemed to lift you out of yourself?' Five per cent reported that such experiences had occurred often. The triggers that emerged from this project gave greater weight to church services, sermons and reading the Bible, but also included childbirth and making love. A similar survey in the USA in 1984 recorded a higher response: 40 per cent had had these experiences and 7 per cent had had them often (Greeley, 1989, pp. 59f.).

In 1980 one in five persons surveyed reported a profound religious experience. In 1987 one person in six testified to having experienced 'a particularly powerful religious insight or awakening'. Research among the rural population found that at least a quarter of adults had had a religious experience (a third of the women, compared to a fifth of the men). A survey of nurses in 1987 found that 66 per cent had had a religious experience, often in connection with caring for the sick or the dying. Hay and Hunt (2000) highlight the theme of a quest for meaning. A salient form of religious experience in their research was the perception of events falling into a meaningful pattern.

Kay asked Catholic and Protestant schoolchildren aged fifteen to seventeen in Northern Ireland whether they had 'ever had an experience of God, for example, his presence or his help or anything else'. Such experiences were claimed by 26 per cent of Protestant boys and 38 per cent of Protestant girls, 34 per cent of Catholic boys and 56 per cent of Catholic girls (Kay and Francis, 1996, p. 120). We note that the question referred specifically to experience of God rather than to religious experience in general, but when a second survey asked about religious experience as such, the figures were even higher (p. 122). Research also indicates that young people who have undergone a religious experience are predisposed by that experience to take a more positive attitude to Christianity (p. 149). Although church affiliation and religious commitment is stronger in Northern Ireland than in the rest of the United Kingdom, the results remain impressive. Kay and Francis point out that their research confirms the widespread prevalence of religious experience among young people. 'Many young people are aware of such experiences, recognize them and are able to name them. Although they may be growing up outside the churches, young people are not living with a totally secular world view.' The challenge facing the churches, they suggest, is to be able to make connections between what young people appropriately recognize and name as religious experience and what the churches themselves stand for and proclaim (Kay and Francis, 1996, pp. 148f.).

The remarkable fact about these findings is that such experiences of the sacred happened independently of the Church (though some research suggests that there is a correlation between religious practice and religious experience: see Acquaviva in Barker *et al.*, 1993, pp. 47–58). Of those who imparted their story to the Alister Hardy Institute, 40 per cent had never before told a soul about what had happened to them – either out of reverence and reserve, or in case they were laughed at. Nearly half of those reporting a religious experience to the Alister Hardy Institute never went to church. They are not included among those whom the Church touches through the usual channels of common religion. Participation in religious worship was the trigger for the experience in only 12 per cent of cases, and in only 3 per cent of cases did the experience lead to participation in the life of a church (Hardy, 1997, pp. 27f.). Hay points out that there are tens of millions of people who seem remote from the churches yet are remarkably close in terms of their inner longing and their interpretation of their experience (Hay, 1990, p. 104).

These explicitly transcendent, sacred or religious experiences suggest something of wider significance about the presence of the divine in the totality of our significant experience. These revelations could not happen in a vacuum. They could not arise out of nothing. There needs to be a substratum of divine presence, of revelation, of the knowledge of God, to some degree, however minimal, to make these impressive specific experiences possible. In his essay 'The Experience of God Today', Rahner insists that there is an experience of God in every person, 'whether consciously or unconsciously, whether suppressed or accepted, whether rightly or wrongly interpreted, or whatever the way in which it is present'. For Rahner, this experience is not to be identified with specific, discrete experiences. Rather it constitutes 'the ultimate depths and the radical essence of every spiritual and personal experience (of love, faithfulness, hope and so on) and thereby precisely constitutes also the ultimate unity and totality of experience'. What is the ground of this depth of common human experience, this quality of existence? It is the universal salvific will of God, no less, touching every human life (Rahner, 1974, pp. 150, 154, 164).

Let me try to sum up the evidence presented in this chapter. There is convincing evidence that most people take spiritual matters seriously. There is currently a rise in indicators of general spirituality. Not less than a quarter – and possibly as many as three-quarters – of all the people we pass in the street, work alongside or meet in the pub have had an experience of a broadly religious nature. It is also apparent that religious belief of a Christian kind remains strong. About two-thirds of the population believes the first two articles of the Christian Creed – God as Creator and Jesus Christ as the Son of God. There are signs that people find it hard to envisage God. Traditional pictures of a transcendent God are hard to handle and many people are not sure whether personal images are appropriate. But the attitude of most of these very people to the third article of the Creed – on the Church – is baffling. They somehow do not feel that it concerns them directly. Many of them certainly claim to belong, but they see little need to translate this passive belonging into active participation. They are content to be represented by others, to take part vicariously. A massive task of education, persuasion and conversion – a task of mission – confronts the churches if they are to attempt to turn this widespread passive Christianity into active commitment and discipleship to any significant extent. But before we launch into ambitious and expensive programmes of mass evangelism, locally or nationally, ought we not to explore more deeply the reasons for this paradox of believing but not belonging? This is the aim of the next chapter.

5

Spirituality and Mission

Identifying common religion

On the eve of the new millennium, Cliff Richard reached No 1 in the pop music charts with his 'Millennium Prayer', a setting of the Lord's Prayer to 'Auld Lang Syne'. As Libby Purves commented in *The Times* on 30 November 1999, this fact presented the astonishing possibility that more people will know the words of the Lord's Prayer than at any time since the 1960s. What does Sir Cliff's amazing success with this song tell us about the influence of Christianity and its churches (the bodies that teach the Lord's Prayer, presumably) in our culture? As Libby Purves put it, this was surely 'another magnificent flat-footed Christian footprint' – a footprint, we might say, on the sands of Matthew Arnold's Dover Beach, where the tide of faith has receded. Like Robinson Crusoe, when he clapped eyes on the single imprint of a man's foot in the sand on his desert island, we might well be transfixed by the sight. However, I am not in the least surprised by the response to Sir Cliff's millennium prayer. There are many such footprints for those who have eyes to see and the skill to respond. Here are just a few of them from my parochial experience:

- You are invited by the local branch of the British Legion to conduct their Harvest Festival service in their hall. You have, of course, taken Harvest Festival services in halls and pubs before, so you take this invitation in your stride. You robe in cassock and surplice behind the bar and squeeze your way between crowded tables where members of the Legion and their families are enjoying a drink, to the narrow space between the harmonium and the table laden with harvest produce which will shortly be auctioned. A

small procession with flags threads its way through the hall
and you receive the colours as reverently as you can in the
cramped conditions and lean them up in the corner. You
announce the first hymn: was it 'Come, ye thankful people,
come' or (more likely) 'All things bright and beautiful'?
After a Bible reading about the lilies of the field, you
attempt a brief and simple address, encouraging folk to
enlarge this moment of thanksgiving and prayer into
a daily awareness of God focused on Christ and leading to
a closer link with the Church. Although you do not make
the mistake of underestimating the quality of their
religious awareness, you know only too well that in very few
cases does it lead them to participate actively in organized
religion. After prayers and an act of remembrance of
deceased comrades, the colour party returns and you
handle the flags with as much dignity as you can muster in
the circumstances. A final hymn is sung: was it 'We plough
the fields and scatter' or 'Now thank we all our God'? After
disrobing behind the bar you join your congregation for a
ploughman's supper and a pint.

- A wife has a new wedding ring because she has lost the old
  one or had it stolen and you are asked to bless it. The
  couple kneels at the communion rail in an empty church
  while you say prayers for their marriage and family life.
- You hold a 'Care of Animals' service and you are pleasantly
  surprised to see people coming along who never normally
  come to church, accompanied by their dogs, rabbits, cats
  in baskets and selected rodents. On another occasion, a
  girl whose pet dog has been run over asks if you will bless
  her new puppy. She sits all through Evensong with the
  animal under her coat and no-one is any the wiser. Just
  before the blessing you invite her to come up to the
  communion rail and, after a word of explanation to
  the congregation, you say a prayer for her care of her
  young puppy and bless both girl and dog.
- In ministering to the dying and bereaved you are
  constantly humbled and encouraged by the hope, comfort
  and trust that they show and by their quiet confidence that
  at death we simply slip into the hands of a loving Creator.
  You are entrusted with confidences about near-death
  experiences of people seeing their Maker and returning to

tell the tale. Another tells you that his last glimpses of this world are transfigured by an unearthly beauty. A man tells you in all seriousness that, like Moses, he has seen the burning bush.

Many parish priests could cap these particular examples, but are they not all moments of common religion and heaven-sent opportunities for the pastoral mission of the gospel?

Defining common religion

The expression 'common religion' stands for a phenomenon that plays a major part in pastoral ministry. It is widely discussed by sociologists of religion, but remains difficult to pin down. I propose a provisional definition of common religion as *the religious beliefs, values and practices of those who are not habitual churchgoers.* These beliefs are residually Christian and, therefore, a better term might be 'common Christianity' if it were not for the fact that there is a perceptible trend or movement away from orthodox Christian belief towards idiosyncratic and amorphous religious aspirations and sacred images. These religious beliefs, values and practices persist outside the communion of the Church, while making contact with it at significant moments in people's lives, especially through the so-called rites of passage: baptism, confirmation, marriage and funerals. My definition of common religion as the religious beliefs, values and practices of those who are not regular churchgoers broadly coincides with that of Grace Davie (Davie, 1994) but needs to be distinguished from several scholarly interpretations of religious phenomena outside of organized religion.

First, my use of the term common religion is different to that of Robert Towler in his book *Homo Religiosus* and in the pioneering work of the Religious Research Project of the University of Leeds Department of Sociology. Towler defines common religion (CR) as 'those beliefs and practices of an overtly religious nature which are not under the domination of a prevailing religious institution' (Towler, 1974, p. 148). I think 'domination' is putting it rather strongly as a description of the authority of any Christian church today, but I agree with Towler that CR gives meaning to people's lives and expresses the transcendent element in their experience. In Towler's work, however, CR embraces superstitions, luck, ghosts and the paranormal. Similarly, Wolfe designates common religion as the area of supernatural beliefs and practices that are independent of institutional religion, distinguishing it from what he calls 'conventional religion' (Wolfe, in Parsons, 1993, pp. 305ff.). While Bruce appeals to the long-term decline of superstition (witches, demons, ghosts, fairies, the power of talismans and amulets) as evidence of secularization (Bruce, 1992, p. 22) others of us are actually alarmed at a current resurgence of interest in occult phenomena and have no wish to domesticate it. It is an area that urgently needs to be addressed by sociologists of religion and theologians, but to my mind, it does not belong within CR. My use of CR is closer to what Towler designates as 'folk religion', which finds expression in Mothering Sunday, Remembrance Sunday and rites of passage.

Second, CR in the present context should also be distinguished from the fruitful idea of 'implicit religion' that Edward Bailey has very much made his own and on which he has carried out and sponsored much useful research and discussion (Bailey, 1997; see also Grainger, 2002). Bailey's concept of implicit religion is rather capacious: it seems to include various forms of ultimate human commitment, secular as well as sacred. He explores issues of identity, selfhood, relationship, community, change and the sense of what is greater than the individual. He is interested in discovering analogues of religious values in structures and activities of human community that are not overtly religious – for example, the implicit religion of the pub or football team. This, it seems to me, is an attempt to explore aspects of human nature, created in the image of God, at a level even more fundamental and elusive than Towler's 'base line' of significant symbols. (The term 'implicit' religion is used to include folk religion, popular religion and civic religion in the report of the ecumenical Mission Theological Advisory Group (MITAG, 1996) *The Search for Faith and the Witness of the Church.*) It is significant that the central conclusion of Bailey's research agrees with Heelas's analysis of the New Age. Both focus on the self as sacred, holy, divine or transcendent. Bailey designates this the 'single greatest underlying certainty, and simultaneously the single greatest integrating value' to have emerged from his research into 'implicit religion' (Bailey, 1997, p. 220; cf. Heelas, 1996). This suggests that the New Age is simply the clearest expression of an assumption – the sacredness of the self – that is now deeply infused in our culture.

Third, CR in the present sense is not the same as Michael Hornsby-Smith's concept of 'customary religion'. Hornsby-Smith, making sociological analyses of Roman Catholicism in this country, applies the term customary religion to those beliefs and practices which are derived from institutional or official religion, normally through the processes of religious socialization in the home, school and parish, but which have cut lose from clerical control. Like Towler, he uses the term 'common religion' for those religious beliefs and practices, particularly of a magical or superstitious kind, that perpetuate themselves independently of the institutional church. But customary religion, for Hornsby Smith, is belief and practice that owes its origin to institutional socialization but has become weakened or diluted by processes labelled by him trivialization, conventionality, apathy, convenience and self-interest (Hornsby-Smith, 1991). Hornsby-Smith predicts that in the future English Roman Catholics 'will select a more individually-chosen form of religious identity' (Hornsby-Smith, in Wilson, 1992, pp. 126–30). Hornsby-Smith's stimulating analysis of customary religion really belongs to the study of Roman Catholicism in England where the specific structures of social-ization of an eclectic religious community take the place of the more diffuse and tacit forms of religious socialization in an intensively territorial church like the Church of England.

Finally, while CR is a term used by some sociologists of religion, many clergy and others tend to speak of folk religion. Are CR and folk religion the same? It depends how the latter is defined. If folk religion is used to refer to the supposed persistence of traces of indigenous, pre-Christian religion in Britain, with connotations of druids, divining, Maypoles, Morris dancing, witchcraft and fortune-telling, then it is something else. But if the term folk religion is used to refer to the community side of human religiosity, with its Harvest Festival, Christmas carols, Remembrance observances and Mothering Sunday, then it is simply another name for an aspect of CR. Bruce Reed seems to use the term in this sense when he remarks that 'folk religion is the outward expression of deep emotions which are kept unexamined through ritualization' (Reed, 1978, p. 108). Helen Oppenheimer lumps together folk religion and CR phenomenologically as 'the kind of religion that is indigenous in whatever society we are talking about' – 'homemade "do-it-yourself" piety, evolved over centuries, resilient, even obstinate, but inclined to be inarticulate and untheological' (Oppenheimer, 1986, p. 52).

Common Religion in our sense is not by any means confined to the Church of England: the point of CR is that it is not denominational. All churches make contact with CR to varying degrees, especially through Sunday schools, youth groups, and rites of passage. But because an established, territorial church tends to be particularly deeply implicated in the life of the local community and, moreover, because the whole community has a claim on the ministrations of that church, CR in England remains a peculiarly Anglican issue. However, the phenomenon of 'believing without belonging' (to return to Grace Davie's suggestive phrase) can be broadly discerned throughout Europe and the English-speaking former dominions. Schillebeeckx, writing from a Roman Catholic continental perspective, observes: 'A new development in our day is the situation in which people continue to believe in God while being alienated from the institutional Church of religion' (Schillebeeckx, 1990, p. 59).

Accounting for common religion

Common Religion (CR) presents us with the paradoxical combination of broad but vague religious belief, derived from the Christian tradition, with tenuous commitment to the institutional Church. This paradox is compounded into a real conundrum when we consider that the majority of the population of Britain regards itself as religious to one degree or another and, what is even more remarkable, feels that it does in fact belong to a Christian church or tradition. I now offer four factors that, I believe, shed light on this perplexing situation. Needless to say, they are not offered as an exhaustive explanation for the intriguing phenomenon of CR.

A legacy of 'Christendom'

The medieval ideal of the unity of church and nation in a single Christian community or commonwealth persisted through the Reformation up to the English Civil War. It received its highest ideological statement in the ecclesiology of Richard Hooker. To be born into English society and to be baptized into the English Church were two sides of the same coin. The nation comprised a Christian commonwealth, with Church and State forming its two integral aspects. You did not need to opt in to the Church and you could not opt out. Conformity and uniformity of religious practice, including baptism, attendance at worship and receiving Holy Communion, was legally enforced and carried sanctions. In practice, however, there was considerable absenteeism, and legislation was patchily and sporadically enforced (see, e.g., Marsh, 1998).

The national aspect of English Anglicanism (as of any other national church) does not mean that Anglican identity can be reduced to a mere function of national identity, as Gilbert suggests when he calls it 'an obvious if merely nominal concomitant of being English' (Gilbert, 1976, p. 207). The complex religious motivations of lay Anglicans cannot be so simplified (cf. Knight, 1995, p. 32). When the legal framework of Anglican monopoly was eroded by the upheavals of the Civil War and finally removed in the early nineteenth century, the necessary link between Anglican and national identities was critically weakened. But it is important to remember that the assumption remained, nevertheless, that everyone belonged to a Christian, though not necessarily Anglican society, even though no-one was required to demonstrate this by mandatory attendance at church. It seems highly likely that, even today, there lingers some corporate folk memory of this assumption and that this helps to shape common religion.

The Church's own failure

The Church itself has undoubtedly discouraged active participation in various ways. It must share the blame for the unpalatable fact that large numbers of thoughtful people with religious convictions of a Christian character do not wish to take part. The process of alienation goes back a long way. At the industrial revolution, when habits of (perhaps reluctant and enforced) conformity and loyalty were broken, the Church of England failed at first to provide churches and clergy in sufficient numbers for the new manufacturing areas. A church that practised a system of pew-rents could not be said to provide incentives for the working poor to attend church. The Church of England is still identified with wealth, privilege and exclusiveness in the minds of many people. Many people assume that the clergy are very handsomely paid – by the Church Commissioners, of course!

Insensitivity and tactlessness on the part of some clergy and laity (not to mention here the pastoral damage done by those clergy who disgrace their calling by sexual or financial misbehaviour) have produced a steady flow of pastoral casualties in the parishes. Strict baptismal policies at the present time and rigid marriage and divorce discipline in the recent past are the chief culprits. The amount of hurt and guilt induced by clergy refusing baptism or admission to Holy Communion (both quite illegal, except in special circumstances) is enormous and one still encounters both. A young wife and mother I know forsook the parish church for the Society of Friends meeting after a well-meaning matron suggested that she should not be (discreetly) breast-feeding her baby in the back pew. Another thoughtful woman, known to me, who had temporarily wandered off, also to the Quakers, was told by her parish priest that if she wanted to come back into communion she would have to make her confession (i.e. as a penitent) in order to be restored.

The amount of pastoral work required to repair this kind of damage in parishes is out of all proportion to the original hurt: whole families become disaffected. The clergy need pastoral antennae sensitive to unspoken messages of unhappiness, and the ability to explain with simple clarity and unwearied patience the reasons for the Church's policy on a given matter. If there is widespread alienation from churchgoing, while Christian beliefs and values continue to be embraced, the Church itself must take part of the blame.

Research on those people (up to an incredible 62 per cent of the population) who had once attended church reasonably frequently and had ceased to do so, summarized in Richter and

Francis (1998) sheds light on pastoral failure. Unfulfilled expectations and life-style changes, rather than loss of faith, were the main causes of people leaving church. In the case of the disenchanted, it was largely the failure of the church to offer acceptance, affirmation and a sense of belonging that led to disaffection. Those who left because they felt driven by a search for personal authenticity were least likely to return. But many others had ceased to attend church by default rather than by intention. If they were visited by a representative of the Church within six to eight weeks, they were more likely to be restored. Talking over the difficulties they had with the Church was cathartic and healing. But 92 per cent of those surveyed had not received a visit within the crucial period.

An intellectual disenchantment

Several recent surveys help us to build up a picture of what unchurched people believe and think (see Avis, 2003), but I do not know of any empirical work that has been done on what they think the Church believes and teaches. Pastoral experience suggests to me that there is a very considerable barrier to the Church's mission in the outmoded perception that many people still have about the Church's message. Again and again one finds people, who ought to know better, making the assumption that the Church still insists on a pre-Darwinian interpretation of Genesis and that the Church resists anything that science can tell us about the origins of the world and of humankind. Young confirmation candidates, who are doing science at school, often assume that you believe that the world was created in six days and that Adam and Eve were historically the first humans and that you think that the stories of Noah's flood and Jonah's whale are literally true. They find it difficult – almost impossible – to get their minds around the idea that the Church could interpret the Bible symbolically and that we do not take many Bible stories in a crude literal sense. Most adults have no inkling that there is such a discipline as biblical criticism or that many clergy and lay Christians interpret (rightly or wrongly) items of the Creed, such as the virginal conception of Jesus and the ascension, symbolically (see on this area Avis, 1999).

At the beginning of 2000 the BBC made much ado about a survey it had commissioned (on whose advice I am at a loss to imagine) as to whether practising Christians and 'church leaders' believe in the 'literal truth' of a collection of Bible stories and credal statements. The creation of the world in six days, Adam and Eve, the virginal conception of Jesus, and the resurrection are lumped together as though the first two and the last two were of the same order. I could hardly believe my ears when I heard the announcer on Radio Four say that it was surprising that so many church leaders did not believe in the divine creation of the world. How is it that we have allowed the assumption to prevail that the theological myths of the Old Testament and the mysteries of the Christian faith are *meant* to be taken in a crudely literal, that is to say, grossly physical, simplistic, fundamentalist way? In the more than a century since theological orthodoxy and Darwinian evolution were reconciled in the work of the *Lux Mundi* school, the message has not got through that not even the *authors* of the Genesis stories took them in a literal sense! I am convinced that such misapprehensions as these, fomented by the media, keep many people away from active participation and in a state of common religion. They feel unable, with any integrity, to commit themselves to an institution that they regard as intellectually discredited.

Once again we have to admit that we, the clergy, are largely to blame for this situation. We have been unduly nervous about airing principles of biblical criticism or non-literal reinterpretations of Christian beliefs. We have been more afraid of upsetting loyal churchgoers, many of whom do not welcome disturbing questions, than concerned to dispel misunderstandings that create a barrier to faith. The pulpit may not be the appropriate place in which to raise strictly academic theological questions. But veracity and integrity demand that, when we preach on a text or passage, we spend at least a few moments setting it in context, touching on authorship, genre and historicity. We do not need to labour the point, but we can, as it were, turn the corner of the page for those who want to go on thinking. Questions of scholarship, which are threatening if presented abruptly, can be pursued in a secure context with those who want to know more, in Bible study and discussion groups.

In her analysis of Christian culture in England, based on the MORI poll that she commissioned, Rosalie Osmond deplored the theological illiteracy of lay Christians and blamed the clergy and bishops for this state of affairs. 'At the heart of much preaching and religious teaching lies a terrible condescension' (Osmond, 1993, pp. 20f.). Whether condescension or cowardice, the result is a massive barrier to faith and an impediment to the Church's mission.

Moral objections to Christianity

I hazard the view that 'the problem of pain', of undeserved or disproportionate suffering – especially the suffering of children – is the reason most frequently encountered by the clergy for thoughtful people not making a full Christian commitment. The argument is familiar, but no less formidable for that: 'I don't understand how a loving God could allow this to happen.' 'There is just too much suffering around.' 'There is so much wrong in the world.' The shadow of suffering blights the faith of many on the fringe of the Church. A woman who had been coming to church twice a month for twelve years, since I ministered to her husband dying of cancer and continued to support her in bereavement, gave this as the reason why she could not take the step of being confirmed.

Common religion (and much practising churchgoing too, for that matter) holds to the disastrous combination of divine providence (understood in a rather mechanical sense) and the *lex talionis*. The combination amounts to a belief in rewards and punishments, meted out by the interventionist justice of God. This fallacy needs to be particularly combated at Harvest Festival where traditional harvest hymns reinforce the assumption that bountiful crops are a direct gift of God (together with the implied corollary that crop failure is a withholding of divine blessing, an act of judgement). Newman suggested cynically that the doctrine of providence was the only Christian doctrine to which the English gave real, as opposed to notional, assent (Newman, 1903, p. 57). The Book of Common Prayer reinforced this interventionist worldview for centuries with its very specific prayers for the aversion of divine judgement on our sins and of thanksgiving for divine deliverance from plague, blight, invasion or sickness. The widespread notion that adversity is mysteriously 'sent' – as in the hackneyed saying 'These things are sent to try us' – dies hard. The clergy can explain until they are blue in the face that God does not want God's children to suffer and cannot be the author of evil, but it will not shift the deeply ingrained prejudice that the only way in which suffering can be given a meaning is to ascribe it to the hand of God.

Some familiar forms of misguided piety reinforce this error when they teach that those dying prematurely – perhaps tragically – have been taken by the Lord for a higher purpose and that God was in control of every detail. When an excellent young missionary volunteer, known to me, lay dying beside a crashed vehicle on an African bush road it seemed more urgent to his uninjured colleague, with her simplistic interventionist theology, to have a word of prayer about the situation than to seek immediate medical assistance. When he shortly died, the tragedy was interpreted by his devout colleagues as woven into the mysterious texture of God's purposes which control all that happens. Within the framework of their admirable confidence in the faithfulness and purposes of God, there was little room for genuine created contingency, of God allowing natural causes to take their course, of God giving real freedom – and therefore genuine responsibility for their own welfare and that of others – to human beings.

Common religion lacks that difficult, sophisticated understanding of tragedy that holds that God permits suffering because that is how God has made the world and that we can, with God's help, find meaning in the midst of apparent meaninglessness by the way that we respond constructively and compassionately to pain and wrong. Common religion does not have a suffering God. A crucifix is not at the centre of its faith. As a result, the intellectual disenchantment with the Church that revolves around the supposed conflict between science and the Bible, is compounded by a moral alienation which justifiably revolts against the assumption that Christianity complacently teaches that 'God's in his heaven, all's right with the world.' As Helen Oppenheimer has pointed out, the doctrine of providence is bitter and insulting to people who know that the agony they are going through, physical or mental, is destructive, rather than morally improving. She rightly judges that 'there are ethical and theological misunderstandings at the root of our troubles' (Oppenheimer, 1986, p. 56). To combat this disastrous moral alienation, we need, I suggest, to relate the cross of Christ, not only to the sin of the world, as we try to do in season and out of season, but to its suffering also. We need to infuse our preaching of the gospel with a credible theodicy.

Why take common religion seriously?

Why should the Church take the phenomena of common religion seriously? Surely it has far more urgent and proper tasks of mission to occupy it? Why attempt to accommodate the patently inadequate expressions of belief or practice that are manifest in CR? That question can be answered, I believe, in two ways: first, that the Church is responsible for fostering CR; second, that CR challenges our pastoral competence.

It is the Church that, over the centuries, has had the making of CR. It is what the Church itself has made it and the Church cannot disown it. When a couple, who do not normally darken the doors of the parish church, hesitantly approach their vicar and ask for their baby to be 'christened', they are obeying an impulse that has been inculcated by the Church's pastoral practice for centuries. The rubrics of the Book of Common Prayer service of the public baptism of infants states: 'The ministers of every parish shall often admonish the people that they bring their children to baptism as soon as possible after birth and that they defer not the baptism longer than the fourth, or at furthest the fifth Sunday unless upon a great and reasonable cause.' At the end of the sixteenth century, Richard Hooker solemnly warned the clergy that by placing impediments in the way of the baptism of infants, they were in danger of casting away their souls and bringing their own ministry into judgement (Hooker, 1845, vol. 2, p. 373: *Of the Laws of Ecclesiastical Polity*, V, lx, 7). Before the Civil Registration Act of 1837, which for the first time required the civil registration of a birth, baptism and entry in the parish baptism register was bolstered by legal as well as religious considerations. The Civil Registration Acts (which eventually affected marriage and burial as well as birth) were probably 'a crucial factor in the Anglican adjustment from national church to denomination' (Knight, 1995, p. 105). But the Acts also led to the clergy stressing the importance of the rites of passage for purely religious reasons. So CR is not alien to the Church but belongs to its historical identity. It is a part of itself which the Church needs to acknowledge and come to terms with.

It is very tempting, especially for the parish clergy, to be dismissive of common religion. Its beliefs are vague, its practice is tenuous, its observances are spasmodic and its community dimension is weak. It seems to debase the currency of Christian faith to include the inadequate gestures of CR. It seems to lower the threshold of required religious commitment to go along with the expectations of CR. It is undoubtedly frustrating for the clergy to grapple with CR week by week. We do not, by and large, find it at all easy to handle. It often seems to take the Church and the clergy for granted. It seems to want to make use of us for its own purposes and then to discard us. It does not seem to value the central sacramental action of the Church, the Eucharist, except perhaps on Christmas Eve. It does not usually follow up its contact with the Church with any lasting commitment. It just does not love the things that we love or want to do the things that we do.

How then do we – mainly the clergy – cope when people turn out of the pub and into the church on Christmas Eve, a little too merry for our liking? How do we react when the young men who have felt obliged to come along for their younger brother's or sister's baptism, smirk and nudge one another instead of knuckling down to sing the children's hymn? How do we feel when people who are not habitual churchgoers troop into church for a wedding and then sit around chattering gaily instead of saying their prayers to prepare themselves for the worship of God? We are usually far from happy! The temptation is to disapprove and to show it. These incidents that are hard to handle make us want to turn with relief to the committed group of worshippers who share our values, whose behaviour is usually predictably conformist and with whom, most of the time, we know where we are. We find ourselves questioning the value of spending so much time with so-called 'outsiders', especially in the ministry of the occasional offices or rites of passage.

I suggest that we need to examine our reactions rather carefully. Could the familiar psychological mechanism of projection be at work here? Perhaps we are simply displacing our own feelings of unease, our lack of assurance about how to cope, on to the stranger. Our professionalism has been dented. We were not trained for this, we think. (What courses or modules are currently offered in ordination training on the interpretation of common religion and the pastoral response to it?) However, we need to see that our Jonah-like jealously on behalf of God is misplaced. God is not offended. The problem is within ourselves. When we acknowledge these projections we find ourselves wrestling inwardly. But if we learn to offer up our confusion, struggle and inadequacy to God we can find release and power to cope. We can work constructively with CR, leaving the outcome to God. CR does indeed challenge our pastoral competence and we should not seek to evade the challenge.

Evaluating common religion

We now come to the tricky task of attempting a critical evaluation of common religion. How valid, theologically speaking, are the basic religious beliefs, practices and values of people who do not habitually attend church? I propose to approach this question in two ways: first, by attempting a suspicious reading of common religion, pointing out its shortcomings, and then by trying out a positive reading, attempting to make the best of it. First, then, a suspicious reading.

The idea of the Church as the carrier or guardian of common religion is absent from the New Testament. As far as our knowledge goes, the first-century Church showed no interest in hallowing the cycle of the seasons or the stages of human life. While it is almost unthinkable that the first Christians should not have marked and sanctified birth, puberty, marriage and death, we have no knowledge of how they did so. 'That mode of the Church's existence, which still colours its whole being, even where it exists in post-Christian social settings, makes virtually no appearance in what we know of the churches of the first century' (Houlden, 1997, p. 80). This observation sets the scene for a sceptical evaluation of CR.

The first move in effecting a critique of common religion is to ask whether it can pass muster as 'religion' at all. Certain essential components of religion are widely recognized. Scholars in religious studies have discerned a common pattern comprising four elements: cognitive beliefs, ethical practice and behaviour, ritual or liturgy and a community dimension (Smart, 1971, pp. 15ff.; Whaling, 1986, pp. 38ff.). How does common religion fare when measured against these criteria?

- Common religion includes a cognitive component. These beliefs exist on a sliding scale from the general to the specific and are held with varying degrees of certainty. At their strongest, they include belief in a transcendent ground of the world, of human life and of moral obligation. Where beliefs are substantial and include the credal articles concerning God as Creator and Jesus as God's Son, they are often bound up with a cognitive framework that is less than fully Christian, one orientated to meritorious good works, rewards and punishments. This is amply borne out by the revealing question that so many sufferers still ask: 'Why has this happened to me?' or 'What have I done to deserve this?' Common religion is not a religion of grace and redemption, but one of merit and 'getting what we deserve'. The idea of a suffering God who bears our sins and sorrows is hard for it to grasp.
- Common religion also involves practice or ethical behaviour. This is diffused throughout the lifestyle of individuals and communities rather than channelled into specific religious observances. It often reflects a minimal ethical insight and is embodied in the universal Golden Rule. The form that this takes in common religion is found in sayings such as 'Do as you would be done by,' 'He never harmed a soul,' 'She led a good life,' and (notoriously) 'God helps those who help themselves.' As we have noted already, half the population believes that the most important part of religion consists in how you treat other people. Common religion is stronger (at least in theory) on the second part of the dominical summary of the Law ('Love your neighbour as yourself'), but weak and uncertain about the first part ('Love the Lord your God with all your heart and soul and mind and strength').

- A ceremonial or liturgical component is also present in common religion, but it too is minimal. Such ritual observance as there is tends to be seasonal (Harvest Festival, Remembrance Sunday, Mothering Sunday, Christmas Eve Midnight 'Mass') or linked to the rites of passage (baptism, marriage and funerals). We shall consider these substantially in the following chapter.
- The community or social dimension of common religion appears to be particularly weak, except in traditional rural parishes. When people come together in community, it is not generally religion that draws them but family ties or recreational conviviality: hobbies, sport, drinking. However, there are certain sacred values implicit in community (as Edward Bailey has helped us to see: Bailey, 1997), particularly the relational nature of personhood, the spirit of reconciliation and the readiness to bear one another's burdens.

Since, then, the beliefs of common religion are either attenuated or vague, its practice is tenuous, its ceremonial aspect is spasmodic and its community dimension is weak, it can hardly qualify as a religion, as exponents of religious studies would define that. There is no point in attempting to disguise the inadequacies of CR. The more interesting and more constructive question, however, is to ask whether CR represents a decline from the Christian religion or an approach to it? Does it contain faint echoes of Christian faith or dim intimations of it? Is it travelling away from religion or moving towards it? My own hunch, based on pastoral experience, is that, in some cases, CR has the potential to form a basis for a more adequate and complete faith and practice, while in other cases it has the potential to dwindle still further until it no longer counts in a person's life, depending on the balance of influences and components that make up an individual's appropriation of CR.

We can explore that question a little further by asking whether CR can serve as a preparation for Christian faith. There is, of course, a well-established tradition in Christian theology of recognizing a *praeparatio evangelica*, preparation for the gospel. The Old Testament is the paradigm *praeparatio evangelica* since for Christians it points towards and is fulfilled by the gospel of Christ. But in the Old Testament the elements of belief, practice, ceremonial and community are pronounced. It includes, as a positive content, an acknowledged revelation in history and prophecy. Early Christian Fathers, such as Justin Martyr, recognized a *praeparatio evangelica* in the Greek and Roman philosophies and the search for truth among the higher minds of antiquity. St Paul's preaching in Athens, at the altar to 'the unknown god', validated this approach. But we have to say that here there was at least an altar: worship was offered and individuals devoted themselves to a serious search for truth – a far cry from most common religion! The same might be said of non-Christian religions today. On an 'inclusivist' reading, they may be seen to contain elements that may serve as a preparation for the gospel, but they usually involve a commitment or practice that is foreign to CR. So I have to conclude that CR is an inadequate preparation for the gospel – though that is not at all to dismiss it: it is worth a good deal to be able to presuppose belief in God as Creator and in Jesus Christ as God's Son.

A related question, helping us to evaluate CR, is to ask whether CR has a *theology*. Let us, for the sake of argument, define theology as 'critical and coherent reflection on religion in its context'. How reflective is CR? How critical is it of itself and how coherent as a body of beliefs, values and attitudes? We should distinguish here between tacit and explicit reflection. CR may well be reflective at a tacit level – in 'the tacit dimension' (to use Polanyi's phrase) of thinking below the threshold of consciousness (Polanyi, 1967). No-one can avoid ruminating on experience, trying to make sense of their life, wondering whether what they have struggled for was really worthwhile, and so on. About one-third of people, according to the polls, frequently reflects on the meaning of life, and one in seven thinks often about death. However, that sort of tacit reflection, which is largely uninformed and unstructured, is not the same as theology. It needs to be articulated, ordered and criticized in order to be dignified with that name. Although our faith resides at a deep and inaccessible part of our being, and is not fully susceptible of rational explication or justification, Christian discipleship demands that at some point the tacit should become explicit. We have to 'confess with our lips that Jesus is Lord' as well as to 'believe in our hearts that God raised him from the dead' in order, as St Paul puts it, to 'be saved'

(Romans 10.9). If CR is not reflective, critical and coherent, it cannot have a real theology. Our conclusion further reinforces our assessment of CR as essentially inchoate and incomplete.

While admitting the glaring inadequacies of CR, it is also possible to read it in a more positive and constructive way. This interpretation is actually demanded, in my opinion, for three reasons: pragmatic, pastoral and theological.

First and at the lowest level, there are purely pragmatic and practical reasons not to dismiss CR out of hand. CR, however inadequate it may be from the point of view of genuine Christian discipleship, contains areas of common ground, points of contact, with the faith and practice of the Church. It acknowledges the reality of sacred values. It is theistic and, therefore, preferable to explicit agnosticism or atheism. Surely it is better that parents should request a baby's baptism for inadequate reasons than that they should not ask at all; better that couples should wish to be married in church for inadequate reasons than that they should take such a momentous step without regard for God and the Church; better that people should enter the church for worship once or twice a year than never. Even on purely pragmatic grounds, CR is not to be sneezed at. But pastoral considerations are not far away. In our pastoral response to CR, we are dealing with some of people's deepest and most cherished, albeit inchoate convictions. They are not to be trampled on simply because they are often misplaced. Let us take care not to 'break a bruised reed or quench a smouldering wick' (Matthew 12.20).

Common religion also provides vital pastoral opportunities. The penumbra of those who have had some past contact with the Church, and retain some residual religious belief, is the source of most fresh Christian commitments. By acknowledging CR, rather than condemning it, by building on it before we try to correct it, we can maximize the pastoral opportunities of the Church, especially through the occasional offices. In these rites of passage (as we shall see later), the sacredness of human personhood and of significant human relationships is affirmed at symbolic points of change and transformation (liminality). Through its pastoral ministrations, the Church can help to articulate the inchoate sense of the sacredness and God-givenness of life by making connections with the Christian doctrines of creation and redemption. The report *Faith in the City* recognized this possibility even in urban situations: 'The most urgent task facing the Church is that of nurturing this common belief [*sic*] in God towards an authentic Christian faith' (ACUPA, 1985, p. 66). Its sequel *Faith in the Countryside* affirmed the parochial system as the base for the Church's mission through its pastoral work. It acknowledged the spiritual hunger evinced in CR. It warned against a rigorous baptismal policy, especially in the countryside, and pertinently suggested that evangelism will be most effective through family and personal contact (ACORA, 1990, pp. 143f., 266, etc.).

A theological validation of CR might be constructed using the concept of natural theology. I would define natural theology as 'theological reflection on the totality of significant human experience'. It stands for a principle of openness to the whole environment of theology, to all the sources of insight that light up the realm of the sacred in human life. Openness to the sacred might be the key to understanding CR. Let us explore this approach from natural theology, as I have defined it, a little further.

The sacred is that realm of ultimate value that is constituted by human encounter with and response to the divine mystery and to the products of that response, the 'artefacts' of traditions, sacred writings, myths and stories, rituals and sacraments. The idea of an intrinsic human openness to a realm beyond has been developed by the Roman Catholic theologian Karl Rahner and the Protestant theologian Wolfhart Pannenberg. They understand this openness in an existential sense to refer to the transcendental capacity of human beings to go out of themselves in order to establish a rapport or relationship with other people, the physical world and God (Rahner, 1968; Pannenberg, 1970). Our lives are given significance and meaning when we can establish contact between the values we prize and reverence in our hearts and consciences, on the one hand, and realities outside of ourselves, whether they be other people, animals, works of art, nature, human projects, or even God, on the other.

This act of making connections between subject and object, of colouring the external world with the hues of the imagination, was labelled 'creative apperception' by the psychologist Donald Winnicott. He commented that it is 'creative apperception more than anything else that makes the individual feel that life is most worth living' (Winnincott, 1971, p. 65). Developing this theme, Anthony Storr suggests that the mind is so formed that a new balance or restoration within the subjective, imaginative world is felt as if it were a change for the better in the external world, and vice-versa. The imaginative hunger that drives us to seek new understanding and new connections in the external world is also a hunger for integration and unity within ourselves. Storr stresses that 'the discovery, or perception of order or unity in the external world is mirrored, transferred, and expanded as if it were a discovery of a new order and balance in the inner world of the psyche' (Storr, 1989, pp. 124, 200).

Clearly artistic creation and the aesthetic appreciation of those works of art both depend upon this correlation. Since the aesthetic is also a vital – if frequently overlooked – factor in the act of faith (cf. Avis, 1999), a similar pattern of correlation between the internal and the external, the subjective and the objective, can be expected in the human construal of the sacred. By working with the grain of CR, the Church and its ministry can help to facilitate the making of that vital connection.

Since there is no-one (except the psychopath) to whom nothing is sacred, perhaps we can say that CR, with its openness to the sacred, has the potential to develop a readiness for overt religious expression when – and this is the vital proviso – these forms of religious expression, such as worship and sacraments, are seen to be embodiments and enhancements of what is already treasured deep within. By confessing the reality of sacred values in the lives of all people, we are acknowledging, I suggest, a tacit link with God the Creator and Redeemer of all. More importantly, we are bringing to light the neglected doctrine of the *imago Dei*, that human beings are created in the image and likeness of God (Genesis 1.26–7). This image or likeness I take to be more than simply rationality, but the capacity to relate to one another and to God, to live out the social constitution of human nature which reflects the divine community and communion (*koinonia*) that is the Blessed Trinity. This truth provides the most theologically fundamental point of contact and of access for mission. The Swedish Lutheran theologian Gustav Wingren affirmed: 'There is not a single living soul who does not have dealings with God every day and in every action' (Wingren, 1964, p. 43).

Common religion is probably the most substantial manifestation of the persistence of the sense of the sacred in our supposedly secular society. Moreover, it is a sense of the sacred that is still informed and structured by a broadly traditional Christian faith. It contains components of credal belief and religious practice. It entails a set of moral values, derived historically from Christian teaching, that guide and shape the way people behave. Even when belief is vague, religious observance is tenuous and moral standards are fragile, CR constitutes a framework for the lives of many people in our society that is certainly sacred and even in some sense religious. This sacred canopy (cf. Berger, 1973) may well be less firm – diminishing in strength and influence – as a new generation of young people arrives at adulthood without the benefit of a Christian grounding in Sunday schools, church youth groups, and a distinctively Christian religious education and worship in school (in spite of the rearguard action of the 1988 Education Act). CR is certainly being diluted by the admixture of Eastern, New Age and occult religious ideas and images – a *pot-pourri* of vague, sub-Christian, shallow mysticism. But the fact that this framework appears to be gradually eroding is not a good reason for failing to take CR and all its pastoral opportunities seriously – broadly Christian as it still is – in the Church's mission. It is still where many people are, spiritually.

6

Transformations of Being

Four funerals and a wedding?

It is safe to say that the majority of those who approach the clergy for the 'occasional offices' of baptism, marriage and funeral rites, and to a lesser extent confirmation, are not regular churchgoers. Common religion (CR) provides the Church with crucial pastoral opportunities. If our constituency for the occasional offices were to be confined to the regular congregation, we would be desperately short of business! In some sparsely populated parishes, the clergy are thankful when a customer turns up. In densely populated parishes, the clergy could wish for more baptism and confirmation candidates, and more weddings, while the quantity of funerals can be oppressive. 'Four funerals and a wedding' just about sums it up!

We might assume that lack of Christian commitment, linked to a decline in church attendance, is a recent phenomenon. Far from it. Diocesan records tell a different story. At the very time when Richard Hooker was expounding the doctrine of the identity of church and nation, at the turn of the sixteenth century, the priest of Eastwell, Kent, Josias Nichols, lamented that only one in ten of the parishioners of communicable age understood the basics of Christian doctrine. A century later, the curate of Queenshill in the Diocese of Worcester reported that he had no congregation at all, even on a sacrament Sunday. The failure of the 1689 Comprehension Bill and the passing of the Toleration Act reduced the sanctions that supported churchgoing. Significant numbers of people interpreted the right to attend a licensed place of dissenting worship, rather than their parish church, as an excuse to absent themselves from public worship altogether. In the mid-eighteenth century, the Rector of Bapchild, Kent, informed his Archbishop of the appalling religious ignorance of the lower classes and servants. Hardly one in three of those he had talked to, he reported, had a clue about who Jesus Christ was and why he had come into the world (Gregory, 1998, p. 312; Holmes, 1973, p. 25). On Easter Day 1800 there were six communicants at St Paul's Cathedral. (When I did a visitation of a new parish in 1980, an elderly resident told me that he had been moved to attend the parish church for the first time for many years on an Easter Day some years earlier. Finding himself one of eight people in the congregation had convinced him that the parish church was not a going concern and he had not been back since. A few years after my visit, Easter Day communicants were running at 70 or more in this parish.)

The occasional offices have long been the mainstay of the parochial ministry, and their use by non-regular churchgoers appears to be of long standing. Frances Knight suggests that the greatest parochial achievement of the Church of England was the popularity of its occasional offices. Many more people came to church for these than for Sunday worship. Many who attended for baptism, churching of women, confirmation, marriage or burial probably had no other formal links with Anglicanism. 'It was in its role as provider of these rites of passage that the Church was able to impinge to some extent on the lives of the hundreds of thousands of people who would not have considered regular Sunday church-going' (Knight, 1995, p. 86).

There was a long-standing resistance to Holy Communion: in some areas only a few per cent of the population were communicants. The 'churching' of women was popular among poorer families and became overlaid with superstitions. It was thought to have contraceptive properties and to prevent miscarriages. Confirmation was regarded as a cure for rheumatism and some made sure that they were 'touched' by the bishop on several occasions. But most confirmees never became communicants. Altogether the rites of passage were thought to do you good and perhaps to bring good luck (Knight, 1995, pp. 89–95).

Although even in deep urban culture the rites of passage (RP) provided an opportunity for the Church to reach the unchurched, the occasional offices were adapted by the recipients to their own agenda. Cox writes of Lambeth between 1870 and 1930: 'The British people remade these rites into popular ceremonies on their own terms, and in that sense were both in touch with organised religion and indifferent to the claims of organised religion' (Cox, 1982, pp. 268f.).

Clearly, the frustrations and disappointments of CR are nothing new. For centuries the rites of passage have been the point at which the Church has delivered its pastoral ministrations. In this chapter I want to ask whether these rites of passage can become vehicles of the gospel. Let us examine the dynamics of the RP from the pastoral point of view (cf. Carr, 1985a, for a perceptive interpretation from a similar standpoint; and Grainger, 1988a).

Symbolizing existential realities

Baptisms, marriages and funerals have the effect of compelling us to face up to the basic realities of our existence. Infant baptism is the rite that celebrates and consecrates the birth into the world of a newly created person. It speaks eloquently, to all who take part in or witness this sacrament being performed, of our total dependence on the creative power of the God who 'calls into existence the things that do not exist' (Romans 4.17). In baptism the new life is manifestly contingent, vulnerable and dependent. It, therefore, becomes a representative symbol for the contingency, vulnerability and dependence of all human life – of every one of us. 'Naked I came from my mother's womb and naked shall I return there [i.e. to the earth]', cried Job in his affliction (Job 1.21). William Blake, one of the greatest interpreters of Job, wrote in 'Infant Sorrow':

My mother groand, my father wept.
Into the dangerous world I lept.

(Blake, 1977, p. 129 [*sic*])

Parents experience a surge of emotion as they are taken back to the wonder and trepidation of those days when they first held a child of their own in their arms. Infant baptism – the celebrating and consecrating of a new life – speaks as nothing else does of the priceless value of the human being, created and redeemed, loved and treasured by God.

People who work in the visual media tell us that the most potent image that can be shown on the television screen is that of a new-born baby. Its sacredness is self-evident to us. The sociologist Edward Shils argues that the sense of the sanctity of life goes deeper than Christian theology and belongs to a 'proto-religious natural metaphysic'. He claims that 'the idea of sacredness is generated by the primordial experience of being alive, of experiencing the elemental sensation of vitality and of fearing its extinction'. Humanity stands in awe before its own vitality and creativity of mind and body (Shils, 1975, pp. 222f.). The profound sense of the sanctity of life, natural and inherent though it may be, is an avenue into the central affirmations of Christian theology, the doctrines of creation and redemption. The new-born baby reflects back to us, as in a mirror, our own selfhood in all its vulnerability and its potentiality. It saddens us with the remembrance of lost innocence and inspires us with hope for the future. Our sensibilities of reverence for the unborn have been brutalized by permissive abortion practice and embryo technology with its built-in waste of potential human life. Nevertheless, protesters such as pro-life pressure groups know that confronting us with the picture of an embryo in the womb or a new-born baby that might not have been allowed to live is still the most effective weapon in their armoury.

The marriage service celebrates and consecrates another aspect of the elemental reality of our existence, that of the union or conjunction of two persons. The institution of marriage tells us that, in order to find deep interpersonal fulfilment and to perpetuate the human race securely, individuals need to come together in an interpersonal union. It speaks of the incompleteness of the separate individual, of our capacity for fuller personhood in relation, in a new whole that is greater than its constituent parts. Marriage is the rite that brings out with peculiar eloquence the relational character of Christian anthropology. In Christian understanding this union is essentially covenantal. All who are present as the public witnesses of the solemn marriage vows are reminded of the vows that they themselves have taken or will one day take in a binding commitment that is like no other. We see our joys and our sorrows, our hopes and our failings reflected back to us as the marriage bond is formed 'in the sight of God and in the face of this congregation'.

The funeral service brings home to us another aspect of our elemental existence that we do not like to think about all the time, our mortality and the cost of this for those who will be 'left behind'. We cannot gaze down into a freshly dug grave as the coffin is lowered, or watch as the curtains close around the catafalque in the crematorium, without being made acutely aware that our turn must come. The term 'celebrate' is hardly appropriate for a funeral, unlike baptism and marriage. The rite, even when imbued with Christian hope, contains rather than celebrates the fact of death. But it certainly also consecrates it, by bringing it into connection with Christ's death and resurrection: 'Blessed are those who die in the Lord.'

The occasional offices concentrate the minds of the participants on the deepest realities of life. But as T. S. Eliot famously said, 'Human kind cannot bear very much reality.' A young man, a mourner sitting in the front row, rushed out of a crematorium chapel with unseemly haste before we had finished the service. He could not stand it any longer. It belongs to the role of the clergy to make these things as bearable as may be. Bruce Reed says cryptically: 'Folk religion is the outward expression of deep emotions which are kept unexamined through ritualisation' (Reed, 1978, p. 108). Liturgical words and actions, that in essence go back to time immemorial, help to make these potent symbols bearable. They tame them by universalizing the experience, lifting it into a broader framework of meaning.

That act of universalization is particularly important at a funeral and is effected, for example, by the words of the Book of Common Prayer 1662: 'Man that is born of a woman hath but a short time to live.' But it is equally vital at marriage and baptism services. The marriage vows have the feeling of having been worn smooth like pebbles by generations of use. Their words stand out above the emotions of the occasion. They do not romanticize, neither do they encourage sentimentality. They are rugged, realistic and take a long view ('till death us do part'). They incorporate the couple into something that has been going on long before they came on the scene and will continue long after they are gone (cf. Cockerell, 1999).

The service of baptism for those who are not old enough to answer for themselves needs to be universalized by being grounded in the doctrine of creation or 'nature'. According to Catholic theology, 'Grace perfects nature; it does not abolish it.' In order to progress we have to start from where we are. We need, therefore, to celebrate and consecrate the gift of a new

life. That is why, when I conduct the baptism of infants, I
include in the service a reminder that one of the reasons why
we have come into God's house is to offer thanksgiving for a
precious and unique gift that only God can give. In the
Alternative Service Book baptism service the moment of
Christian initiation was not adequately universalized. The
context was too narrow. The *Common Worship* initiation services
show little improvement over the ASB in this respect. While
they acknowledge that children need to be nurtured and
supported as they grow up, there is no recognition within the
baptismal liturgy itself that they have first *been born* and that
their sacramental new birth in baptism corresponds analo-
gously to their natural birth. The baptismal imagery of John 3.4
makes the connection explicitly: 'Can one enter a second time
into the mother's womb and be born?'

An ancient font also helps us to universalize what is
happening. I might ask the congregation gathered around the
font just to look for a moment at the font itself (say in Stoke
Canon parish church). I would remind them that it is a
Norman font and dates from about a century after the
Domesday Book. But it also has pre-Norman (Saxon or Celtic)
designs on it, depicting wild beasts devouring Christian martyrs
and some bishops or apostles with books, keys and a chalice. It
is eight hundred years old. 'Just think of all the generations of
children of this parish who have been baptized at this font –
and adults too!' This helps us to feel part of something that has
been going on almost as long as there has been a community in
that place and to link ourselves up with the first Christians, not
just in words, but three-dimensionally, as we strain to make out
the figures of the martyrs and bishops in the worn stone.

Giving direction to the human journey

The idea of the transformation of being through various stages
of a spiritual journey has a deep historical background in
the Christian culture of Western Europe. In medieval times the
stages of life, imprinted with an indelible sacramental
character, were successively accomplished within the
framework of an all-embracing sacred world administered by
the omnicompetent Church. The idea of the unique self or

soul, given by God in an act of creation, dies hard even in these secular times. It lies behind modern notions of individualism, self-fulfilment and self-expression. The Christian soul has become transposed into the secular self. Instead of the soul making its Christian journey from baptism and confirmation, through matrimony, to a final passing over the threshold of death accompanied by Christian burial rites that sanctify our mortality, we have the secular self following a stereotyped life-course dictated by society-wide economic and political institutions. We follow a largely predictable path from birth and infant socialization, through education and the gaining of credentials, to a career or careers, followed by planned retirement and pension and suitable recreations for those whose services are no longer required as producers by the economy (cf. Meyer, 1987).

So here we have two main rival paradigms for the destiny of the individual: the pilgrim Christian soul passing from one sacramental milestone to another as it runs its earthly course; and the secular self promoted from one socially-imposed stage of the life-course to another until it has fulfilled its usefulness. These two models are in tension, but are not, I think, fundamentally opposed. The secular model still respects the value of the individual. 'The rationalisation of western society over recent centuries does not simply submerge the individual as a cog in the machine – the machine itself is organised in part to reflect and give meaning to a neatly staged and sequenced individual life' (Meyer, 1987, p. 246). The idea of a staged and sequenced life (though much less certain today, in post-industrial society) is a legacy of the ecclesial model of Christendom. A fundamental Christian value has been transposed into secular terms to meet the economic exigencies of modernity.

However, the evolution of the subjective self in relation to the life-course which, even in its present weakened form, is mandated and reinforced by society, tends more and more to take place in abstraction from Christian nurture and from the milestones provided by the sacred rites of passage. Contemporary culture encourages identification with vague and ill-defined macrocosmic or global collectivities such as 'the human community', 'society', 'mankind', at the expense of local, given communities of kinship, locality or affinity, such as the family or the parish. Collectivities which are less susceptible to rationalization are unfashionable and less psychological virtue is attached to them (Meyer, 1987, p. 259). The notion of rites of passage helps us to build a bridge between the Christian sacraments and the secular life-course. Baptism should be always explicitly related to natural birth. This can be done through prayers and acts of thanksgiving for the priceless gift of a new life. Confirmation often fits fairly neatly into the transition from primary to secondary schooling – though this traditional positioning for confirmation has become problematical as the average age of confirmation candidates has reduced. Marriage relates to the life of a couple who have set up home and are hoping to raise a family, in conformity with the expectations of society. The predominance of the retired among the most active and useful members of our parish churches suggests that the Church manages – more by accident than design perhaps – to give meaning and purpose to the years of retirement. This particular transformation of being (retirement) is a modern phenomenon and it could be further developed in more explicit ways. The wisdom of the Church is to accommodate itself pastorally to the primary patterns of individual and social existence, evolving and fluctuating as they are in a rapidly changing society, which are dictated by biological and economic necessities. That approach should be seen not as a form of syncretism, but as a justifiable pastoral strategy that relates the doctrines of creation and redemption to each other.

Paying a pastoral premium

The ritual or enacted symbolism of baptism, marriage and burial carries numinous power. As those who are set apart and given authority to handle these potent symbols, we, the clergy, pay a price and are revealed as wounded healers. Our involvement raises searching questions about our own integrity. How are our own children growing up in the faith (the children of clergy families are notoriously recalcitrant)? How is our own marriage fulfilling those wonderful nuptial aspirations of our wedding day (clergy are no more exempt from marital failure than is the rest of the population, it seems)? And how are we coping with the knowledge of our own vulnerability and mortality and the fact that our work must one day come to an end and be subject to divine scrutiny (we often give all the indications of highly repressed personalities and of those who cannot admit their common humanity)? To help sustain others in these crucial areas of life we need a profound self-knowledge, a disciplined rule of life, and the ability to take time off from work to spend with our spouses and children. The more we give of ourselves in the dangerous work of sacramental celebration and consecration, the more we need to retreat into recreation. We deny 'nature' at our peril, however much we may exalt 'grace'.

The ministry of the occasional offices requires a 'hard slog' from the clergy. The time and effort involved, particularly in visiting and preparation classes, seems disproportionate to the results. The 'output' is not commensurate with the input. These rites of passage raise in an acute form the question of clerical productivity. They make us ask, 'Is this the best use of my time?' and 'Is this really worth the effort?'

When I had an article on common religion published in *The Times* a few years ago, I received a clutch of letters. Most of them were supportive of the line I was taking (which I am elaborating in this book). But there was one in particular that gave me pause for thought. It was from a parish priest who had been ordained for eight years and was working in an outer London suburb. He confessed that, while he had tried to give generous pastoral care through the occasional offices, he had hardly ever found such contacts to lead, as far as he could tell, to any deeper involvement with the Church or the Christian faith. As a result, he had come to feel very sceptical about CR and now considered that it probably had little to do with Christianity. He did not consider CR to be a suitable basis for presenting people with the challenge of the gospel. He had come to believe that in all probability we should now proclaim the Christian message as though no-one had ever heard of it before.

My own experience is much more positive. I can think of many examples of individuals or families, previously unchurched, who have stayed within the orbit of the parish church, and in some cases have become key members of the Christian community, as a result of being brought into contact with the Church through baptism, confirmation, a wedding or a blessing on a second marriage, or following the funeral of a relative. The congregations of my previous parishes were full of such people. It is one way in which ageing congregations are renewed. When our ministry in the sphere of CR seems to fall on stony ground, we need to remind ourselves of the biblical principle that one sows and another reaps (John 4.37f.; 1 Corinthians 3.6).

John Finney's research into patterns of conversion shows that, for two-thirds of Christians, their journey to faith was a gradual rather than a sudden one. I take comfort from the case of the person who reported that it had taken him forty-two years! (Finney, 1992). Our pastoral contact with individuals, their families, and even whole communities, as their parish priest or minister, is rather like walking in the hills of Scotland, Snowdonia or the Lake District. The traveller, looking for the right path in sometimes disorientating terrain, comes across a cairn of stones raised by those who have passed that way before, and adds a stone or two to the total edifice. As Newman used to insist, great acts of God take time. Pastoral ministry, especially in connection with the occasional offices, calls for faith in the God who is working his purposes out. As St John of the Cross put it, the grace of the sacrament of baptism is given all at once, 'at God's pace', but it becomes ours at our human pace 'and so little by little' (Matthew, 1995, p. 15).

The dearth of tangible results in the ministry of RP is undoubtedly discouraging. But the immature state of expectation in those who request the occasional offices is also depressing. Certainly they expect to receive something of significance and value, but they generally have an extremely hazy idea of what it is. They seem to simply expect some blessing of their lives by contact with the Church and its sacraments. But the sacraments of the Church involve so much more than this. For example, baptism may well be a suitable opportunity to give thanks for the birth of the child and to pray for wisdom to be given to the parents and godparents as they bring up him or her in an uncertain world. Those aspects give you your *entrée*. But they cannot compare with the mighty act of God that incorporates us into the death and resurrection of Christ and thus into his body the Church.

Parents often have an idea that baptism means introducing the baby into the Church, but they have no grasp of the christological meaning of the Church as the mystical body of Christ. It is discouraging when, as the officiating minister, you have to accept that there is little that you can do about this. You may well try to make a connection with the vague expectations of the applicants by explaining that baptism brings us near to God and that Jesus will bless this child just as in the gospels he takes little children in his arms and blesses them. Clergy who manage to get that simple message across, have succeeded in a key part of their pastoral task.

In the occasional offices, we can only skim the surface of sacramental meaning. We cannot hope to bring the sacrament to light in its fullness. For example, the baptism of a small child witnesses to the prevenient grace of God who calls us from the womb (cf. Jeremiah 1.5), but it cannot speak as effectively of the conscious faith of the individual and his or her commitment to Christian discipleship. On the other hand, adult baptism makes concrete and vivid the baptismal promises to turn to Christ, to repent of one's sins and to renounce evil. It is a moot point whether the sovereign prevenience of divine grace or the appropriate human response is the more important aspect to get across. The sacraments of the Church cannot be tailor-made for a particular individual. On any given occasion, only a few facets of a stupendous reality will shine out. Pastoral skill lies in drawing out what speaks most directly to the candidate's spiritual condition.

An aspect of our pastoral role that is particularly difficult to cope with is that the relationship with applicants for the occasional offices is not under our control. The applicants for baptism or marriage tend to set the agenda and our role is assigned to us. The date for the baptism has often already been agreed in the family before we are brought in. It leaves little time for preparation or attendance at suitable church services. The godparents have very likely already been asked and it has not occurred to some parents that godparents have to have been baptized themselves, let alone confirmed. Our pastoral skills come into operation as we manoeuvre within circum-scribed limits to help the applicants, who have usually acted in good faith, to do greater justice to the requirements of the Church, while not antagonizing them. In a marriage, on the other hand, you are a small cog in a large and complex operation. It is costing the couple or their families a great deal of money, of which the Church sees comparatively little, yet our responsibility is enormous. Whether the wedding is a triumph or a disaster depends largely on us.

It helps to remember that Jesus did not insist on being in control of his ministry. He did not demand to set the agenda, nor did he stand on his dignity. As his Passion approaches, he is portrayed in the gospels as delivered up by the Father to his fate and as passive in the face of circumstances (cf. Vanstone, 1982). Now the ordained minister of the Christian sacraments can never be the pliable tool of clients for that ministry, but given that our role is largely assigned to us, we can certainly use those expectations to create a rapport with our parishioners before we go on to gently correct some of their assumptions. We cannot negate their expectations but, once we have established a pastoral relationship that responds as far as we can to those expectations, we can go on to question some of the more patently inadequate assumptions, while we let much else that may also be inadequate go by. We must not mind being stereotyped. As we go further, pastorally, with individuals, we will break out of the straitjacket.

In the sphere of CR we have to deal with inarticulate and inchoate spiritual intuitions. Parents often cannot tell us why they are asking for a baby's baptism. I have given up putting them on the spot about that. But if we explain very simply what we think baptism is about, beginning of course with the theme of thankfulness for the new life, their faces will often light up because we have put into words what they obscurely felt but could not adequately express. Part of our pastoral role is to understand and to interpret the genuine but inarticulate spiritual instincts of individuals who do not have the received Christian vocabulary on the tip of their tongue.

Powerful hopes and gnawing fears surround the transformations of being that are celebrated and consecrated in the rites of passage. The vicar is the safe pair of hands, the one who by spiritual qualities, gained through prayer, training and the authority of his or her office, can be trusted to handle sacred power and threatening feelings. Appropriate words of interpretation can be the key that unlocks the door and gives a glimpse of Christian meanings that make sense, perhaps for the first time. But words should never be allowed to obscure the given symbols or sacraments which are themselves the vehicles of transforming power. Let us now look more closely at the symbolic aspect of the occasional offices.

The threshold of Christian meaning

When a congregation takes part in the liturgy, whether it is the Eucharist or one of the occasional offices, it is dramatizing its faith in a corporate way. It is renewing the meaning that is its reason for existing and doing so in a way that is therapeutic. The function of liturgy, with its ritual element, is to give shape to life in terms of meaning. It enables us to inhabit our beliefs bodily, so to speak. It fixes fleeting time by suspending it in a series of *rites de passage* and focal points that embrace past, present and future, as the Eucharist so patently does. It reflects back to us our vulnerability, pain, aloneness and guilt in a way that can be faced because it holds them in a frame of wholeness, totality and universality. They are bearable because they are only a part of the picture and they are our common human lot. There is also the reality of grace, understanding and forgiveness, and these are real because they are not private predilections but universal possibilities. Ritual that respects the natural rhythms of earth, body and community has therapeutic potential. Even ritual that is not overtly religious points to the sacred dimension of life and to ultimate wholeness. 'To present movement, gesture, sounds, objects and words in ritual form is to perform a healing action' (Grainger, 1994, p. 109).

C. G. Jung wrote to a Protestant pastor on the subject of Christian baptism:

> Every epoch of our biological life has a numinous character: birth, puberty, marriage, illness, death, etc. This is a natural fact demanding recognition, a question wanting an answer. It is a need that should be satisfied with a solemn act, characterising the numinous moment with a combination of words and gestures of an archetypal, symbolic nature. Rites give satisfaction to the collective and numinous aspects of the moment, beyond their purely personal significance ... to unite the present with the historical and mythological past. (Jung, 1973, p. 208)

Jung added that such rites should be 'archaic' in both language and gesture.

Van Gennep's celebrated early twentieth-century work *The Rites of Passage* has provided a framework and a vocabulary for interpreting the occasional offices of the Christian Church – though Christian sacraments can never be reduced to mere rites of passage for they are, above all, means of grace. According to Van Gennep, transitions from one state of existence to another – from the womb to the world, from childhood to maturity, from singleness to the married state, from life to death – were acknowledged to be sacred even in the basically secular modern world. Van Gennep distinguished three stages in the symbolic effecting of the transition from one state of life to another. There is first of all a rite of separation from the former state (preliminal); then a rite of transition towards the new state (liminal); and finally a rite of incorporation firmly into the new state (postliminal). Marriage includes, in addition to rites to which the parties are subject as individuals, also a rite of union for the couple. Funerals, he demonstrates, involve brief separation rites, extensive transition rites and – most important – substantial rites intended to incorporate the deceased into the world of the dead (Van Gennep, 1960, pp. 11f., 116ff., 146ff.).

Van Gennep's insights have been developed by Victor Turner, notably in *The Ritual Process*. Turner points out that, during the transitional or liminal state, the characteristics of the ritual subject (or 'passenger') are ambiguous: he passes through a cultural realm which has few of the attributes of either his past or his future state. Thus candidates for ordination go into silent retreat, cut off from their families and communities and each other. Liminality is frequently likened to death, being in the womb, darkness, invisibility, bisexuality, dwelling in the wilderness (like Moses, Elijah, John the Baptist and Jesus), and the eclipse of the sun or moon. Liminal persons, who are in the process of making the transition, are stripped of possessions, relationships and individual identity – as though ground down to basic human material from which they will be remade at a new level. Ordinands at a Church of England theological college in the 1970s were reputedly told on arrival: 'First we want to break you and then we want to remake you.' As Turner writes: 'Liminal entities are neither here nor there; they are betwixt and between the position assigned and arrayed by law, custom, convention and ceremonial' (Turner, 1969, p. 95). It is while they are allocated to this state of liminality that candidates for a new state or life or a new status in society acquire sacredness. Turner's comments originally applied to the initiation of a village elder or a tribal chief, but they seem relevant to the making of a priest or bishop (ordination too is one of the Church's occasional offices). He suggests that something of the sacredness of that transient humility and malleability carries over and tempers the pride of the incumbent of a higher position or office. 'Liminality implies that the high could not be high unless the low existed, and he who is high must experience what it is like to be low' (Turner, 1969, p. 97).

Prophets, artists and writers are often liminal persons, living on the margin of society, on the edge of the community. That is a condition of their calling and facilitates their work. 'Liminality, marginality, and structural inferiority are conditions in which are frequently generated myths, symbols, rituals, philosophical systems and works of art' (Turner, 1969, p. 128).

Rites of passage or 'life-crisis rites' are those in which the subject of the symbolic ritual moves from 'a fixed and placental placement within his mother's womb, to his death and ultimate fixed point of his tombstone and final containment in his grave as a dead organism – punctuated by a number of critical moments of transition which all societies ritualise and publicly mark with suitable observances' (Lloyd Warner, cited in Turner, 1969, p. 168).

Durkheim defined ritual as 'the totality of practices concerned with sacramental things'. It welds together the community that imparts strength and vitality to its members. Ritual cannot be separated from symbol and myth. Ritual recalls the founding myth of the community and entrenches it in the consciousness of participants (Pickering, 1984, pp. 329, 347, 336). Geertz suggests rather neatly that sacred meanings are stored in symbols, dramatized in rituals and related in myths (on literary symbols and myth see Avis, 1999). But our concern here is with the particular ritual or stereotyped symbolic action that is enacted in the sacraments and occasional offices of the Church. Ritual action, enacted corporately, reinforces and redirects identity by rehearsing in dramatic form a system of meaning. It thereby engraves this corporate meaning-system or worldview on the hearts of the participants.

The Church's sacramental actions set forth the revealed form of Christ as Saviour and Lord. He who is the way, the truth and the life imparts his form to us salvifically. This insight from anthropology suggests that the occasional offices are one of the most effective ways of imparting and reinforcing Christian identity. They have a vital part to play in conforming individuals and families to the Christian worldview. Because they are corporately enacted, not just interiorized individually, and use the media of drama, symbol and action, as well as words, they are far more powerful than sermons. They are (in sociological jargon) our chief means of socialization within the Church. It is, therefore, in missiological terms, short-sighted to disparage or downplay the role of the occasional offices. Ritual, wherever it is found, is identified as 'consecrated behaviour' (Geertz, 1973, p. 112). Symbols have the power to 'consecrate certain styles of life' (Duncan, 1968, p. 22). In fact, symbolic ritual is both consecrated and consecrating. In the occasional offices of the Church we add also the element of celebration.

In the worship and sacraments of the Church, liminality is curbed and controlled. In the occasional offices, only traces of it remain. The crucial point is that in liminality there is movement, flux and change. The rites of passage celebrate and consecrate the significant milestones in a journey of life that is orientated to the sacred. They speak of unfolding selfhood, of transformations of our being as it receives the imprint of Christian meanings, of the change that is effected in our mode of existence as we are brought into an enhanced relation to the Christian community and through that community to the one who is the Saviour of the Church and its Lord. I hope to show that this whole matter is a christological one. To do this we need to switch the emphasis from ritual to symbol.

Symbols of the sacred

A living spirituality is sustained through the mediation of symbols. Symbols are the vehicles of the process whereby we become incorporated into the life of the Church and simultaneously incorporate and internalize its meanings into our deepest being. Symbols are the bearers of value and the currency of identity-formation. They unite the particular and the universal, the individual and the community. There are verbal symbols or constellations of symbols in prayers, hymns and creeds; tangible symbols in gestures such as kneeling or making the sign of the cross; and enacted symbols performed corporately in sacraments and other liturgical acts. Our most important symbol is the symbol of the self. As we have already noted, C. G. Jung held that the symbol of the self and the symbol of God were clinically indistinguishable in analysis, both being manifestations of the unconscious archetype of wholeness (on Jung see further Avis, 1995, ch. 6: 'God or the Unconscious?'). The symbol of the self is thus the most sacred symbol in the human psyche. It is profoundly implicated with the question of the source, purpose and destination of our existence. This is surely where our half-Christian society still finds mystery and sacredness. But, as we have seen, there is no self without a community of some sort. The self is formed through various transformations of being, the most significant of which are celebrated and consecrated in the rites of passage. These all have a corporate and public dimension. In baptism the self is celebrated and consecrated as a gift of God, unique and priceless. But at the same time it is incorporated into the Body. In marriage the self unites with another in an affirmation of sociality and in hope for the future of humanity. As the law recognizes, marriage is a public act that is of concern to society. In death, marked by Christian funeral rites, the self suffers its ultimate transformation and returns to the source of its being. It is perhaps in death that we are least autonomous and most dependent on others, the family and the community.

What is the connection, in understanding, in meaning, between the self and the God to whom we relate the self in the occasional offices? Once again we can take our cue from Jung who suggested that in analytic material the symbols of the self and of God were both – in a Christian culture, at least – christomorphic, that is to say, identified with the figure of Jesus Christ. As a symbol, the Christ stands for the once-for-all unity of God with humanity. This unity is manifested in what the Gospels tell of the narrative sequence of the destiny of Jesus of

Nazareth, who is believed in by his people as the Christ of God. The great christological milestones correspond to the rites of passage that have sacramental status for the Church. The paramount christological events of incarnation, crucifixion and resurrection correspond to the milestones of human existence: birth, suffering and passing through death to God. These milestones of the transformation of being are both celebrated and consecrated through baptism and funeral rites – the beginning and the end of the Christian's earthly journey – while the ongoing unity of Christ and his Church, which is the inner meaning of the Eucharist, is an analogy of marriage. With the mention of the Eucharist we are moving away from the rites of passage, but the Eucharist must be allowed to be paradigmatic for our understanding of all Christian symbolism. Let us pursue this a little further by first jumping to a non-Christian context.

As an example of a non-Christian symbol which has a sort of 'sacramental' value within its own sphere of spirituality, let us take the Buddhist mandala. Jung has helped to make the mandala known in the West as a symbol of integration and perfection. It is an effective symbol which has to be used, if not ritually, at least almost sacramentally, as an outward and visible sign of an inward grace or spiritual state. Using it for meditation, as Jung himself discovered during his period of profound psychic turmoil in his late thirties, can centre the self, knitting together the conflicting aspects that are driving towards disintegration. The mandala also draws the self towards the ideal, towards perfection, whether that is thought of as transcendent and 'out there' or as located in the depths of the psyche. At the centre of the mandala is a human form. The symbol of the self (the human form) and the symbol of divinity (the complex patterns creating harmony and integration within the perfect circle) are united. We are reminded of Blake's expression 'the human form divine' (Blake, 1977, p. 111).

It is difficult not to see a connection between this and what happens at Holy Communion or Mass. There we receive a small white disc, the wafer or host, as likely as not bearing upon it at the centre the embossed form of a crucified human figure. We take that powerful symbol of the union of humanity and deity, of our oneness with God through Christ, into ourselves as we allow it to dissolve on the tongue. Of course, there are other conjunctions of symbolism at work here, not least that of maternal nurture. But what more striking example of intro-jection – of taking the symbols of ideal identity, with which we seek to be united, into ourselves so that we may be more fully conformed to them – could there be? Von Balthasar quotes William of St Thierry's exhortation: 'Come closer to the form that gives you form' (Von Balthasar, 1982, vol. 1, p. 288).

At the consummation of Dante's journey, at the moment of the beatific vision when his desire was fully redeemed and became one with the love that moves the perfect and uncor-rupted spheres, he saw a three-dimensional symbol of three concentric and superimposed circles, representing of course the Holy Trinity, and in the centre of the second was a human form, the Son of God, Jesus Christ, the Word made flesh (Dante, 1981, pp. 498f.: *Paradiso* XXXIII, ll. 115–32). I must confess that I find the conjunction of Dante's symbol, the host at the Eucharist, and the mandala quite arresting. It reinforces once again my contention that the rites of passage, in the context of the sacramental life of the Church, have an ultimately christological meaning.

The liturgy in mission

In liturgy the Church sets forth in heightened language, symbolic gesture and enacted drama the story of salvation, the faith of the Church. Liturgy does this more effectively than preaching and more explicitly than compassionate service to the needy. Those non-churchgoers who participate in the occasional offices may be said to be 'trying out a church'. There is a perceptible sense, in many a baptism party or wedding congregation, of dipping a toe in the water to test the temperature, a tentative foray into something that just might have something very important to offer. In his study of the dynamics of the local church, *Congregation*, Hopewell empha-sizes that potential members are 'testing their own symbolic expression against that of the prospective church. Silently they ask of the congregation: What does this place say about us? What does it signify about our values and the way we see the world?' (Hopewell, 1987, p. 6). In the symbolic rapport that needs to be established between client and congregation, the style of the liturgy has a vital role to play. As Bridget Nichols demonstrates, the liturgy expresses an invitation that calls for acceptance, makes a proposal that requires consideration and establishes a threshold that may be crossed (Nichols, 1996). 'Out of the fullness of the heart, the mouth speaks.' Does a liturgy aptly articulate what we want to say to God and to each other in church: about birth and rebirth, about getting married, about death and sorrow, about forgiveness and hope? The liturgy is a bridge between the inchoate and unarticulated religious aspirations of the people gathered in church and the God who has the good things of salvation to bestow. The bridge needs to be kept in good repair. Familiar expressions, that once performed their office admirably, can come to seem unsuitable. They no longer say what the faithful heart wants to say to its God. They may be perfectly sound theologically, but they strike the wrong note. The general confession in the Book of Common Prayer (1662) Holy Communion service is a piece of liturgy that many people today find difficult to make their own.

Modern alternative liturgies are, however, not always successful. The Church of England's Alternative Service Book 1980 met with accusations of contrivance, banality, woodenness and absence of transcendence (see Martin and Mullen, 1981; for an analysis of theological strengths and weaknesses of the ASB, see Nichols, 1996). The ASB baptism service (now thankfully largely superseded) was a particularly abysmal example of these attributes. Conducting this service for a congregation largely made up of non-churchgoers was extremely hard work. Sometimes it felt like driving a car full of passengers uphill on four flat tyres. Its combination of matter-of-fact statements with a didactic tone and sexist language was pastorally lethal. The text read in places like the instructions on an electrical appliance.

Vivid metaphors, which are also doctrinally sound, are richly present in the initiation services published in 1998. These are a world away from those of the ASB 1980 and seem more pastorally effective. The language is concrete, dynamic, uplifting and biblical. The involvement of the church community in the service is integral. Candidates for baptism (and confirmation) are not grilled but participate in the faith of the Church. The distribution of theological symbolism is well thought out and explained in notes. A prayer of thanksgiving for the birth of the child is available. However, the 1998 initiation services are not beyond criticism. The baptism service suffers from theological overload as biblical image is piled upon biblical image to an extent that can become oppressive. And any occasional office with thirteen unnumbered sections is open to criticism on grounds of pastoral practicality.

The functions of the liturgy

The irreducibly symbolic character of liturgy is underlined if we attend to the distinction between two functions of liturgy: the explicit and the tacit, the manifest and the latent. The liturgy says certain things about God and ourselves. But it also does certain things to us – to our perceptions, our feelings, our attitudes. The tacit, latent function is particularly vital because it connects with the unarticulated, largely unexamined demands made by the submerged nine-tenths of the human psyche, the unconscious – and it is the unconscious that always wins out in the end. The faith of most people today, whether regular worshippers or not, is still instinctive, intuitive, and unthought-out, just as it was in earlier semi-literate ages. This faith is sustained by richness of imagery and association, by a sense of mystery and an awareness of unexplored depths which are evoked by Bible readings, prayers and hymns.

The modern Church has been seduced by the mirage of a supposed higher state of rationalized belief and self-conscious practice that will probably never be typical of most believers. The trauma often produced by liturgical change bears little relation to the respective liturgical merits of the rites. Rather, it points to the deep personal and emotional investment that worshippers make in the words and symbols of the service. These are important, not for what they actually say (which is not fully understood), but for what they represent. Neglect of this fact has taken its toll of the language of worship which so often fails to nourish the deep longings of the worshippers. In following this strategy, the modern Church is, I believe, acting against its own best interests. In principle, it is obviously good to know what we are saying, to understand what we are reading, and to clarify and examine our beliefs. But it is doubtful whether most worshippers do rationalize what they are doing in that explicit way. Pastoral experience suggests that modern liturgies do not make things very much clearer to most church-goers – how much less then to those who experience the Church's worship and ministry mainly through the occasional offices of Harvest Festival and Remembrance Sunday. People do not use liturgy in that way.

However, people may comprehend what they do not fully understand. They may know much more than they can artic-ulate. Polanyi suggests that the worshipper 'indwells' the fabric of the liturgy, becoming completely absorbed in it, and that Christian worship sustains an heuristic vision and spiritual longing that leads ever further:

> The dwelling of the Christian worshipper within the ritual of divine service differs from any other dwelling within a framework of inherent excellence, by the fact that this indwelling is not enjoyed. The confession of guilt, the surrender to God's mercy, the prayer for grace, the praise of God, bring about mounting tension. By these ritual acts the worshipper accepts the obligation to achieve what he knows to be beyond his own unaided powers and strives towards it in the hope of a merciful visitation from above. The ritual of worship is expressly designed to induce and sustain this state of anguish, surrender and hope. (Polanyi, 1958, p. 198)

With their emphasis on the birth-pangs of transformation, Polanyi's comments provide a salutary corrective to the current emphasis on celebration and feeling good.

The latent function of the liturgy should not be overlooked. David Martin has pointed out (in a paper in connection with a Consultation on Common Religion at St George's House, Windsor Castle: Martin, 1994) that, though the churches are not the only institutions that care for individuals, they are 'the only repositories of all-embracing meanings pointing beyond the immediate to the ultimate. They are the only institutions that deal in tears and concern themselves with the breaking points of human existence.' Martin went on to claim that 'out of the varied situations in which people find themselves, there emerge dumb requests for those things which are already present in the sacred narrative and the repository of Christian sign and gesture'. Occasional worshippers in particular should be helped to recognize that the Church offers something that corresponds to their deepest needs. The liturgy requires, therefore, the sort of language that acknowledges and articulates the deepest, common human concerns, not language that merely mirrors the private preoccupations of what is, in this perspective, an in-group.

In accordance with the paradigm of incarnation, the Church seeks to be involved in all aspects of human life, showing thereby how God is present as Creator, Redeemer and Sanctifier. But the Church cannot hope to do this unless all aspects of life are reflected in the liturgy. It is a theological truth that God's presence is not far from any one of God's children, but it is the role of the liturgy to illuminate this for individuals. We need to go further than *Common Worship* does in this respect. Bruce Reed has finely said:

> The strength of the Christian movement depends on its capacity to generate a vocabulary of symbols which could be co-ordinated to cover all the contingencies of human existence. Its power would be demonstrated if there were no deep concern of the human psyche which could not respond to the gospel, and no lofty aspiration of the spirit which it could not irradiate like the sun glancing on the wings of a kingfisher. (Reed, 1978, p. 220)

The music of familiar phrases and arresting rhythms, richness of metaphor, symbol and myth, echoes of associative intimacies, and glimpses of what is beyond our ken, are the vehicles of sacred values and shared meanings. In this tacit and indirect way, the obscure background of human consciousness, where the deepest reflection goes on, is brought into contact with the mysterious ground of all reality. It is vital for the language of the liturgy to have a texture that corresponds to the transcendent and ultimately ineffable nature of the reality that it hopes to evoke.

The language of liturgy is in fact poetic without being lyrical (see further Avis, 1999, ch. 8: 'Liturgy as Literature'). It is a disciplined poetry and its *raison d'être* is not a function of individual artistic subjectivity. Rather, it exists to mediate the experience of a great community, the Christian Church, that extends through time and space. The lyric, by contrast, is the apparently spontaneous expression of the feeling, the affectivity of an individual. Liturgy needs to be restrained enough to avoid offending the sensitivities of worshippers by being too shrill or specific emotionally. As well as requiring sacred places (churches) and sacred persons (priests and other ministers), liturgy demands sacred space – personal space, so that worshippers are not expected to wear their hearts on their sleeves. It should leave worshippers unmolested to think their own thoughts and use the common prayer as a vehicle for their own prayer. This space makes it possible for the God who is supremely personal to be encountered through a mutual indwelling of personal space. It is significant that, of those whose religious experiences have been studied by the Alister Hardy Institute, most had received their encounter with the holy in stillness and solitude. At the same time, however, liturgy needs to be expansive enough to accommodate the emotions of many persons of diverse educational and cultural backgrounds and of various degrees of Christian maturity. It allows them to indwell its language. Liturgy gives the Christian religious affections 'a local habitation and a name'.

7

The Cross in the Community

Community in perception and reality

'Community' is a chronically over-used word that has undergone currency-depreciation. It is a 'feel-good' word whose bluff has now been called. Not all so-called communities are beneficial: some are oppressive or claustrophobic. Community is not an unmixed good. The term is ideologically suspect: it purports to be straightforwardly descriptive but in fact entails a value judgement. At the micro-level of general usage, many rural parishes (let's keep on calling them parishes, not villages) still have a sense of community. But at the other end of the spectrum of usage, the macro-level, the term 'the international community' is almost completely prescriptive, far removed from the real state of affairs – the international scene being, in most respects, anything but a true community. It is sometimes argued that public life does not – and by definition should not – possess the attribute of community, because that depends on intimacy (Cochran, 1990, pp. 63, 75), but that seems to me to be a rather Procrustean approach. In wartime and other emergency situations there can be a sense of national community and even a feeling of community among allies who are undergoing the same trials and sufferings. However, the point is well made that 'community' is much too easily and too frequently invoked.

Even as far as the countryside is concerned, the term 'community' should be approached with our sceptical antennae quivering. Rural parishes have a useful modicum of communal authenticity, but they are far from being utopias. However, many urban parishes lack even basic communal viability. As Steven Croft has pointed out, until recently the parish priest was dealing with people who were already shaped into a community by other circumstances of their lives. Now the priest sometimes finds no pre-existing community. One of the crucial tasks of mission then becomes 'the creation of primary communities in a desert of isolated lives' (Croft, 1999, p. 20). In the process of industrialization during the eighteenth and nineteenth centuries, families and individuals migrated to the towns and cities in search of a better livelihood than they could obtain in the country. Rural existence was often wretched. The eighteenth-century parson-poet of Aldeburgh, Suffolk, Thomas Crabbe, set out to expose centuries of ideological mystification of the rural community in the pastoral idylls of English poetry. In his narrative poem *The Parish* Crabbe resolved to portray the distressing reality, stripped of all idealization.

No longer truth, though shown in verse, disdain
But own the Village Life a life of pain.

(Williams, 1973, p. 87)

In the affluent parts of the West, the process of migration from country to city has been partly reversed as those who can afford to do so move back to the countryside and commute to the cities to work, or retire to the countryside in search of the community life they lacked in the anonymous conurbations, or become part-time members of rural communities when they visit their holiday homes at weekends. Though this trend puts house prices in country areas beyond the reach of many native first-time buyers (who find themselves forced to move into the towns), it provides work and other economic benefits for those who remain. Rural church life benefits from the influx of capable, comfortably-off, public-spirited professional people who often become parish treasurers, secretaries or churchwardens and form the backbone of parish organizations and of discussion and Bible study groups.

There is, in historical perspective, an interchange, a flux and reflux between the urban and the rural. They stand for different qualities of life, as much in people's perceptions as in reality. Lewis Mumford suggested that 'human life swings between two poles: movement and settlement'. The city is stereotypically identified with movement and dynamism; the country with settlement and permanence. In the modern imagination, the city stands for mobility, vitality and variety, but it pays a price for these attributes in alienation, anonymity and disorientation. The countryside represents, in the modern imagination, a more wholesome existence, lived closer to nature and in real community, but it pays the price of isolation, cultural deprivation and inconvenience. These are stereotypes, serving ideological needs. The countryside has acquired the idea of a natural way of life: one of peace, innocence and simplicity. The city, on the other hand, has acquired the idea of a centre of energy and achievement: of learning, communication, culture. 'Powerful hostile associations have also developed: on the city as the place of noise, worldliness and ambition; on the country as a place of backwardness, ignorance, limitation' (Williams, 1973, p. 1).

This was not always the case. Until early modern times (say the late sixteenth century), the city or town represented the ideal of community and of civilized existence – hence the dominant imagery of the city of God in the Bible, patristic writing and Christian hymnody – while the country stood for barbarity and boorishness. As Keith Thomas puts it, 'The town was the home of learning, manners, taste and sophistication. It was the arena of human fulfilment.' In 1700 over three-quarters of the population of Britain lived in the countryside. Only about 13 per cent lived in towns of over 5,000 inhabitants, large villages by today's Home Counties standards. By the mid-nineteenth century the majority lived in towns and cities (Thomas, 1984, pp. 242ff.: 'Town or Country?'). It rather looks as though the more we lived in cities, the less we liked them. But the converse seems to apply too. We tend to idealize the place where we do not happen to live. The grass is always greener on the other side of the fence. As Gorringe says, the country is really no more natural than the town (Gorringe, 2002, p. 122).

A symposium on location and identity *Space and Place* takes a critical look at the promotion of glamorous urban living. In spite of the political rhetoric of renewal and regeneration, the authors maintain, urban regeneration schemes are not the harbingers of an urban renaissance. They are in fact simply recycled visions. They express a yearning for an idea of urban life that is no longer sustainable, and are characterized by a vocabulary of nostalgia and loss. Nineteenth-century Romanticism created an idealized image of rural life to pit against the debased and alienated life of the great cities. The new urban romanticism also looks for a cosy, cleaned-up version of city life that avoids the conflicts and stresses of urban existence (Robbins, in Carter *et al.*, 1993, p. 321). Praise of community must not fall into these stereotypes. It must not presuppose a fictional, static, unchanging rural paradise. 'The rural idyll actually comprised social misery, unhealthy housing, political injustice and institutional deference' (Norman, 2002, p. 113). The ideal of fixed settlement was achieved at the expense of disregarding the victims of the Poor Law, enclosures and unemployment. Economic factors, not sentiment, have made both countryside and city what they are. An analysis of the phenomena of identity and location concludes that 'places are no longer the clear supports of our identity' (Morley and Robbins, in Carter *et al.*, 1993, p. 5). The sense of permanent location, of a home and a community, may not give the support to identity that it once did, but it is still integral to it, even as merely a home-shaped hole in the heart. Sheldrake defines 'place' as 'space that has the capacity to be remembered and to evoke what is most precious' (Sheldrake, 2001, p. 1).

The power of the home-place can be seen at work in the struggle of Israelis and Palestinians for land that is regarded as sacred, however barren. 'Though the "homes" which ground and house identities can be denied people physically by enforced exile or lost through chosen migration, they still continue to resonate throughout the imaginations of displaced communities' (Carter *et al.*, 1993, p. vii).

But the idea of the home-place can also be applied, much less dramatically, to the tug on the heart-strings exerted by thoughts of where we once belonged, an experience powerfully evoked in autobiographies of childhood. As Raymond Williams comments: 'around the idea of settlement . . . a real structure of values has grown. It draws on many deep and persistent feelings: an identification with the people among whom we grew up; an attachment to the place, the landscape among which we first lived and learned to see' (Williams, 1973, p. 84). 'Familiar landscapes are the geography of the human imagin-ation' (Sheldrake, 2001, p. 14). In *Landscape and Memory*, Schama asserts: 'Before it can ever be a repose for the senses, landscape is a work of the mind. Its scenery is built up as much from strata of memory as from layers of rock' (Schama, 1995, pp. 6f.).

By tracing expressions of nostalgia back from one generation to another, Williams shows that lament for a lost rural innocence or urban intimacy is a matter of perception and of rationalization. We are rationalizing a longing for community. 'It is not so much the old village or the old back street that is significant', he writes. 'It is the perception and affirmation of a world in which one is not necessarily a stranger and an agent, but can be a member, a discoverer, in a shared source of life' (Williams, 1973, p. 298). It seems inevitable that we should be romantic when we talk about community – we all have so much invested in the identity that comes through belonging – but let us not be too starry-eyed: let us be realistic and critical too.

For all its drawbacks, 'community' is a word that we cannot do without. It stands for an ideal that is honoured and praised by almost everyone. A community is usually (but not necessarily) an established, localized society, made up of a web of relationships between individuals and families that are of varying degrees of formality or intimacy and are governed by patterns of mutual expectations, duties and conventions. A community seeks to benefit its members and to perpetuate itself. To this end, it welcomes others into its midst provided that they honour its code of expectations, duties and conventions. A community preserves traditions, celebrates its identity and supports its members. There is no community that does not have to define its boundaries, but to be healthy it welcomes interaction, on its own terms, with its environment, that is to say, with contiguous communities. Thus a vital community can be described as an open system, drawing energy from outside and exporting its products to other communities.

Almost every community has three foci. It has focal places (buildings and spaces), focal persons (leaders, representatives, officers) and focal occasions (times and seasons). These help to structure the life of a community, both giving it a centre or heart and setting inevitable parameters or boundaries. The three foci and their connection with each other are affirmed and celebrated in symbolic social performances that knit a community together and redefine the boundaries. The boundaries (parameters) are crucial.

A community is prescriptive. There are things that are 'done' and things that are 'not done'. You cannot get away with just anything, as you can in individualistic, anonymous atomized cultures where communities have disintegrated. Communities limit choice because they know that increasing choice saps loyalty and undermines continuity. Communities share a common purpose, broadly defined, but argue over the best way of implementing that purpose. In order to survive, they must be capable of containing conflict and somehow sublimating the energy it generates towards the common good.

There is currently a groundswell of concern, on both sides of the Atlantic, that is reaffirming the value of community. This is much more than the product of illusion and nostalgia implied by Norman when he remarks that 'the whole texture of assumptions about the importance of "community" is woven from insubstantial threads of social myth' (Norman, 2002, 114). It is in fact a reaction against the tide of individualism and the privatization of values so unsparingly denounced by Norman. The communitarian movement in the United States and the swing back to affirming civic responsibility, a sense of the common good and the need for a collective ethic in Britain are responses to untrammelled individualism and the ethic of personal fulfilment and unreciprocated rights (see Etzioni, 1995; Selbourne, 1994; Atkinson, 1994, for down-to-earth practical forms of community regeneration).

As those know who have lived and worked over a substantial period of time in fairly well defined, basically stable communities (not least parochial clergy and other ministers), you cannot have community without tears! Community is bound up with identity, territory and tradition. These are prime sources of disagreement and conflict of interest. Conflict – the breakdown of consensus – is brought about by the scramble for the good things we seek: not merely the physical, material necessities of life, but perhaps above all the elusive goods of privilege, reputation, esteem. Conflict is generated because not everyone can have all these things at once. The limelight is limited. The spotlight does not fall on everyone. There is thus a problem of scarcity: scarcity of physical or moral goods that individuals, families and whole communities work and struggle for (cf. Shils, 1975). In its hierarchies, deferences and inequalities a community is a sort of low-key ant heap. There is a constant scurrying to and fro and intense transactions of energy, but it is all held together by a hidden structure of command that informs social assumptions and expectations.

Church and community

There is a deep Christian instinct that God and community are intrinsically connected. Theologically, it can be said that community is inherently ordered to the blessedness of the life of God. T. S. Eliot wrote:

> What life have you if you have not life together?
> There is no life that is not in community,
> And no community not lived in praise of God.
> (Eliot, 1974, p. 168: chorus from *The Rock*)

A life not lived together, a life not shared, is not a life worth living. In truth, such an existence is impossible. So far, Eliot's claim is incontrovertible. But can we go further and make the bold theological claim that every true community serves to glorify God, even when it is entirely unconscious of so doing? We can begin to explore Eliot's dictum in *The Rock* that there exists 'no community not lived in praise of God' by exploring the relationship between the Christian Church and the idea of community.

The relationship between the Church and 'community' is a complex one. The Church is itself a community and a patently imperfect one. It is set in the midst of a community which is currently subject to a number of counter-communal pressures. Its ultimate *raison d'être* is the creation of a qualitative kind of community – what the New Testament calls *koinonia* – that reflects and embodies the perfect community that is the life of God.

Church AS community

The Church itself exists in the mode of community. The word community here is not a sociological descriptor, like 'region' or 'state': it is a value judgement grounded in eschatology. In the ministry of Jesus the Church is the 'little flock', the chosen, faithful, but fragile remnant. It is, as it were, a corporate messianic person gathered and restored by his words and deeds for the last days, the time of fulfilment of God's purposes (Lohfink, 1984, p. 71, etc.). That eschatological action of Jesus in constituting (or more correctly reconstituting) the Church in himself and by means of his destiny, is the unchanging foundation of the Church. His incarnation, ministry, passion, resurrection and ascension, with the ensuing gift of the Holy Spirit, incorporate the Church into the triune life of God.

The European churches of the Reformation recently stated: 'In receiving the justifying grace of God in Jesus Christ through the Holy Spirit people are joined in community with each other... The Spirit is the power of community originating from the oneness of the Father and the Son' (Leuenberg Fellowship, 1995, para. 1.3). The Church itself is a community because it derives its existence from the triune life of God, worked out in the unfolding of salvation history. The deepest meaning of the Church is a Trinitarian one. The *koinonia*, the communion, fellowship or mutual participation of the Church, is created by the Holy Spirit through all the means of grace: principally the preaching of the gospel, the administration of the sacraments and the exercise of pastoral care and oversight. Thus the Acts of the Apostles says of the first Christians that 'they continued in the Apostles' teaching and *koinonia*, the breaking of the bread and the prayers' (Acts 2.42). St Paul pictures the Church as community in a twofold manner: in a fraternal way, as a loving family, and in an organic way, as the 'body of Christ' (Banks, 1994). The Letter to the Hebrews and 1 Peter prefer the image of God's priestly people. The Second Vatican Council dwelt on the biblical image of the Church as the 'people of God'.

Though the worldwide Church is perhaps more aptly described as a society than as a community (in applying the latter term we would be coming dangerously close to the vacuity of the common expression 'the international community'), it rejoices in the bonds of communion that make it one, as far as its divided state permits. These bonds of communion are, for example: the Bible; the apostolic faith in the ecumenical creeds; our common baptism, mutually recognized; the Lord's Prayer; and fragmentary and incomplete forms of a common ministry, a common Eucharist and shared structures of conciliarity. Within these vital bonds of communion, representative persons such as the Pope, the Ecumenical Patriarch and the Archbishop of Canterbury, take their place. As a community itself, the Christian Church well understands what is essential to its communal life. It exhibits the same logic or structure as 'secular' communities: the network of relationships of various degrees of formality or intimacy, sustained by shared beliefs and values; living tradition as a resource for adaptation to new circumstances; the importance of territory; established patterns of expectation, duties and conventions. The Church has its own focal persons (the clergy, ministers and bishops), focal places (churches, chapels and cathedrals) and focal times and seasons (Sundays and the Christian Year). These provide the essential constituents of the rite (or sacred performance) which constitutes the liturgy: time, place and relationship (to use Grainger's terms again).

The liturgy of the sacraments gives embodiment and shape to the meaning and significance of life for Christians. That meaning and coherence seems always at our fingertips, but at the same time just beyond our grasp (for what follows see the suggestive insights of Grainger, 1994).

- *Time:* the rite invests the fleeting moment with salutary meaning by enclosing it in a series of rites of passage that unite us with the destiny, the journey, of Jesus Christ in salvation history. The rite has the power to convey healing of body, mind and spirit because it unites the spiritual drama of descent and ascent, death and resurrection, with the natural rhythms of the body, of day and night, light and darkness, and of the seasons (the rhythm of the cosmos). Even the Eucharist is a rite of passage in a sense, though it is regularly repeated, because it marks our journey and transition from one state of being to another, 'from glory to glory'.
- *Space:* sacred space, like sacred time, is therapeutic. It is a set-apart, bounded space where no harm can come. There it is safe to take the risk of allowing oneself to be touched by a power that can make one whole. Our vulnerability, pain and guilt are held and healed within this matrix. There may be something intrinsically therapeutic about the symbolic words and actions of ritual, even when it is not specifically Christian. Perhaps all rites have the power

to knit lives together in the context of community and tradition, even when that integration is then put to uses motivated by fear or hate, like witchcraft. If so, this must be mainly due to the potential of symbols to unite the individual and the group, the particular and the universal, the immanent and the transcendent (see Avis, 1999). Grainger seems to make these claims for ritual as such, rather than for the rites of the Church: 'To present movement, gesture, sounds, objects and words in ritual form is to perform a healing action' (Grainger, 1994, p. 109). That is very probably the case, but how much more so when the words tell of divine redemptive acts in human history and the symbolic actions are instituted by the historical person of the Saviour with his gospel promises attached!

• *Person:* the facilitating role of focal persons equates to Grainger's 'relationship'. It is personal mediation that brings people together in sacred time and sacred space. Someone has to facilitate it, to be the catalyst. Wholeness is not effected by impersonal processes, but when heart speaks to heart. Though this is a genuinely mediating role, it is not sacerdotal, and it is certainly not magical. Relationality is the key, and that cannot occur without a basis in the life of a distinct community and an outreach into networks of wider community around. Let us explore this a bit further.

Concerted communal actions, in a liturgical sense, are profoundly embodied. 'In ritual we use our bodies to get as close to God as we can without our minds getting in the way,' says Grainger (1994, p. 113) with thought-provoking overstatement. But it is true that all our senses, not least that of touch, are involved in liturgy and sacraments and that they are the gateway to the spirit. The Psalms evoke tasting, smelling and touching as well as seeing and hearing. What else could we do but use all the faculties of our embodied spirits (or pneumatic bodies) when we are responding to 'This is my body. Do this is remembrance of me'? (On the pastoral value of participation in the liturgical action see Moody, 2000.)

Wholeness is only possible as far as the therapeutic relationship is possible. The potential scope of healing is the potential scope of relationship. The connecting role of the wounded healer is therefore pivotal. As Grainger emphasizes, rites express and embody experiences of wholeness in the only way such experiences can be expressed: that is to say, in the language of a conscious relationship with another. Because ritual needs people in order to express itself, it is capable of great subtlety of meaning; 'and yet its meaning is clear to us when we approach it on its own terms. We learn by involvement' (Grainger, 1994, p. 107).

I think I need to emphasize once again that the determinants of Christian community are not simply sociological. They are ultimately and decisively theological in the sense that they are grounded in revealed knowledge of the nature and purposes of God. They take their rise from what the kingdom of God, embodied and focused in Jesus, demands of us. That demand is social but not merely sociological. It is the vocation to a corporate ethic. As Lohfink puts it in his exposition of the theme of community in the ministry of Jesus: 'Isolated individuals are simply not in a position to exemplify and to live the social dimension of the reign of God' (Lohfink, 1984, p. 72).

The three *foci* (sacred places, sacred persons and sacred seasons) should therefore not be regarded as three huge monolithic political pillars, holding up the Church, but they should be seen as emerging from the organic vitality of the body of Christ. In the tension between dynamics and structure in the life of the Church, there can be no dynamics without structure, but equally, no structure without dynamics. Structures are historically, culturally and socially contingent and therefore vary from one context to another. Moreover, they are dependent on the dynamics that give rise to them in the first place. Whenever we say that the structured means of grace (such as sacraments and ministry) are God-given, we should acknowledge that the sovereign Spirit blows where it wills.

We often take the historic structural foci of the Church for granted, treating them as a sort of benevolent accident and imagining that the Church's real vitality lies elsewhere. If we reflect for a moment, however, on the reality of pastoral encounters – and on the roles played by church buildings, the ordained ministry and the Christian year in those – we will see, I think, that the historic foci are essential conditions of pastoral mission. Even in our highly mobile, fragmented society, in which parish structures mean little to most people, pastoral mission would be severely curtailed without these foci, for all their supposed historical impedimenta and cultural liabilities. Although the structures can get out of proportion and become obstacles to the pastoral flexibility required by mission, it must be admitted that in experience they are precisely what facilitates most pastoral interactions.

Church IN community

Bosch lays down that 'the Christian faith never exists except as translated into a culture' (Bosch, 1991, p. 447). A key aspect of the inculturation of the gospel is its translation, with all the risks and compromises that such translation entails, into the social, economic and political fabric of human life. Just as humankind cannot flourish without such structures, so the gospel itself somehow remains up in the air, disembodied, elusive and lacking purchase on our lives until it is so entextured. The community of the gospel exists – and can only exist – within the structures of civil society. As Sheldrake emphasizes, every encounter with the sacred is rooted in place and therefore takes the form of a narrative (Sheldrake, 2001, p. 17)

As a community itself, the Church is set within a wider community which constitutes its significant environment and helps to define how the Church actually understands itself. The Church respects the established contours of human identity because its view of the world is informed by its doctrines of creation, incarnation and redemption. As Gabriel Hebert SSM said, 'The things done and said in church must have a direct relation to the things done and said everywhere else' (Hebert, 1935, p. 8). Christianity is disposed to work with the grain of broader community structures, both local and national. The Church seeks to relate to the focal persons of the community (leaders and representatives in local community, region, nation and state). It wants a presence in the focal places, especially the institutions of civil society (universities, hospitals, schools, community centres, cultural facilities, industrial plant and business networks). It is inclined to respect the focal times and seasons of the wider community (national anniversaries, holidays, festivals, terms). The Church seeks to avoid two extreme positions with regard to the wider community. One is to withdraw into itself as a ghetto, sealed off from the life of the community around it. The other is to become absorbed and dissolved in that community, with the loss of its own distinctive identity. The middle path of enhancing distinctiveness through committed engagement should be its aim.

In his study of secularization, Gilbert argued that 'churches as social organisations are effective only when their own structures mirror those of the societies which they seek to serve'. 'In order to thrive,' he continued, 'they must adapt themselves to the basic social divisions and settlement patterns of their constituencies.' The developed medieval parochial system, where church and community structures were coterminous, provides an obvious example of the ideal relationship between church and community (Gilbert, 1980, p. 80). The Church is predisposed to mirror, in its own organization, the established contours of social identity.

However, the progressive urbanization of Britain during the past two hundred years, to the point where 90 per cent of the population lives in cities and towns, has created an environment that militates against traditional models of religious community. We seem to spend an increasing proportion of our lives passing through spaces that are not real places, such as supermarkets, shopping malls, airports, motorway services and railway terminals. They are mere holders of transience, providing a framework for fluidity. Those who pass through them leave no mark upon them. They struggle to achieve a value in themselves and not simply in relation to further destinations. They cry out for people, even the staff themselves, who will give them some enduring identity.

Mobility creates rootlessness, damages community identity, disperses families and undermines loyalty to place. The social identity of the commuting urban dweller is only minimally territorial. This fact obviously weakens the appeal of the churches and the purchase they have on the population, since they remain primarily territorial in organisation and ethos. I regard this rooting in place not as something merely incidental, but as something of permanent importance and value in human life, which the Church stands for over against socio-economic trends that may prove to be short-term in the long history of society. Simone Weil said that to be rooted was perhaps the most important and least recognized need of the human soul. Human beings, she pointed out, had roots by virtue of their active participation in the life of a community that 'preserved in living shape certain particular treasures of the past and certain particular expectations for the future'. 'Uprootedness', Weil believed, was 'by far the most dangerous malady to which human societies are exposed' (Weil, 1952, pp. 43, 47).

Brueggemann, writing on the theme of 'the land' in biblical faith, insists that 'a sense of place is a primary category of faith' and concludes that the central issue is 'not emancipation but *rootage*, not meaning but *belonging*, not separation from the community but *location* within it' (cited by Davey, in Rowland and Vincent, 1995, p. 65). These are perennial human spiritual needs and the Church understands them profoundly.

Nevertheless, it is no good the Church indulging in nostalgia for a more settled society, sticking its head in the sand while waiting for the currents of social mobility to pass. Writing more than twenty years ago, Gilbert castigated the churches for failing to adapt to the new situation. Organized religion had failed to cope with the decline of the territorial community and the emergence of pluralistic, partial communities. The idea of territory remained central to Christian strategy and church leaders still tended to think of work among newer, functional communities as the exception (Gilbert, 1980, pp. 84f.). In response to this challenge, I would make two comments.

First, rootlessness may be a fact but it is not something to celebrate. Everyone needs roots and many people devote a good deal of time and effort to tracing them (incidentally, this often brings them into useful contact with the Church and the clergy, as they visit parish churches, consult registers and try to identify headstones). Territoriality is an integral aspect of human identity, as sociologists have recognized (Shils, 1975). Edwin Muir wrote:

> Seek the beginnings, learn from where you came,
> And know the various earth of which you are made.
>   (Muir, 1984, p. 169: 'The Journey Back')

Furthermore, the life of the Church provides, even temporarily, stability, security and support in highly dynamic urban cultures. Although the sense of continuity in relation to place is undoubtedly weaker in the urban situation, it is not unchallenged in the countryside either. The influx of urbanites into rural communities means that there are many individuals who have acquired an adoptive loyalty. They are grafted into existing patterns of continuity. Sometimes, however, they prove more ardent defenders of local identity and traditions than the natives. Any contrast between urban and rural contexts is relative. Continuity and stability have to be worked at in both country and city.

My second comment, in response to Gilbert's criticisms, is to affirm strongly that opportunities for chaplaincies or sector ministries should be seized with both hands. Where they do not already exist, the churches should be proactive (as some already are) in creating them in partnership with civil or other institutions. Such ministries should be funded as a priority – even, to some extent, at the expense of parochial ministry. One of the reasons why dioceses need a strong parochial power-base, in terms of numbers, activities and finance, is to enable them to fund mission outreach through sector ministries. Developing patterns of collaborative ministry, where lay people and clergy work together in benefice-wide ministry teams, may eventually help to release some funding for this purpose.

In many 'secular' institutions, it is Christian lay people, rather than ordained chaplains, who must bear the brunt of witness and ministry: they need to be increasingly equipped and motivated for this. However, there will always be a need for the Church's 'official representatives', the clergy, who have the calling, training and commissioning to minister word, sacrament and pastoral care on behalf of Christ's Church. I have a hunch that, on the whole, and with some conspicuous exceptions, it is recognized chaplains or sector ministers, rather than the so-called 'ministers in secular employment' (members of the workforce who are ordained with a view to witness and ministry at work) who are the publicly identifiable agents of the Church's mission outside the parochial structures.

Church FOR community

The celebrated Archbishop's report on the Church in Urban Priority Areas *Faith in the City* affirmed a noble ideal for the relationship between the Church and its environing society: 'A

Christian community is one that is open to, and responsible for, the whole of the society in which it is set, and proclaims its care for the weak, its solidarity with all, and its values which lie beyond the mere satisfaction of material needs' ([ACUPA], 1985, p. 59: para. 3.22). This statement – admirable as it is – puts only one side of the picture, however. The relation between society and church is actually reciprocal. Their destinies are linked together. The Christian community and the wider community are in the same boat. Their interests are interdependent. The fortunes of religion are linked to the fortunes of community. Whatever else religion may be, it is at the very least 'the ideology of community' (to use Bryan Wilson's phrase once again). As non-Christian communal activities, such as clubs, societies, political parties and team sports, experience a decline in their membership and support in areas where community structures are under threat, so too the Church has to work harder to gather support for its Sunday schools, youth groups, uniformed organisations and women's or men's groups. This suggests that the Church is inevitably on the side of all salutary forms of community.

The Church, by its nature, has an inbuilt bias towards community. It exercises a 'preferential option' in favour of community (cf. Jon Davies, 'A Preferential Option for the Family', in Barton, 1996). It wants to throw its weight behind all beneficial forms of community. The Church has a major stake in the sustaining of community. Although the sustaining of community entails privileging continuity over discontinuity and therefore a predisposition towards social conservatism, 'community' here is not code for nostalgia for a past way of life nor does it necessarily imply a stable society, low on mobility. It does not automatically imply the notion of settlement. The Christian faith does not have to endorse all social structures that call themselves communities. Nor should it have a predisposition towards rural rather than urban existence. Its relation to given forms of community must always be one of 'critical solidarity'. The Church is committed to the creation of true community because that belongs to the essence of Christianity as a corporate faith. Christian community (*koinonia*) is a sign, instrument and foretaste of the 'peaceable kingdom'.

Community is the first casualty of those deep-seated factors in modern society (differentiation of institutions in society, the society-wide organization of services, the impersonal character of social relationships, globalization and all its works) that, as we noted earlier, give rise to secularization, and religion is the second. Where community succumbs, the fate of religion is almost decided. So Christianity has a vested interest in community. It is on the side of all those social bonds that support or enhance human flourishing but against those that oppress or enslave human beings. Christianity affirms families, incomplete families and faithful relationships. It encourages loyalty toward place, custom and tradition, but it is not chauvinistic and also teaches the virtues of tolerance, sympathy and hospitality. The Christian faith knows that it is not good for humankind to be alone (cf. Genesis 2.18). It affirms that it is the will of God for humanity to live in community.

The Church cannot be neutral about community. Clearly it must be committed to building community. It is therefore fitting that the Church should work through community structures and community projects in carrying forward its mission. Without those structures based on kinship, affinity or common economic interests, the Church lacks purchase among the population for its mission. Community projects are one of the most effective vehicles of mission. They can unite a local Christian community, broaden its horizons, give a new purpose to pastoral care and provide the indispensable 'stepping stones' to participation in the life of the Church for those outside. David Sheppard points out that, if the gulf between most urban working-class people and the organized Church is ever to be bridged, there is a need for many 'stepping stones' – events, groups, projects, together with all the pastoral opportunities offered by common religion – to make the initial contact. 'The gap is so great,' he adds, 'that for some people it will take a generation to bridge it' (Sheppard, 1983, p. 218).

The door is open for mission through community projects. Because it is in intimate touch with local human and social needs, the Church can take the initiative and invite people into partnership in projects that will benefit the whole community. It can do this without dissolving its identity as the Body of Christ into that of an agency for social amelioration. Out of this partnership, opportunities for sharing in (unthreatening) worship may well arise. From the experience of worship and service, some will experience a call to discipleship (Fung, 1992; Morisy, 1997).

We can bring these three aspects of the Church's relation to community (*as*, *in* and *for*) together in O'Donovan's suggestive notion of the Church as 'a gathering community' (O'Donovan, 1996, p. 175). A gathering community is a body that exists with its own integrity, but it is not complete without those who do not yet belong. The gathering church is actually the antithesis of the 'gathered church', in spite of the similarity of language. Its catholicity implies that it has both a centre that is given and a circumference that is continually enlarged. 'To speak of a "gathering" church ... is to speak of a community which, for all the permeability of its skin, has a sharply defined core' (p. 176).

In search of true community

Christianity is not uncritical of the notion of community. It recognizes intuitively the difference, defined by Bellah, between mere 'lifestyle enclaves' and true 'moral communities'. Whereas lifestyle enclaves are established by consumer spending power and are transient, moral communities are built by a shared sense of identity and are enduring. They embody such values as historical continuity, mutual respect, tolerance, participation, and the integration of individuals into the whole. The essential moral well-being of communities – which marks them off from mere aggregations of convenience – lies in 'the enhancement of fellowship', that is to say, the intensification of mutual concern and respect (cf. Selznick, 1992, pp. 32ff., 357ff., 361ff.: key values in community). Robert Bellah and his fellow authors of *Habits of the Heart* tried to define the difference between 'lifestyle enclaves' and true moral communities. A lifestyle enclave was formed by people who shared aspects of their private lives. Members of a lifestyle enclave expressed their identity through shared patterns of personal appearance, consumption and leisure activities, which often served to differentiate them sharply from those with other lifestyles. Their lives were not truly interdependent, they did not act together politically and did not share a history. Bellah and his colleagues defined a moral community, on the other hand, as a group of people who were socially interdependent, who took decisions together and who shared certain practices that both defined the community and were nurtured by it. Such a community, they added, could not be quickly formed. It almost always had a history and so was also a community of memory, defined in part by its past and by its memory of its past (Bellah *et al.*, 1986, pp. 72ff.). To define the two phenomena as distinctly as this is, admittedly, to delineate stereotypes. It is also to imply, I think, that there is something of the lifestyle enclave even in supposedly Christian moral communities today!

These insights about the nature of moral communities owe a good deal to the seminal work of Ferdinand Tönnies *Gemeinschaft und Gesellschaft* (ET *Community and Association*). Tönnies defined *Gemeinschaft* as constituted by personal relationships – intimate, private and exclusive – in real organic community, 'the lasting and genuine form of people living together'. *Gemeinschaft* could have a basis in physical location or in intellectual affinity. In either form, the relationship is sustained by empathetic understanding (*Verstehen*): an intuitive grasp of the experience of another, of their joys and sorrows. The context is that of a shared tradition. The highest manifestation of *Gemeinschaft* is the idea of the family, and its most extensive manifestation is in towns with a fellowship of work and fellowship of culture, including its religious aspects, when the religious community, comprising its constituent families, becomes coterminous with the sphere of work and recreation (Tönnies, 1955, pp. 37ff., 48, 54, 266, 57).

In *Gesellschaft*, on the other hand, relationships are notional or mechanical, public life is superficial or transitory, and people come together for convenience, forming not a community but a mere aggregate of individuals. Their relations are dictated not by tradition but by convention and they remain fundamentally alienated from one another. The paradigm of *Gesellschaft* is the city (Tönnies, 1955, pp. 37ff., 74, 87, 266). To sum up: in the *Gemeinschaft* people 'remain essentially united in spite of all separating factors, whereas in the *Gesellschaft* they are essentially separated in spite of all uniting factors' (p. 74).

Moral communities such as churches are bound together by a common story, the narrative of the journey that they and their forebears have made together, by gatherings for communal practices in the presence of the transcendent source of the purpose that unites them, and by a constellation of sacred symbols that focus their identity, are woven into the story and are reverenced in communal gatherings. The Christian story is, of course, that of salvation history, beginning with the call of Abraham, continuing in the exodus and the history of Israel and culminating in the coming of Christ, the cross and resurrection, the sending of the Spirit and the commissioning of the Church. The communal practices of the Church are focused on sacraments in the context of worship and fellowship. The symbols that unite the community with its transcendent source are the cross, the Bible, the water of baptism, the bread and wine of the Eucharist, the Lord's Prayer, the church building and churchyard, the priest and the bishop, among others. These stories, rites and symbols generate, perpetuate and sustain both the spiritual vision and a set of moral values. They attract unreflecting loyalty and are more readily affirmed than explained.

There is gathering interest today in the Church as a moral community (see the survey of some recent studies in Gill, 1999, pp. 1ff.). The discipling of Christians in the moral teaching of the churches (though the churches are not agreed about some aspects of morals) is an essential form of mission and is intrinsic to the nature of the Church. World Council of Churches studies have emphasized that ecclesiology and ethics are inseparable and interact. While Christian ethical engagement is an expression of our deepest ecclesiological convictions, that ecclesiology must be informed by our experience of ethical engagement in the complex situations of the world (Best and Robra, 1997, p. ix). To see the Church as a moral community means to see it as a community that wrestles, in the light of the gospel, with issues of 'moral formation'. This formation is centred in worship where the history of salvation is re-enacted in prayer, proclamation and sacrament (Best and Robra, 1997, pp. x, 66, 68; cf. Mudge, 1998, p. 90).

The visual media are hostile to moral communities and their value-sustaining role. As McDonnell points out, 'At the heart of the modern media is a vacuum of meaning' and in this the media faithfully reflect modern society. He suggests that 'one of the urgent tasks of the Christian Churches today is to offer the possibility of integration of personhood and wholeness of spirit to people who are living in fragmented and incoherent societies'. McDonnell shows how 'unreflecting immersion in media consumption tends to increase the difficulty of finding a coherent vision of life. The messages are so diverse and contradictory' (McDonnell, in Montefiore, 1992, pp. 180f.; for a more nuanced evaluation of the moral significance of the media see Tilby, 1999; and more broadly Carr, 1990).

A true society is not a concatenation of atoms but a woven fabric of relationships: natural and elective, given and chosen, permanent and temporary, local and regional. Those relationships are acknowledged to be essential first for survival – as a small child needs parents – and then for fulfilment, for drawing out what we are capable of in the sphere of mortal virtue, in the realms of work, the arts, recreation, and so on – in other words, for all the 'value-added' aspects of life. A society that does not privilege the bonds of relationship in its public doctrine and its economic regime is cutting off the branch it is sitting on. Our fragile society, with its high mobility, its economic stresses on marriage and the family, its multiple choices of lifestyle, needs to safeguard those social relations that make for community and build up the fabric of society. This is where the sacramental ministrations of the Church relate directly to the idea of community.

All significant meanings are expressed symbolically, and the values that attach to relationships are no exception. Sacred symbols have the effect of earthing transcendent values in the natural realm, uniting the ideal and the mundane, transforming and transfiguring our ordinary lives in the light of eternity. Symbols are not empty signs, mere theatrical gestures, but truly participate in the realities that they symbolize. Sacred symbols are constellated in narrative form to create the myths of the origins and destiny of a people. Genesis 1–11 and parts of the book of Revelation are just such myths of origin and destiny. Sacred symbols are enacted in stereotyped dramatic ways in the performance of sacred rites, such as the liturgy and sacraments of the Church. The stories, the symbols and the foundational rituals of the community comprise the tradition that unites people across time in a common purpose. The Christian Church is by nature a traditional body, conservative in its ethos, slow to change and committed to the conservation of the teachings and values that it has received. These are expressed and affirmed above all in its sacramental life, including the occasional offices.

The occasional offices, considered as *rites de passage*, sanctify and affirm the bonds of community. They are all concerned with relationships: parents, child and the community in infant baptism; individual and the community in adult baptism and in confirmation; wife, husband, children not yet born and the community in marriage; the deceased and the bereaved, both the family and the community, in the funeral service. They sanctify these ties of relationship, of union, by bringing them into connection, sacramentally, with a transcendent purpose and meaning. The occasional offices set those sanctified relationships in narrative sequence, as stages on the journey of life, and thus they incorporate or re-incorporate us into the Christian story, the grand narrative of salvation history.

The occasional offices also help to root relationships in the locality. The narrative of the Church, its symbols and rituals are not free-floating but are earthed in particular localities with their local traditions and their networks of relationships and loyalties. This rooting of the Christian mystery in what is particular and local demands a specific purchase on the phenomenon of locality in the form of sacred places (churches and cathedrals), sacred persons (the clergy) and sacred times (church services and the Christian year). Such places, persons and times are regarded as sacred because they are set apart from the profane or secular world in order to serve as signs of another, greater and better world beyond this life but impinging on it. This earthing, it seems to me, is in keeping with the distinctive ethos of the Christian faith which is incarnational and sacramental. The Church works like rooting powder to help bind individuals, couples and families to the community. Since it is actually baptisms, confirmations, marriages and funerals that bring families together more than almost anything else – and, moreover, bring them together in church – this ministry testifies to the Church's commitment to community. Thus the sacramental ministrations of the Church relate not merely to individuals but to communities and thence to society. They are the means whereby communities can be connected to salvation history, that is, to God's redemptive purpose for the world.

The occasional offices take their place in the Church's overall mission. There is bound to be an element of reciprocity, of give and take, of exchange, in mission. Mission is not firing off a missile and diving into the bunker. It is conducted in the personal mode, person to person, face to face. We need to listen as well as to speak; to receive as well as to give. A 'take it or leave it' attitude is unbecoming the Christian Church and actually futile. We have to win a hearing by taking to heart people's most vital human interests and anxieties and thus establishing an area of common concern. This builds up trust which is the prerequisite of all effective pastoral ministry.

Let me take a specific example of traditional practice, the reading of Banns of Marriage (now modified but not completely abolished by the General Synod), and try to show how it exemplifies my argument. An engaged couple come into the church where perhaps they will shortly be married and where they may well wish their children to be baptized in the future. Perhaps, however, they are to be married in another church and have come simply to check that their banns are actually read. Nevertheless, they are sufficiently motivated by the approaching marriage to cross the threshold of the church and to attend worship – something that they might not often do. In either case, the couple find themselves surrounded by an atmosphere of prayer and worship; they glimpse true Christian fellowship; they hear the gospel preached; they see the cross and resurrection of Christ set forth in the sacramental action of the Eucharist. They find there, albeit imperfectly understood, a source of guidance, strength and blessing for their future life and have the motivation behind their marriage vows strengthened. What they are experiencing is a form of preparation for the marriage service that will shortly take place. They are getting in tune with God's purpose for their marriage.

The Church, for its part, is making good use of a pastoral and evangelistic opportunity. We work so hard to encourage people to come to church. When they do come, some of us, it seems, want to turn them away again! Handling banns calls for pastoral skill. Reading them need not be an intrusion on the service. A few kind words of welcome from the minister, before and after the banns, can break the ice, indicate to the congregation how they should regard the visitors, and commend the couple to the prayers of the Church.

By publishing banns of marriage, however, the Church is also making a public statement about its own values. It is showing once again that it is working to build community, in the form of lifelong marriage and stable families – in other words, that it has at heart the best long-term interests of the community and of the individuals and their relationships that comprise the community. By simply doing that, the Church is commending its mission. It is making it easier for people to approach the Church and the clergy by showing itself to be a welcoming and hospitable community. What the parish priest and the people do at this point is not lost if the couple is never seen again: they have sown the seed of a harvest that another parish, another priest may one day reap. Even if the harvest is never apparent to human eyes, to minister to those preparing for marriage is a privilege and is always worthwhile. A pastoral church would not doubt the value of banns. There is an alarming trend in the Church: the perverse compulsion to renounce unilaterally the pastoral opportunities provided by the Church of England's traditional role in society.

In promoting its pro-community stance on the national stage, the Church can act (as far as possible ecumenically) to justify in well-researched and rigorously thought-out reports its instinct that resources put into local facilities, such as schools, health-centres, recreational facilities and locally identifiable policing, are actually cost-effective in reducing delinquency, crime, child-abuse, vandalism, truancy, vagrancy and various forms of substance abuse. Such initiatives can help to achieve this precisely by creating a climate of mutual responsibility and collective security in which people are encouraged to be true neighbours and to take responsibility for one another's well-being. Governments desperately seeking short-term economies must be helped to see that the decay of the social fabric must be costed too and that adequately resourcing it repays the investment.

The churches also lead by example – by their own commitment to building community (as in the case of the Church Urban Fund, following on from the Archbishop's report *Faith in the City*). The most effective example that a territorial church like the Church of England can give is to make the maintenance of its parochial structure, whereby the Church is profoundly and inextricably involved in the community, a major priority. The parishes are the building blocks of the Church and the 'power-base' of national religious leadership.

Territorial churches such as the Church of England and the Church of Scotland have more reason than most to 'love the local'. The challenge they face in our shifting culture is not merely to shore up the threatened fabric of a common life, but to plant the cross of Christ at the heart of the community. To do that, however, they must first be committed to building community and must have its well-being at heart.

8

The Primacy of the Pastoral

Mission in the pastoral mode

In our strangely mixed-up culture, with its traditional, modern and post-modern elements, the inchoate spiritual needs and aspirations of generic spirituality, deeply infused with Christian meanings as they are, confer an obligation on the Church (cf. Romans 1.14-15). In late modernity the Church's mission is carried forward largely in this context. That mission has a distinctive character: though it includes vital prophetic and priestly elements, the ministry of word and sacrament, it is fundamentally pastoral. The cutting edge of mission is not words. Without living proof that we love and care, words will fall on deaf ears. Nor is it the celebration of holy mysteries. Without pastoral contact and all kinds of pastorally sensitive stepping-stones to worship, liturgical performance seems remote and even alien to many people. Pastoral care stands in the vanguard of mission. It is the John the Baptist that prepares the way of the Lord.

Who will heed the gospel if they do not trust the preacher? Who will come forward for baptism, confirmation or a church marriage unless they already know that the pastor is a friend to all such? Who will be brave enough to cross the threshold of the church for the first time in many years if its clergy are not known in the community? Who will even consider that the Church might have the answer to their questions and needs unless it impinges on their consciousness? Who will turn to the Church unless its most obvious representatives, the clergy, are easily visible in the community? Personal, practical, loving care and support in the name of Christ, extended to individuals, households, institutions and communities, opens the way for the ministry of word and sacrament. The fact that about half of the population has drifted away from earlier links with the Church is surely bound up with the decline of systematic pastoral outreach in recent decades.

This thesis raises a crucial theological question. The question is whether the church can work with, can accommodate the patently inadequate responses of generic spirituality without compromising its integrity. Can the Church reach out in ways that are patently welcoming, generous and hospitable without diluting its core identity as a divinely commissioned, apostolic community? Can it respond to the largely private, rather domesticated expressions of contemporary spirituality, half-baked and incoherent as it generally is, without colluding with the privatization of values and undermining its own conviction that the Christian message is public truth or it is nothing? For example, what of the Eucharist, that is crucial to ecclesial identity but does not figure centrally in the spirituality of those who remain beyond the committed, worshipping congregation?

The answer surely must lie in the discovery by Christian communities of a purpose beyond themselves, in the realization that they exist for the sake of others, and that (as the old revivalist saying puts it) the Church lives by mission as a fire lives by burning. A church that is keenly aware of its obligations to those 'outside', far from having its identity and integrity undermined, can find its sense of communal purpose strengthened. A church that gathers its energies and focuses its aims to love, serve, win and save those who do not yet share the blessings of the Christian gospel will be knit together and focused in its aims, but without becoming inward-looking or exclusive (cf. Habgood, 1983, p. 90). Where identity is discovered in mission, we have identity with integrity. Late modernity offers powerful challenges and great opportunities to the Church in mission.

Belonging before believing

The relationship between our two main variables, believing and belonging, of what it means to be a religious person in a largely secular and significantly plural culture, is far from straight-forward. In England the equation is dominated by the phenomenon of common religion that Grace Davie has called 'believing *without* belonging', when the broadly Christian beliefs, practices and values of the majority of the population fail to lead them to commit themselves actively to the life and worship of the Church. We face the paradox that many people seem to want a church from which, with a fairly clear conscience, they can stay away. They choose to participate, if at all, at arm's length, as it were, in two ways: first, through the rites of passage (the church's occasional offices of baptism, marriage and funeral, and to a less extent, confirmation); and second, through the special services that have overtones of family solidarity, such as Remembrance Sunday, Mothering Sunday and 'Midnight Mass' on Christmas Eve – these are the liturgies that particularly have a bridging function. Others may not even get this far, but nevertheless have a residual sense of participating and belonging vicariously – being genuinely glad to know that a few actually attend church, and feeling that, provided someone goes, it need not be them!

The phenomenon of common religion thus creates a penumbra around the committed Christian community and a pool of persons that have some dealings with the Church and a degree of socialization into the Christian tradition, from which new active members tend to be drawn. In Church of England parishes this tends to overlap with the Church Electoral Roll and is a reason why administration of the Roll should not be too rigorous. Where it is a factor in assessment of parochial share for the diocesan common fund, there is pressure to curtail the membership of the Roll and therefore to constrict the pastorally crucial penumbra of parishioners who are potential committed worshippers and workers. The so-called 'membership' figures of the Church of England took a sharp dip in 1990 when Electoral Rolls had to be freshly subscribed.

In reality, this distinction between those who both believe and belong and those who believe without belonging is not at all clear-cut. It is not a division between members and non-members, for the Church of England's understanding of membership is intentionally flexible. Ecclesiologically, all baptized parishioners should be regarded as members of the Church of England unless they overtly opt out. The Church Electoral Roll is not a membership list but a device for regulating the governance of the church at parochial level and facilitating participation in synodical structures. Its ecclesiological significance is minimal. There are shades of belonging and gradations of commitment and involvement on a sliding scale, from those who have an apparently one-off encounter with the Church and its ministry through baptism, marriage or funeral rites and are seldom seen again, to those who form the active core of every parish. The reality of parish life is that there is a continual two-way traffic across the fictive boundary between active participation and non-involvement. Committed Christians from time to time slip back in their discipleship, become disaffected or take a rest from energetic parish activities. The previously not-so-committed move further towards the centre as changes in circumstances bring corresponding spiritual changes in their inner lives. The clergy, assisted by lay ministers, have the delicate task of negotiating this two-way traffic, not letting those who are moving away from the centre feel condemned or abandoned, but maintaining a pastoral link with them until they are ready to start moving in the other direction again, and gently holding out encouragement to those who are dipping a tentative toe in the water of active church life, giving them to understand that they are wanted and needed, dispelling fears that they are 'unworthy', but not pushing so hard that people over-react and 'back off' under pressure.

Participation in community creates a sense of belonging, and belonging is the prerequisite for believing. We sometimes tend to assume that church attendance has dropped because people have lost faith and that if we could win them back to faith they would return to church. That assumption is belied by recent research (Richter and Francis, 1998). Some popular forms of evangelism treat potential converts as free-floating individuals, detached from a community, devoid of a tradition, autonomous Cartesian thinking atoms. Such persons, if they existed in that stereotyped form, would be incapable of belief anyway. Belief is the articulation of trust that arises out of the deep patterns of meaning that have made us what we are and lend significance to our lives. Those meaningful patterns are imprinted on a person's being primarily by living in community, sharing its tradition and participating in its symbols. In practice, as Robin Gill's recently proposed 'cultural theory of churchgoing' makes explicit (Gill, 1999), attendance at church services is not the least part of this participation.

Religious practice should be understood in a holistic way. Wittgenstein has taught us that religion is neither an individual nor a cerebral matter but is a 'form of life ... language embedded in action'. Religion, he insisted, 'is not agreement in opinion but in form of life' and a form of life means the practice of a culture ('language game') within a community. To do that you have to participate, to commit yourself, to take a risk. 'A language-game is only possible if one trusts something.' Here we touch merely the tip of an iceberg of epistemology, of the relation of knowing to being and of theory to practice. What comes into view here is epistemology in the so-called fiduciary tradition – a rich vein of thought from Coleridge to Polanyi that I have explored elsewhere. It is perhaps enough simply to state that our pastoral instinct that faith is a matter not primarily of believing but of belonging can be justified philosophically as well as theologically (Wittgenstein, 1968, para. 241; Kerr, 1986; Avis, 1999, ch. 4).

Just as the doctrine of creation is theologically prior to the doctrine of redemption, so the gospel makes contact with all that is already most important to us. It impinges on those commitments that reside in the depths of our lives and make us the persons that we are. Though they are not easy to articulate, they are values that we hold dear and know ourselves to be sustained by. They are essentially interpersonal and relational and belong to the wider purpose of our lives. Looked at in christological terms, they are the forms of truth, beauty and goodness, of which Jesus Christ is the archetype. They do not float around the universe like patches of mist: they are embodied precisely in communities of people. That is why, in its mission, the Church ministers to the whole person.

People cannot respond to God's loving purpose for them unless they have basic identity, basic dignity (cf. the extended exposition in Sugden, in Samuel and Sugden, 2000, pp. 236–60). To take an extreme stereotype of human need: a homeless, abandoned, abused and starving victim is incapable of belief until he or she has been befriended, fed, housed and the framework of trust has been created or restored. There is an African saying from missionary times: 'Empty bellies have no ears.' By building salutary forms of community the Church is creating the climate of moral values, actualized in human relations, within which people find it possible to believe the essential Christian message. God's revelation was originally given to a community of people, the nation of Israel. The faith of Israel was a corporate faith. Jesus Christ was not a freelance religious pundit but a prophet of Israel to Israel, though rejected by his own people (John 1.11). His prophetic words and deeds reconstituted faithless Israel in himself and in his community of the last days which, through his final sacrifice and vindication, blossomed into the Christian Church. Christianity cannot exist except in community, since by its nature it is a corporate faith.

Though there are exceptions – and the sovereignty of the Spirit must always hold sway – for most of us belonging comes before believing. As a pastoral rule of thumb, it is true that without belonging there is no believing. By the many fine threads of compassionate service, pastoral ministration, social amenity, Christian education and moral prophecy, the Church binds to its fellowship the questioning, searching, wistful half-believers who aspire to a better world for themselves and their families and who sense that this cannot come about without the life of fellowship. They can be helped to come to see in the Christian Church a fellowship that has its anchor in the covenant love of God, the source of the values we hold dear. Thus, through faith, they may reach out at last to the one whose body the Church is.

Only connect

The fact that the phenomenon of generic spirituality, which we have tried to interpret in earlier chapters, is the sphere in which the clergy do much of their pastoral work raises a serious issue of principle for the Church: how should the Church handle the patently inadequate response that most people with whom it has dealings make to the gospel? Should it adopt counsels of perfection and treat inadequate believing and inadequate belonging alike with disdain, so hardening and sharpening the edges of the Christian community and aiming for quality rather than quantity? Alternatively, should the Church acknowledge that an inadequate response may, in fact, comprise that faith like a grain of mustard seed which Jesus assured us has the potential to grow into the largest of all trees? Should we rest content with a church with blurred edges and a permeable boundary with less resistance to people passing in – and, therefore, also out? Should the Church opt for quantity before quality, bear the frustration that this brings and seek, as Archbishop Robert Runcie put it in his last Presidential Address to the Church of England's General Synod in November 1990, to fan the smoking flax into the flame of faith?

There is a temptation, to which some of us clergy are prone to succumb at times, to allow ourselves to become discouraged with the meagre results of our work and, as a result, to turn our attention away from the apathetic world outside to the more congenial worshipping community (though that is certainly not without its problems!). In that mood we may exaggerate the inroads that secularization has made into our culture and see the Church as a safe haven in a hostile environment. But to concentrate on the comparatively faithful worshipping community and to neglect the source from which its members are largely drawn is short-sighted in the extreme. To pull up the drawbridge that connects the Church and the world, though it would afford some temporary relief, would drastically curtail our evangelistic opportunities. It would make the Church into a closed system, cutting it off from the interchange of energy and information with its environment. As we have noted in Chapter 2, systems theory tells us that a closed system lacks resistance to entropy: it runs down until equilibrium, which means sterility and death, is reached. (On systems theory see Laszlo, 1972, and for an accessible introduction see Capra, 1983. Systems theory is applied to religion in Bowker, 1987, appendix.)

On the contrary, we should do all we can to intensify the exchanges between the Church and its environment. We should not write off those who have left the Church, or abandon them (cf. Richter and Francis, 1998). We should try to hold on to them by any means that we can: requesting their help with social and fundraising activities of the parish, for example, if they do not wish to come to church; encouraging them, through the public signals we give, to believe that they have received something of real and lasting value through their nurture in the Church (particularly through baptism and confirmation); and making it clear that they can return at any time and resume worship and gradually be restored to full participation. It would be a serious mistake to dismiss their reasons for leaving as naive or fallacious. Instead we should listen with open heart and mind to the reasons that they give and attempt to interpret those reasons (or rationalizations) in order to inform our ongoing mission. I find that the reasons people give are generally to do with intellectual or moral difficulties with Christian belief (focusing on the more patently miraculous articles of the Creed and the problem of suffering), or arise from a feeling that they need to widen their spiritual horizons in the direction of greater intimacy, inwardness and spontaneity. As people generally live longer, there is a sense of deferring a decision until there is more time to think or become committed. This attitude should not be interpreted as mere apathy or as hostility to the Christian faith. It sometimes reflects a serious weighing up of the challenge of Christian discipleship.

There is ample evidence that many people participate in the life of the Church at second hand, representatively or vicariously: by identifying with those who attend, by simply being thankful that the parish church or nonconformist chapel is there, and sometimes by making a contribution to the repair and maintenance of the building (cf. Reed, 1978, p. 55). Many of those who do not regularly attend services believe that they have a vital stake in the continuance of the Church and what it stands for.

The various ways in which the sense of the sacred still manifests itself, including the diverse phenomena of common religion and the fact of widespread religious experience outside of the churches, indicate a potential basic receptivity to the mission of the Church in a culture that is still far from completely secular. How can the Christian Church connect with this submerged iceberg of inchoate, inarticulate spirituality, the nine-tenths of spiritual awareness that is not expressed in overt religious practice? Clearly the Church cannot uncritically 'baptize' all human spiritual aspirations, disregarding their inadequacy or incompatibility with the gospel. It must discriminate between differing values and make judgements. It must refine the raw material of human spirituality in its manifold forms. But it cannot do that – and has no right to do that – unless it has a basic respect in principle for all manifestations of the human sense of the sacred which leads it to make

contact and establish an initial rapport that provides the
context for dialogue, theological evaluation and pastoral
engagement. The strategy that is required is first of all to
multiply points of access – access to the life of worship, witness,
fellowship and service.

Christian theology teaches that there is a work of God's Holy
Spirit taking place in the lives of many – ultimately in the lives
of all – who are not in direct contact with the Church and its
means of grace. There is no-one who is completely untouched
by the grace of God. All human beings have a fundamental
relationship to God through their creation in the image
of God, through natural revelation and through the voice of
conscience. St John of the Cross said that each person is 'a most
beautiful and finely wrought image of God'. He pointed out
that God treats each one 'with order, gentleness and in a way
that suits the soul' (Matthew, 1995, p. 15). Just as Philip the
Evangelist came upon someone already prepared by the Spirit
of God in the desert, to whom he could show the way of
salvation (Acts 8. 26-40), so also all of us engaged in Christian
ministry need the faith to believe that God has not left himself
without witness even in the most apparently spiritually arid
secular environment. To step into such a context is to draw
near in faith to God's hidden presence.

Karl Rahner stressed that humanity as a whole is addressed by
God in 'primordial divine revelation'. On the basis of God's
universal salvific will, the grace of God is at work far and wide
in the world, conveying God's 'universal standing invitation' to
relationship with himself. God is continuously revealing himself
to all humanity in a way that is received tacitly and unreflec-
tively. 'Humanity as a whole, under God's universal salvific will,
is the first addressee of divine revelation.' Though this divine
communication to every human being as such is prone to
distortion, Rahner said, 'popular religion is continually being
unconsciously inspired and carried by original revelation'. We
do not need to subscribe to all the technicalities of Rahner's
theology to endorse his vision of the generous grace of God
impinging on every human life (Rahner, 1991, pp. 144f.).

Having acknowledged that God is 'out there' in the world, as
well as 'right here' in the Church, we must set about strengthening the network of connections between the two. These
connections are only partly 'given' nowadays – we cannot take

the old socio-political integration of Christendom for granted any more – and they need to be exploited and worked at. The opportunities to connect are there to be grasped: in the local community, at the national level, and at various levels of civil society in between. In this way, we can learn to work with the grain of common religion, responding to people's expectations without gratifying all their assumptions. A predisposition to pastoral generosity can lead to opportunities for critical engagement. Here are some practical, concrete examples:

- At Harvest Festivals we can take our cue theologically from the inarticulate impulse of thankfulness and the sense of ontological dependence that are not far beneath the surface at such times. Schleiermacher made this sense of ultimate dependence fundamental to his systematic theology, regarding it as synonymous with a relationship with God that was ready to be shaped by the experience of redemption through Christ (Schleiermacher, 1928, pp. 12ff.). At Harvest Festival we should take the opportunity to correct superstitious assumptions about blessings in this life being God's rewards for 'the righteous' and the absence of them God's punishments for 'the wicked'. Then we can go on to make St Paul's point in our own way: 'the goodness of God is intended to lead you to repentance' (Romans 2.4).

- In services of infant baptism we can begin with words of thanksgiving for the priceless gift of a new life and link this to a prayer for wisdom and strength to be given to the parents and godparents to enable them to fulfil the responsibilities that this brings. But we should go on from this starting-point to speak of faith, commitment and discipleship, though of course it demands pastoral skill to make the transition without jarring.

- The marriage service shows that the Church and the Christian faith are on the side of the happiness of human beings and that God wants their flourishing and fulfilment within the community. It speaks of hope for the future through human communion and its creative potential to bring new life into the world – precisely because hope and creativity belong to God's purpose, revealed in Christ's love for his bride the Church, for whom he gave himself (Ephesians 5).

- In funeral services, as we recall with thanksgiving the life of the deceased, we implicitly place it in a Christian frame of reference which reminds us that our lives are a gift and a trust from God, that we are answerable to our Maker for our stewardship of it and that the only safe path through life is to follow Christ who is 'the way, the truth and the life' (John 14.6) – just like the first Christians who were called 'followers of the New Way' (Acts 9.2). If it has been a tragic or premature death, we gently remind the congregation that, while God permits suffering to free and responsible human beings in a world that is causally determined, God does not send or inflict it and has shown us in the cross of Christ that God is involved in the bearing of suffering and shares our afflictions with us.

Essentially, the pastoral method in mission is to work with whatever people bring, within reason, but to transcend it. If the presenting motive is patriotism and people want to sing Blake's 'Jerusalem', that is fine, provided that we then try to build on that starting-point. If the presenting motive is family solidarity, generosity to the Church, pride in a beautiful historic building or wanting to do something useful in the local community, the same principle applies: respond as positively as you can to people's expectations before you begin to question their assumptions. You can only take them further if you respect the place at which they start.

Helen Oppenheimer has coined the suggestive expression 'making God findable' (Oppenheimer, in Ecclestone, 1988, pp. 65ff.). Multiplying points of access in order to make the Church 'findable' involves seeing the Church as an open system, interacting with its environment and making exchanges of information and energy with it through a permeable boundary. It is primarily lay people who cross and recross that boundary. Unlike the clergy (who are inevitably stereotyped as set apart and different, however much they may wish it were otherwise), lay people are identified, through many 'secular' commitments of work and community life, with the world as well as with the Church.

Without making the disastrous assumption that we have to find God before God can find us, or the arrogant assumption that God's presence and activity are confined to the Church,

Oppenheimer's phrase is suggestive for our method in mission. From it we can infer the pastoral imperative of making *the Church* findable. 'Findability' is a passive term: it implies active seeking. It needs, therefore, to be complemented by a proactive strategy for placing the Church's representatives where they cannot help being encountered. It entails making the clergy and other public ministers of the Church readily accessible. To be accessible, the Church needs publicly accredited ministers. As Wesley Carr has rather brutally put it, in the popular mind the world is divided rather unequally into vicars and non-vicars! The current tendency for clergy to creep about incognito much of the time, in contravention of the Canons, militates against the findability of the Church and its ministers. Leaving off the 'dog collar', except for services and formal meetings, and going about the parish by car makes the clergy invisible and drastically curtails the sort of unsought pastoral encounter that is the life-blood of parochial ministry. I sense from the way that people in central London look at my clerical collar out of the corner of their eyes, that it is a rare sight, usually seen only on television, where the clergy are invariably objects of ridicule. John Wesley and George Whitefield were stared at in areas where the established church was weak, as though clergy were almost unknown. 'Why did you not come before?' the miners of North-East England demanded of Wesley (Rack, 1989, p. 172). A young woman, reading a devotional book, introduced herself to me on a train. 'It's so unusual to see a fellow Christian on a train,' she said. 'One you can recognize, I think you mean,' I replied. Findability depends on visibility. A senior lay person in a parish seeking a new priest said to me: 'See and be seen – that's the crucial thing.' In truth it is the *sine qua non*.

Of course the clergy alone cannot make God or the Church findable to the vast majority of the population. Getting alongside people in the office or the works canteen, at the corner shop or outside the school gate, is something that only lay Christians can do. They will not usually be perceived as representing the Church as an institution, but they can be identified with the Church and be ambassadors for Christ (2 Corinthians 5.20). Nevertheless, however effective the witness of lay Christians in their daily calling may be, there is still, in my view, a need for a significant increase in the number of recognized representatives of the Church and of its ministry. Sector ministries are becoming increasingly essential (see Legood, 1999) and there is room for the creative deployment of 'niche ministries', both lay and ordained. There is a special connecting ministry for the diaconate, whether 'distinctive' or 'sequential' (described in the report *For Such a Time As This*, 2001).

Ministry in mission

As culture has become pluralist, eclectic and ephemeral, so the task of pastoral care has become 'bewildering, multifaceted and complex' (Goodliff, 1998, p. 6). The radical pluralism or fragmentation of the fabric of society demands imaginative flexibility on the part of the Christian mission. It suggests that a whole range of 'niche ministries' may need to be brought into being (with suitable training, commissioning and supervision) in order to tap in to the enormous diversity of sites in which the sense of the sacred and of the divine impinge on human life today. These niche ministries will include, but not be confined to: lay parish assistants, evangelists, healers, children's and young people's workers and those who can communicate the gospel through art, music, sculpture, multi-media events, etc. The sheer diversity of expressions of the gospel in Christianity is itself an instrument of mission because it represents a proliferation of points of access to individuals and groups in their distinctiveness and diversity.

As stipendiary clergy become fewer and their ministry becomes more thinly spread across multi-parish benefices and team ministries, it is natural to ask how they might be augmented by non-stipendiary clergy, readers, evangelists, lay parish assistants and retired clergy in order to keep the show on the road. There is pressure to reduce the provision of ministry to ministry to 'members', whereas the mission of the Church demands that it should be also ministry to non-members. The concept of the local ministry team of clerical and lay ministers can carry tacit assumptions that it exists to enable services to happen on Sundays in church buildings. The Church's mission demands a broader vision and rationale for the local ministry team. The core activities of the ministry, in word, sacrament and pastoral care, properly understood, are instruments of mission, outreach and evangelism.

- The ministry of the word of God is an instrument of mission. The word is ministered in schools, children's organizations and youth groups; in hospital wards, prison chapels and among the armed services; in house groups and adult training; in baptism and confirmation classes and marriage preparation. Lay ministers of the word, especially Readers, can preach and teach with support and supervision from the clergy.

- The administration of the sacraments is an instrument of mission. The sacrament of baptism should not be tightly restricted but should be offered (as the Canons require) to all who are willing to undergo preparation (adult candidates and the parents of infants). Baptism is a means of grace and something that Jesus Christ commanded his Church to do. Similarly, confirmation is an integral part of the Church's mission as a pastoral provision to enable those baptized in infancy to claim their baptism, make it their own in an act of personal faith, and receive the strengthening of the Holy Spirit. Confirmation leads normally to first communion. The Eucharist is an instrument of mission because, as a means of grace, it binds baptized and confirmed Christians closer to Christ and to one another – whatever stage they are at on their journey of faith. John Wesley regarded Holy Communion as a 'converting ordinance' (assuming that, like himself, a person could be baptized without being converted). Recent ecumenical theology has stressed the need for 'continual conversion' of all Christians to Christ.

- The provision of pastoral care is an instrument of mission. It is still possible to offer pastoral care, in the form of visiting the sick, the bereaved and those in trouble, provided that clergy and lay representative ministers work together and churches collaborate in this, as in other areas of mission. Lay people and clergy between them can visit those who have moved into the parish as an expression of interest, care and welcome. In many rural parishes clergy visit all parishioners who are in hospital or ill at home or otherwise in need, whether or not they attend church, whether or not they are Anglicans. Parishioners will continue to expect this – and such priority visiting is certainly practicable in rural communities. But mission-orientated local ministry teams can make essential visiting possible even in highly populated urban parishes where the clergy could never cope single-handed.

The wealth of opportunities that exists for the threefold mission of word, sacrament and pastoral care needs a strategy at the appropriate level (which in the Church of England is the diocese) to provide representative ministry in every viable community. Resources available for lay and ordained forms of representative ministry include Readers, churchwardens, evangelists and lay parish assistants; stipendiary and non-stipendiary priests and deacons and the active retired clergy. In order to maximize points of access in the form of appropriate persons, places and occasions, the Church should try to fill every sort of niche in terms of ministerial opportunities, so that people in their homes, at work, in education, at leisure and in community activities can encounter not simply Christian witness by lay people – that is fundamental and presupposed in everything else – but representative Christian ministers who can provide the ministry of word, sacrament and pastoral care. The radical diversification of society must call forth from the Church a corresponding diversification of recognized ministries – 'niche ministries' if you like – so that the Church can touch the whole range of sub-cultures and lifestyles with its mission (cf. Nazir-Ali, 1995, p. 25).

Parishes and their churches

If our criteria are identifiability, accessibility and availability, the parish system remains probably the best way of meeting these – though not the exclusive way of doing so. Sector ministries are also essential, and here the chaplain has his or her own 'parish': a defined and structured community of people, for whom he or she has pastoral responsibility. For their part, they know to whom they can turn. The Church of England's Canon C 24 sums up the pastoral imperative for the priest who has the cure of souls: 'He shall be diligent in visiting his parishioners, particularly those that are sick and infirm; and he shall provide opportunities whereby any of his parishioners may resort unto him for spiritual counsel and advice.'

What the parochial system ultimately means is that every

person who does not opt out is assigned to the pastoral care of a parish priest. Everyone is fully entitled (by law in the last resort) to the ministry of the clergy and to attend their parish church. Either they know who their vicar is or, by taking a little trouble, they can find out. Conversely, the clergy are not freelance spiritual consultants, waiting for their clients to approach them, but are commissioned to offer, in a proactive way, the ministry of word, sacrament and pastoral care to all who are willing to receive it. In the abstract, this is a daunting, perhaps an impossible task. But the responsibilities of the clergy are delimited by geographic and demographic boundaries. It is not that they are uninterested in anyone outside the parish or that they will turn away a person who is not a parishioner. It is rather that these given factors constrain the task and make it bearable. The work of the clergy and those lay ministers who assist them is earthed and rooted in a specific community (one that often coincides with spheres of civic responsibility). Their work receives shape and focus by being linked to a defined cure.

One can hardly hear a good word spoken about the parish system today. It seems to be regarded as an impediment to mission rather than as a primary vehicle of mission, and there are pressures to weaken it. Edward Norman can speak for many (for once) when he remarks, 'The more the emphasis is on the parish the less the prospect of addressing the world' (Norman, 2002, p. 118). However, social mobility, commuting to work, informal interest networks and eclectic congregations do not in fact negate the principle of territorial ministry. Even where parish boundaries are blurred in the minds of parishioners and churchgoers, the defined area of a parish represents a specific quantum of pastoral responsibility – and the limits of that responsibility – for the Church, its clergy and its local councils. Looking in from the outside, as it were, the parish structure looks outmoded; looking out from its heart, it makes sense. With its legal reinforcement of the clergy's primarily moral obligations to baptize, marry, and conduct the funerals of parishioners, the parochial structure still provides a framework for mission that has not been superseded and a salutary pastoral discipline for those who are engaged in it.

Writing in *The Times* on Christmas Eve 1997, Simon Jenkins spoke of the exceptional power that some parish churches have to bring the sceptic to his knees and send the atheist on his way enveloped in doubt. No believer himself, Jenkins acknowledged that such churches 'shift the burden of proof' as far as faith is concerned. Quoting William Morris's phrase 'sacred monuments of the nation's growth and hope', he concluded that these parish churches 'embody the continuity of human imagination evolving over centuries'. Edward Bailey's researches into 'implicit religion' suggest to him that the parish church has a unique place in what he calls the sacramental language of the identity of a community, the language of its buildings. The parish church 'makes the parish what it is', gives it its distinctiveness, its uniqueness, as far as the inhabitants are concerned. It helps to make a parish a community and a personal, relational entity. Its history, as usually the oldest building, and its status, as the most public building, function as myth in symbolizing the elusive sense of the identity of a community (Bailey, 1997, pp. 225ff., 257). An estate agent likes to be able to say that a property is in a street with a church in it!

That, however, is not how many in the Church see it. A group of students, training for ordination, volunteered in my hearing that church buildings were the greatest obstacles to mission. It would raise serious questions if their training still left them with that impression. I would expect many of them to change their minds once they had become fully inducted into parochial ministry and discovered for themselves how pivotal parish churches are in local ministry. Though buildings are a financial burden, and there are some that are unquestionably white elephants, parish churches are more often than not a privilege to care for and a means of outreach. Their very fabric, with its wealth of architectural and artistic detail, bears witness to Christian truth and to the enduring quality of Christian tradition. They are visible, public expressions of the core meaning of the Church as *ekklesia*, the community called together for worship. Churches and chapels constitute centres of Christian activity and witness: worship, teaching, pastoral care, fellowship, stewardship of resources.

In my previous parishes, the largest church building could accommodate the three smallest congregations put together. But the quantity of Christian commitment, devotion and service distributed through several buildings and their surrounding communities was far greater than it would have been if they had all been concentrated into one. The same principle applies to the Parochial Church Councils and church meetings that maintain them. To place the responsibility where it belongs – as locally as possible – shares out the work, motivates individuals and recognizes their calling. Proposals to merge parishes, combine PCCs and close church buildings are usually profoundly misguided. Centralized paternalism is a stock recipe for decline.

What of the services that these buildings accommodate? Clearly, pastoral mission cannot be fully carried out through the offices of Morning and Evening Prayer and the Eucharist. The staple diet of the liturgy nourishes the faithful but leaves many untouched. To maximize the impact of the ministry of word and sacrament, one must supplement routine forms of ministry with special services that have a central interest or focus: family services, healing services, care of animals services, Mothering Sunday, Christingle, lessons and carols, pram services, Plough Sunday, uniformed organizations' parades, sacred concerts, mystery plays and much else. All parishes do this to some degree and cathedrals excel at it. What we are in fact doing is 'niche marketing' of pastoral ministry, and there is nothing to be ashamed of in that. It enables us to reach numerous individuals and families who would otherwise remain untouched.

We often assume that there are many people who would not under any foreseeable circumstances willingly darken the doors of a church. But the large number who flock with a will to church funerals suggests that this is not the whole truth. Men, who are normally heavily outnumbered by women in Sunday services, are a striking presence at funerals, especially of work colleagues. There must be a 'funeral factor' that is not operative in other church services. There is a sense of obligation: people know that their place is there. There is a sense of purpose: they are there to honour the deceased and support the bereaved. And there is a satisfying sense that something is being achieved: necessary work is being done in marking the end of a life, commending the deceased to their Maker, and saying prayers for the sorrowing – for prayer is seen as never more appropriate than at such a time. There is also, perhaps, an unacknowledged element of 'insurance': while we honour and mourn the dead now, the time will come when others will honour and mourn us.

Obligation, purpose, productivity, self-interest – all these produce a sense of well-being and together probably comprise the elusive 'funeral factor' that motivates those who would normally be classed as non-churchgoers to attend church. In those four elements, none of which should be despised, we have perhaps the crucial recipe for motivating people to come to church. Clergy who try to find a task, a role, for everyone and who encourage their key workers to find someone with whom they can share their duties, understand this secret.

Evangelism is most effective when it takes place face-to-face. As Newman once said, nothing anonymous will ever convert. For its mission to be fruitful, the Church has to commend itself. There has to be a basic rapport, a set of mutual expectations. Above all, the Church's ministers have to be known and trusted. Close encounter over a sustained period is the *sine qua non*. But the alarming fact is that on both scores (relationality and continuity) we now weak. Plainly the Church is now more remote from the lives of most people than it has been since Christianity first came to Britain. Moreover, for various reasons its preoccupations are more immediate and short-term than for many centuries.

Bill Vanstone pointed out that the clergy need to dwell long in a parish in order to become aware of the depth and detail of the social fabric and community dynamics. (Even working out who is related to whom in rural parishes takes a couple of years, and woe betide the parish priest who puts his foot in it!) Intimate acquaintance with a parish, achieved over time, has the effect of blurring and softening the distinction between worshippers and parishioners, insiders and outsiders, the committed and the peripheral (Vanstone, in Martin and Mullen, 1981, p. 143). The parish priest becomes a friend to the whole community and scrupulously makes no distinction between one and another.

Conclusion

The burden of this book has been the paradoxical one that mission is, on the one hand, personal and relational and, on the other hand, public and communal. I have advocated the primacy of the pastoral because, in our culture, it is the pastoral that, more effectively than any other aspect of ministry, brings together the personal and the public. If mission is understood in the pastoral mode – as the leading edge of the ministry of word, sacrament and pastoral care – it must be offered on as broad a front as possible, through a multiplicity of points of access: sacred persons (clergy and other representative ministers); sacred places (parish churches and chapels of ease, chapels in secular institutions, etc.); and sacred times (not just Sunday worship in the rhythm of the Christian year, but on every occasion that is significant for the values of the community, in season and out). The Church is called to take the risk of exposing its gifts of grace all along the boundary with society, so enabling individuals to make the vital connection between their most deeply cherished moments and the Christian gospel. In many diverse contexts, through various different media, the Church can speak to the heart of individuals who experience intimations of the reality of God, but have not yet identified those glimmerings with the gospel of Christ.

When it is seen to be deeply involved in the structures and hopes of society, the Church will be perceived also as welcoming the spiritual aspirations of individuals, couples and families, of communities, organizations, institutions and societies. While committed lay people establish the vital networks of communication wherever work and leisure take them, the publicly available channels of the Church's ministry consist of its sacred places and sacred persons. These are the publicly identifiable points of access. To help people find God, we must make it easier for them to find the Church and to find the clergy. The Church must draw much nearer than it often does to human needs, questions, and aspirations – and it must be seen as doing so.

Those current tendencies within the Church that make the Church and the clergy less outward-looking, less extended, less visible in our society, are damaging mission. I question whether these trends are compatible with the mission of a national church with an obligation to maintain a territorial ministry. The creeping influence of the 'gathered church' model of ecclesiology, with its eclectic congregations, hardened demarcation between members and non-members, and cavalier attitude to geographical boundaries and historical identity, colludes with the damaging privatization of values in the modern/post-modern world and gives succour to the forces that continue to undermine communities that are not so much chosen as given.

The Christian Church vindicates its place in a society when it is seen to be committed to the healing of human identity through Christ – nurturing the wholeness of human beings, strengthening the bonds of family and community and deploying its pastoral resources where the volume of human need is greatest. This involves ordained and lay ministers working with the grain of common religion and other expressions of generic spirituality wherever possible. Here they act as catalysts and interpreters of those sacred values that are still strong in our society and that point to their fulfilment (and judgement) in the Christian gospel. I cannot stress strongly enough that the riches of Christ far exceed the obscure gropings of common religion and the newer alternative forms of spirituality – but they do not entirely negate them. As Aquinas said, grace does not abolish nature but perfects it.

The mission of the Church offers and presents Christ in many ways, through many people, in many places, not least through lay people in family, community and place of work. But, as a mission that is executed through the ministry of word, sacrament and pastoral care, it comes into focus particularly clearly in sacred persons, sacred places and sacred occasions. The sacred persons are the bishops, priests and deacons (or other ordained ministers) and the authorized lay ministers of the Church who assist them in ministry. The sacred places are the churches, chapels and cathedrals where worship is offered to the Father, through the Son, in the power of the Holy Spirit. The sacred occasions are the wide variety of services where the gospel is proclaimed and the Christian mystery is set forth in words, music, visual symbols and dramatic enactment – primarily in the Eucharist, which is the *sacrament* of the real presence of Christ with his Church in mission.

References

Abelard, P., 1974. *Letters of Abelard and Heloise*, Harmondsworth, Penguin.

Acquaviva, S. S., 1978. *The Decline of the Sacred in Industrial Society*, trans. P. Lipscourt, Oxford, Blackwell.

[ACUPA] The Archbishop's Commission on Urban Priority Areas, 1985. *Faith in the City*, London, Church House Publishing.

[ACORA] The Archbishops' Commission on Rural Areas, 1990. *Faith in the Countryside*, Worthing, Churchman.

Ahern, G., and Davie, G., 1987. *Inner City God*, London, Hodder & Stoughton.

à Kempis, T., 1952. *Of the Imitation of Christ*, Harmondsworth, Penguin.

Alter, R., 1981. *The Art of Biblical Narrative*, London, Allen & Unwin.

Aquinas, T., n.d. *Summa Theologiae*, London, Eyre & Spottiswoode; New York, McGraw-Hill (Blackfriars edn), vol. 16.

Aristotle, 1995. *Politics*, trans. and ed. E. Barker and R. F. Stalley, Oxford, Oxford University Press.

Atherton, J., 2000. *Public Theology for Changing Times*, London, SPCK.

Atkinson, D., 1994. *The Common Sense of Community*, London, Demos.

Audi, R., 2000. *Religious Commitment and Secular Reason*, Cambridge, Cambridge University Press.

Augustine, 1961. *Confessions*, Harmondsworth, Penguin.

Avis, P, 1989. *Eros and the Sacred*, London, SPCK.

—— 1995. *Faith in the Fires of Criticism*, London, Darton, Longman & Todd.

—— 1999. *God and the Creative Imagination: Metaphor, Symbol and Myth in Religion and Theology*, London and New York, Routledge.

—— 2001. *Church, State and Establishment*, London, SPCK.

Avis, P., ed., 2003. *Public Faith? The State of Religious Belief and Practice in Britain*, London, SPCK.

Bailey, E. I., 1997. *Implicit Religion in Contemporary Society*, Kampen, Kok Pharos; Weinheim, Deutsche Verlag.

Banks, R., 1994. *Paul's Idea of Community: The Early House Churches in their Historical Setting* (rev. edn), Peabody, MA, Hendrickson.

Barker, E., Beckford, J. A., and Dobbelaere, K., eds, 1993.

202   *References*

Secularization, Rationalism and Sectarianism: Essays in Honour of Bryan R. Wilson, Oxford, Clarendon Press.

Barthes, R., 1977. *Image – Music – Text,* New York, Noonday Press.

Barton, S., ed., 1996. *The Family in Theological Perspective,* Edinburgh, T&T Clark.

Bauckham, R., and Hart, T., 1999. *Hope Against Hope: Christian Eschatology in Contemporary Context,* London, Darton, Longman & Todd.

Bauman, Z., 1992a. *Intimations of Postmodernity,* London and New York, Routledge.

—— 1992b. 'A Sociological Theory of Postmodernity', in P. Beilharz, G. Robinson and J. Rundell, eds, *Between Totalitarianism and Modernity,* Cambridge, MA, and London, MIT Press.

Baumeister, R. F., 1986. *Identity: Cultural Change and the Struggle for Self,* New York, Oxford University Press.

Baylis, J., and Smith, S., eds, 1997. *The Globalization of World Politics: An Introduction to International Relations,* Oxford, Oxford University Press.

Beckford, J., 1989. *Religion and Advanced Industrial Society,* London, Unwin Hyman.

Beesley, M., 1997. *Mission on the Margins,* Cambridge, Lutterworth.

Bell, D., 1977. 'The Future of the Sacred? The Argument on the Future of Religion', *British Journal of Sociology* 28, pp. 419–49.

Bellah, R. N., Madsen, R., Sullivan, W. M., Swidler, A., and Tipton, S. M., 1986. *Habits of the Heart: Individualism and Commitment in American Life,* New York, Harper & Row.

Benhabib, S., 1992. *Situating the Self: Gender, Community and Postmodernity in Contemporary Ethics,* Cambridge, Polity Press.

Berger, P. L., 1973. *The Social Reality of Religion,* Harmondsworth, Penguin.

—— 1992. *A Far Glory: The Quest for Faith in an Age of Credulity,* New York, Anchor.

Berger, P. L., ed., 1999. *The Desecularization of the World: Resurgent Religion and World Politics,* Grand Rapids, Eerdmans.

Berman, M., 1982. *All That is Solid Melts Into Air: The Experience of Modernity,* New York, Simon & Shuster; London, Verso (1983).

—— 1992. 'Why Modernism Still Matters', in S. Lash and J. Friedman, eds, *Modernity and Identity,* Oxford, Blackwell.

Berry, P., and Wernick, A., eds, 1992. *Shadow of Spirit: Postmodernism and Religion,* London, Routledge.

Best, T. F., and Robra, M., eds, 1997. *Ecclesiology and Ethics: Ecumenical Ethical Engagement, Moral Formation and the Nature of the Church*, Geneva, WCC.

Beyer, P., 1994. *Religion and Globalization*, London, Sage.

Bion, W. R., 1961. *Experience in Groups and Other Papers*, London, Tavistock.

Birnbaum, P., and Leca, J., eds, 1990. *Individualism: Theories and Methods*, Oxford, Clarendon Press.

Blake, W., 1977. *The Complete Poems*, ed. A. Ostriker, Harmondsworth, Penguin.

Blond, P., ed., 1998. *Post-Secular Philosophy*, London, Routledge.

Boeve, L., 1999. 'Market and Religion in Postmodern Culture', *Theology* 102, pp. 28–36.

Bosch, D., 1991. *Transforming Mission*, Maryknoll, NY, Orbis Books.

Bowker, J., 1987. *Licensed Insanities*, London, Darton, Longman & Todd.

Bradbury, N., 1989. *City of God? Pastoral Care in the Inner City*, London, SPCK.

Brown, C., 2001. *The Death of Christian Britain*, London, Routledge.

Bruce, S., 1995. *Religion in Modern Britain*, Oxford, Oxford University Press.

—— 1996. *Religion in the Modern World: From Cathedrals to Cults*, Oxford, Oxford University Press.

Bruce, S., ed., 1992. *Religion and Modernization: Sociologists and Historians Debate the Secularization Thesis*, Oxford, Clarendon Press.

Buber, M., 1937. *I and Thou*, Edinburgh, T&T Clark.

Bunting, M., 1999. 'Sacred Spaces in Secular Culture', in M. Warner, ed., *Say Yes to God*, London, Tufton.

Bynum, C. W., 1982. *Jesus as Mother: Studies in the Spirituality of the High Middle Ages*, Berkeley, University of California Press.

Capra, F., 1983. *The Turning Point*, London, Flamingo.

Carle, R. D., and Decaro, L. A., eds, 1997. *Signs of Hope in the City: Ministries of Community Renewal*. Valley Forge, PA, Judson Press.

Carr, W., 1985a. *Brief Encounters*, London, SPCK.

—— 1985b. *The Priestlike Task*, London, SPCK.

—— 1990. *Ministry and the Media*, London, SPCK.

Carter, E., Donald, J., and Squires, J., eds, 1993. *Space and Place: Theories of Identity and Location*, London, Lawrence & Wishart.

Casanova, J., 1994. *Public Religions in the Modern World*, Chicago & London, University of Chicago Press.

Chadwick, O., 1975. *The Secularization of the European Mind in the Nineteenth Century*, Cambridge, Cambridge University Press.

Church Assembly, 1945. *Towards the Conversion of England*, London, Church Assembly.

Cipriani, R., 1989. '"Diffused Religion" and New Values in Italy', in J. A. Beckford, and T. Luckmann, eds, *The Changing Face of Religion*, London, Sage, ch. 2.

Clark, D., 1996. *Urban World/Global City*, London and New York, Routledge.

Cochran, C. E., 1990. *Religion in Public and Private Life*, New York and London, Routledge.

Cockerell, D., 1999. 'The Solemnization of Matrimony', *Theology* 102, pp. 104–12.

Cohen, A. P., 1985. *The Symbolic Construction of Community*, Chichester, Ellis Horwood; London and New York, Tavistock.

Cohen, A. P., ed., 1982. *Belonging: Identity and Social Organisation in British Rural Cultures*, Manchester, Manchester University Press.

Cohn-Sherbok, D., and McLellan, D., eds, 1992. *Religion in Public Life*, Basingstoke and New York, St Martin's Press.

Connor, S., 1989. *Postmodernist Culture*, Oxford, Blackwell.

Cooley, C. H., 1983. *Human Nature and the Social Order* (1902), New Brunswick and London, Transaction Books.

Cox, H., 1968. *The Secular City: Secularization and Urbanization in Theological Perspective* (1965), Harmondsworth, Penguin.

Cox, J., 1982. *The English Churches in a Secular Society: Lambeth, 1870–1930*, New York and Oxford, Oxford University Press.

Crewdson, J., 1994. *Christian Doctrine in the Light of Michael Polanyi's Theory of Personal Knowledge*, Lewiston/Queenstown/Lampeter, Edwin Mellen Press.

Croft, S., 1999. *Ministry in Three Dimensions*, London, Darton, Longman & Todd.

Dante, 1981. *The Divine Comedy*, trans. C. H. Sisson, London, Pan.

Davie, G., 1994. *Religion in Britain Since 1945: Believing Without Belonging*, Oxford, Blackwell.

—— 2000. *Religion in Modern Europe: A Memory Mutates*, Oxford, Oxford University Press.

Davies, D., Park, C., Seymour, S., Short, C., Watkins, C., and Winter, M., 1990–. *Rural Church Project* (4 vols), Nottingham, Centre of Rural Studies, Royal Agricultural College, Cirencester, and Department of Theology, University of Nottingham.

Davies, D., Watkins, C., and Winter, M., 1991. *Church and Religion in Rural England*, Edinburgh, T&T Clark.

Davis, C. F., 1989. *The Evidential Force of Religious Experience*, Oxford, Clarendon Press.

de Levita, D., 1965. *The Concept of Identity*, Paris and The Hague, Mouton.

Dominian, J., 1987. *Sexual Integrity*, London, Darton, Longman & Todd.

Duffield, I. K., ed., 1997. *Urban Christ: Responses to John Vincent*, Sheffield, Urban Theology Unit.

Duncan, H. D., 1968. *Symbols in Society*, New York, Oxford University Press.

Eagleton, T., 1996. *The Illusions of Postmodernism*, Oxford, Blackwell.

Ecclestone, G., ed., 1988. *The Parish Church*, London, Mowbray.

Eisenstadt, S. N., 1973. *Tradition, Change and Modernity*, New York, Wiley.

Eliot, T. S., 1974. *Collected Poems 1909-1962*, London, Faber & Faber.

Erikson, E. H., 1968. *Identity: Youth and Crisis*, London, Faber & Faber.

—— 1977. *Childhood and Society*, London, Paladin.

Ester, P., Halman, L., and De Moor, R., eds, 1994. *The Individualizing Society: Value Change in Europe and North America*, Tilberg, Tilberg University Press.

Etzioni, A., 1995. *The Spirit of Community: Rights, Responsibilities and the Communitarian Agenda*, London, Fontana.

Evans, G. R., ed., 2000. *A History of Pastoral Care*, London, Cassell.

Fergusson, D., 1998. *Community, Liberalism and Christian Ethics*, Cambridge, Cambridge University Press.

Field, C. D., 1998. '"Its all chicks and going out": The Observance of Easter in Post-War Britain', *Theology* 101, pp. 82–92.

Finney, J., 1992. *Finding Faith Today: How Does it Happen?*, Swindon, British and Foreign Bible Society.

Flanagan, K., and Jupp, P., eds, 1996. *Postmodernity, Sociology and Religion*, Basingstoke, Macmillan; New York, St Martin's Press.

Flannery, A., ed., 1982. *Vatican Council II: More Post Conciliar Documents*, New York, Costello.

Foerster, W., 1971. art. *sozo* in G. Friedrich, ed., G. W. Bromiley, ed. and trans., *Theological Dictionary of the New Testament*, Grand Rapids, Eerdmans, vol. 7.

For Such a Time As This: The Report of a Working Party of the House of Bishops on a Renewed Diaconate in the Church of England, London, Church House Publishing, 2001.

Ford, D., 1999. *Self and Salvation: Being Transformed*, Cambridge, Cambridge University Press.

Forster, P. G., 1995. 'Residual Religiosity on a Hull Council Estate', in P. G. Forster, ed., *Contemporary Mainstream Religion: Studies in Humberside and Lincolnshire*, Aldershott, and Brookfield, VT, Avebury.

Fung, R., 1992. *The Isaiah Vision*, Geneva, WCC.

Geertz, C., 1973. *The Interpretation of Cultures*, New York, Basic Books.

Gellner, E., 1992. *Postmodernism, Reason and Religion*, London, Routledge.

—— 1994. *Conditions of Liberty: Civil Society and its Rivals*, London, Hamish Hamilton.

Giddens, A., 1990. *The Consequences of Modernity*, Cambridge, Polity Press.

—— 1991. *Modernity and Self-Identity: Self and Society in the Late Modern Age*, Cambridge, Polity Press.

—— 1998. *Runaway World: The Reith Lectures* (on internet).

Gilbert, A. D., 1976. *Religion and Society in Industrial England: Church, Chapel and Social Change, 1740–1914*, London and New York, Longman.

—— 1980. *The Making of Post-Christian Britain: A History of the Secularization of Modern Society*, London and New York, Longman.

Gill, R., 1989. *Competing Convictions*, London, SCM Press.

—— 1992. *Moral Communities*, Exeter, University of Exeter Press.

—— 1994. *The Myth of the Empty Church*, London, SPCK.

—— 1999. *Churchgoing and Christian Ethics*, Cambridge, Cambridge University Press.

Gilliat-Ray, S., 1999. 'Civic Religion in England: Traditions and Transformations', *Journal of Contemporary Religion* 14.2, pp. 233–44.

Godfrey, J., 1969. *The English Parish 600–1300*, London, SPCK.

Goodliff, P., 1998. *Care in a Confused Climate*, London, Darton, Longman & Todd.

Gorringe, T., 2002. *A Theology of the Built Environment*, Cambridge, Cambridge University Press.

Grainger, R., 1974. *The Language of the Rite*, London, Darton, Longman & Todd.

—— 1988a. *The Message of the Rite: The Significance of Christian Rites of Passage*, Cambridge, Lutterworth.

—— 1988b. *The Unburied*, Worthing, Churchman.

—— 1994. *The Ritual Image: The Phenomenology of Liturgical Experience*, London, Avon.

—— 2002. *Health Care and Implicit Religion*, London, Middlesex University Press.

Greeley, A., 1989. *Religious Change in America*, Cambridge, MA, Harvard University Press.

Greeley, A., and Hout, M., 1989. 'The Secularization Myth', *The Tablet*, 10 June, pp. 665–7.

Green, L., 2001. *The Impact of the Global: An Urban Theology*, Sheffield, New City Special.

Green, Maxine, and Christian, C., 1999. *Accompanying Young People on their Spiritual Quest*, London, National Society/ Church House Publishing.

Gregory, J., 1998. 'The Making of a Protestant Nation: "Success" and "Failure" in England's Long Reformation', in N. Tyacke, ed., *England's Long Reformation*, London, UCL Press.

Grey, M., 1989. *Redeeming the Dream*, London, SPCK.

Gunton, C. E., 1993. *The One, the Three and the Many: God, Creation and the Culture of Modernity*, Cambridge, Cambridge University Press.

Habgood, J., 1983. *Church and Nation in a Secular Society*, London, Darton, Longman & Todd.

—— 1988. *Confessions of a Conservative Liberal*, London, SPCK.

Hammond, P. E., ed., 1985. *The Sacred in a Secular Age*, Berkeley, Los Angeles, and London, University of California Press.

Hardy, A., 1997. *The Spiritual Nature of Man: A Study of Contemporary Religious Experience* (1979), Oxford, Religious Experience Research Centre.

Harré, R., 1983. *Personal Being*, Oxford, Blackwell.

Hart, K., 1989. *The Trespass of the Sign: Deconstruction, Theology and Philosophy*, Cambridge, Cambridge University Press.

Harvey, D., 1989. *The Condition of Postmodernity*, Oxford, Blackwell.

—— 2000. *Spaces of Hope*, Edinburgh, Edinburgh University Press.

Hay, D., 1982. *Exploring Inner Space*, Harmondsworth, Penguin.

—— 1990. *Religious Experience Today*, London, Mowbray.

Hay, D., and Hunt, K., 2000. *Understanding the Spirituality of People who Don't Go to Church*, Nottingham, Centre for the Study of Human Relations, University of Nottingham.

208 References

Hebert, G. 1935. *Liturgy and Society*, London, Faber & Faber.

Heelas, P., 1996. *The New Age Movement*, Oxford, Blackwell.

Heelas, P., ed., 1998. *Religion, Modernity and Postmodernity*, Oxford, Blackwell.

Heelas, P., Lash, S., and Morris, P., eds, 1996. *Detraditionalization: Critical Reflections on Authority and Identity*, Oxford, and Cambridge, MA, Blackwell.

Henson, H. H., 1929. *Disestablishment*, London, Macmillan.

Hollenbach, D., SJ, 2002. *The Common Good and Christian Ethics*, Cambridge, Cambridge University Press.

Holmes, G., 1973. *The Trial of Dr Sacheverell*, London, Eyre Methuen.

Hooker, R., 1845. *Works*, 3rd edn, ed. J. Keble, Oxford, Oxford University Press.

Hopewell, J., 1987. *Congregation: Stories and Structures*, Philadelphia, Fortress Press.

Horkheimer, M., and Adorno, T., 1973. *Dialectic of Enlightenment*, London, Allen Lane the Penguin Press.

Hornsby-Smith, M. P., 1987. *Roman Catholics in England: Studies in Social Structure Since the Second World War*, Cambridge, Cambridge University Press.

—— 1991. *Roman Catholic Beliefs in England: Customary Catholicism and Transformations of Religious Authority*, Cambridge, Cambridge University Press.

Houlden, J. L., 1997. *The Public Face of the Gospel: New Testament Ideas of the Church*, London, SCM Press.

House of Bishops of the Church of England, 2001. *For Such a Time as This: Report of a Working Party of the House of Bishops on the Renewed Diaconate*, London, Church House Publishing.

James, W., 1890. *The Principles of Psychology*, London, Macmillan.

Johnson, M., ed., 1990. *Thomas Cranmer: Essays*, Durham, Turnstone Ventures.

Jones, A., 2000. *A Thousand Years of the English Parish*, Moreton-in-Marsh, Windrush Press.

Jordan, W. K., 1932. *The Development of Religious Toleration in England*, 2 vols, London, Allen & Unwin.

Jung, C. G., 1954–. *Collected Works*, ed. R. F. C. Hull, London, Routledge.

—— 1973. *Letters*, ed. G. Adler, 2 vols, London, Routledge & Kegan Paul; Princeton, Princeton University Press, vol. 2.

—— 1983. *Selected Works*, ed. A. Storr, London, Fontana.

—— 1984. *Answer to Job*, London, Ark.

—— 1985. *Dreams*, London, Ark.

Kay, W. K., and Francis, L. J., 1996. *Drift from the Churches: Attitude Toward Christianity During Childhood and Adolescence*, Cardiff, University of Wales Press.

Kear, A., and Steinberg, D. L., eds, 1999. *Mourning Diana: Nation, Culture and the Performance of Grief*, London and New York, Routledge.

Kerr, F., 1986. *Theology After Wittgenstein*, Oxford, Blackwell.

—— 1997. *Immortal Longings: Versions of Transcending Humanity*, London, SPCK.

Klapp, O., 1969. *The Collective Search for Identity*, New York, Holt, Rinehart, & Winston.

Knight, F., 1995. *The Nineteenth-Century Church and English Society*, Cambridge, Cambridge University Press.

Kort, W., 1988. *Story, Text and Scripture: Literary Interests in Biblical Narrative*, Pennsylvania and London, Pennsylvania State University Press.

Lacan, J., 1977. 'The Mirror-Stage as Formative of the Function of the I as Revealed in Psychoanalytic Experience', in *Ecrits: A Selection*, trans. A. Sheridan, London, Tavistock Press.

Lambert, K., 1973. 'Agape as a Therapeutic Factor in Analysis', *Journal of Analytical Psychology* 18, pp. 25–46.

—— 1981. *Analysis, Individuation and Repair*, London, Academic Press.

Laszlo, E., 1972. *Introduction to Systems Philosophy*, New York, Harper Torchbooks.

Legood, G., 1999. *Chaplaincy: The Church's Sector Ministries*, London, Cassell.

Leuenberg Fellowship, 1995. *The Church of Jesus Christ*, Frankfurt am Main, Verlag Otto Lembeck.

Lewis, H. D., 1959. *Our Experience of God.* London, George Allen & Unwin.

Lohfink, G., 1984. *Jesus and Community*, Philadelphia, Fortress Press; New York, Paulist Press.

Loughlin, G., 1996. *Telling God's Story: Bible, Church and Narrative Theology*, Cambridge, Cambridge University Press.

Lovejoy, A. O., 1953. *The Great Chain of Being*, Cambridge, MA, Harvard University Press.

Luckmann, T., 1967. *The Invisible Religion: The Problem of Religion in Modern Society*, New York, Macmillan.

—— 1983. *Life-World and Social Realities*, London, Heinemann Educational.

Luhmann, N., 1982. *The Differentiation of Society*, New York, Columbia University Press.

Lukes, S., 1973. *Individualism*, Oxford: Blackwell.

Luther, M., 1967. *Table Talk*, ed. T. G. Tappert, *Luther's Works*, vol. 54, Philadelphia, Fortress Press.

Lyon, D., 1998. 'Memory and the Millennium: Time and Social Change at the Fin de Siècle', in T. Bradshaw, ed., *Grace and Truth in the Secular Age*, Grand Rapids, MI, Eerdmans.

Lyotard, J.-F., 1984. *The Post-Modern Condition: A Report on Knowledge*, Manchester, Manchester University Press.

McFadyen, A. I., 1990. *The Call to Personhood*, Cambridge, Cambridge University Press.

MacIntyre, A., 1985. *After Virtue*, 2nd edn, London, Duckworth.

McLeod, H., 1996. *Religion and Society in England 1850–1914*, Basingstoke, Macmillan.

MacMurray, J., 1961. *Persons in Relation*, London, Faber.

Marchant, C., 1999. 'Take a Walk: Urban Mission in the United Kingdom', in K. Luscombe, ed., *Serving With the Urban Poor*, London, World Vision.

Markus, R. A., 1970. *Saeculum: History and Society in the Thought of St Augustine*, Cambridge, Cambridge University Press.

Marsh, C., 1998. *Popular Religion in Sixteenth-Century England*, Basingstoke and London, Macmillan; New York, St Martin's Press.

Martin, D., 1969. *The Religious and the Secular*, London, Routledge.

—— 1993. *A General Theory of Secularization* (1978), Aldershot, Gregg Revivals.

—— 1994. 'Believing Without Belonging: A Commentary on Religion in England', *Crucible*, (April–June), pp. 55–65.

—— 1996. *Forbidden Revolutions: Pentecostalism in Latin America and Catholicism in Eastern Europe*, London, SPCK.

—— 1997. *Reflections on Sociology and Theology*, Oxford, Clarendon Press.

Martin, D., and Mullen, P., eds, 1981. *No Alternative*, Oxford, Blackwell.

Marx, K., and Engels, F., 1967. *The Communist Manifesto*, with an introduction by A. J. P. Taylor, Harmondsworth, Penguin.

Matthew, I., 1995. *The Impact of God: Soundings from St John of the Cross*, London, Hodder & Stoughton.

Maxwell, M., and Tschudkin, V., 1990. *Seeing the Invisible: Modern*

Religious and Other Transcendent Experiences, Harmondsworth, Arkana.

Mead, G. H., 1962. *Mind, Self and Society* (1934), ed. C. W. Morris, Chicago, University of Chicago Press.

Methodist Church, 1997. *The Cities*, London, NCH Action for Children.

Meyer, J. W., 1987. 'Self and Life Course: Institutionalization and its Effects', in G. M. Thomas, J. W. Meyer, F. O. Ramirez, and J. Boli, eds, *Institutional Structure: Constituting State, Society and the Individual*, Newbury Park, Beverly Hills, London, New Delhi, Sage Publications.

Mission Theological Advisory Group, 1996. *The Search for Faith and the Witness of the Church*, London, Church House Publishing.

Mol, H., 1976. *Identity and the Sacred*, Oxford, Blackwell.

Mol, H., ed., 1978. *Identity and Religion*, London, Sage.

Montefiore, H., ed., 1992. *The Gospel and Contemporary Culture*, London, Cassell.

Moody, C. J. E., 2000. 'Drawing Near', *Theology* 103, pp. 243–50.

Morisy, A., 1997. *Beyond the Good Samaritan: Community Ministry and Mission*, London, Mowbray.

Morris, C., 1972. *The Discovery of the Individual 1050–1200*, London, SPCK.

—— 1980. 'Individualism in Twelfth Century Religion: Some Further Reflections', *Journal of Ecclesiastical History* 31, pp. 195–206.

—— 1989. *The Papal Monarchy: The Western Church from 1050 to 1250*, Oxford, Clarendon Press.

Mudge, L. S., 1998. *The Church as Moral Community: Ecclesiology and Ethics in Ecumenical Debate*, New York, Continuum; Geneva, WCC.

Muir, E., 1984. *Collected Poems*, London, Faber.

Nazir-Ali, M., 1995. *Mission and Dialogue*, London, SPCK.

Newbigin, L., 1991. *Truth to Tell: The Gospel as Public Truth*, London, SPCK.

Newman, J. H., 1903. *An Essay in Aid of a Grammar of Assent*, London, Longmans, Green & Co.

Nichols, B., 1996. *Liturgical Hermeneutics: Interpreting Liturgical Rites in Performance*, Frankfurt am Main, Peter Lang.

Norman, E., 2002. *Secularization*, London, Continuum.

Norris, C., 1993. *The Truth about Postmodernism*, Oxford, Blackwell.

Northcott, M., 1998. *Urban Theology: A Reader*, London, Cassell.

O'Donovan, O., 1996. *The Desire of the Nations*, Cambridge, Cambridge University Press.

Oman, J., 1931. *The Natural and the Supernatural*, Cambridge, Cambridge University Press.

Oppenheimer, H., 1986. 'Mission, Morals and Folk Religion', in P. Turner and F. Sugeno, eds, *Crossroads Are for Meeting: Essays on the Mission and Common Life of the Church in a Global Society*, Sewanee, SPCK/USA.

Osmond, R., 1993. *Changing Perspectives: Christian Culture and Morals in England Today*, London, Darton, Longman & Todd.

Otto, R., 1959. *The Idea of the Holy*, Harmondsworth, Penguin.

Pannenberg, W., 1970. *What is Man?*, Philadelphia, Fortress Press.

—— 1989. *Christianity in a Secularized World*, New York, Crossroad.

Parsons, G., ed., 1993. *The Growth of Religious Diversity in Britain from 1945*, vol. 1: *Traditions*, London, Routledge/Open University.

Pickering, W. S. F., 1984. *Durkheim's Sociology of Religion*, London, Routledge.

Pickstock, C., 1998. *After Writing: On the Liturgical Consummation of Philosophy*, Oxford, Blackwell.

Pocock, J. G. A., 1975. *The Machiavellian Moment: Florentine Political Thought and the Atlantic Republican Tradition*, Princeton, Princeton University Press.

Pohier, J., 1985. *God – in Fragments*, London, SCM Press.

Polanyi, M., 1958. *Personal Knowledge: Towards a Post-Critical Philosophy*, London, Routledge & Kegan Paul.

—— 1967. *The Tacit Dimension*, London, Routledge & Kegan Paul.

Purves, L., 1999. 'Is God still No 1?', *The Times*, 30 November, p. 24.

Rack, H., 1989. *Reasonable Enthusiast: John Wesley and the Rise of Methodism*, London, Epworth Press.

Rahner, K., 1968. *Spirit in the World*, London, Sheed & Ward.

—— 1974. 'The Experience of God Today', in *Theological Investigations*, vol. 11, London, Darton, Longman & Todd; New York, Seabury Press.

—— 1991. 'Theology and Popular Religion', in *Theological Investigations*, vol. 22, London, Darton, Longman & Todd.

Raiser, K., 2002. *For a Culture of Life: Transforming Globalization and Violence*, Geneva, World Council of Churches.

Ramshaw, E., 1987. *Ritual and Pastoral Care*, Philadelphia, Fortress Press.

Reed, B. D., 1978. *The Dynamics of Religion*, London, Darton, Longman & Todd.

Reed, C., ed., 2001. *Development Matters: Christian Perspectives on Globalization*, London, Church House Publishing.

Reed, E., 1996. *A Theological Reading of Hegel's* Phenomenology of Spirit *with Particular Reference to its Themes of Identity, Alienation and Community: Salvation in a Social Context*, Lewiston, Queenston, Lampeter, Mellen University Press.

Repstad, P., ed., 1996. *Religion and Modernity: Modes of Co-existence*, Oslo, Scandinavian University Press.

Richter, P., and Francis, L. J., 1998. *Gone But Not Forgotten: Church Leaving and Returning*, London, Darton, Longman & Todd.

Ricoeur, P., 1984. *Time and Narrative*, vol. 1, Chicago and London, University of Chicago Press.

—— 1988. *Time and Narrative*, vol. 3, Chicago and London, University of Chicago Press.

—— 1992. *Oneself as Another*, Chicago and London, University of Chicago Press.

Robertson, R., 1989. 'Globalization, Politics and Religion', in J. A. Beckford, and T. Luckmann, eds, *The Changing Face of Religion*, London, Sage, ch. 1.

Rowland, C., and Vincent, J., eds, 1995. *Liberation Theology UK*, Sheffield, Urban Theology Unit.

—— 1997. *Gospel from the City*, Sheffield, Urban Theology Unit.

—— 1999. *Liberation Spirituality*, Sheffield, Urban Theology Unit.

Rumsey, A., 2001. 'The Misplaced Priest?', *Theology* 114.818, pp. 102–14.

Runcie, R., 1990. Presidential Address to the General Synod of the Church of England, *General Synod Report of Proceedings*, vol. 21. no. 3, p. 1042.

Russell, A., 1986. *The Country Parish*, London, SPCK.

Sacks, J., 1991. *The Persistence of Faith*, London, Weidenfeld & Nicolson.

Sagovsky, N., 2000. *Ecumenism: Christian Origins and the Practice of Communion*, Cambridge, Cambridge University Press.

Samuel, V., and Sugden, C., eds, 2000. *Mission as Transformation*, Oxford, Regnum Books.

Samuels, A., ed., 1985. *The Father: Contemporary Jungian Perspectives*, London, Free Association Books.

Sassen, S., 1991. *The Global City: New York, London, Tokyo*, Princeton NJ, Princeton University Press.

Saxbee, J., 1994. *Liberal Evangelism*, London, SPCK.

Schama, S., 1995. *Landscape and Memory*, London, HarperCollins.

Schillebeeckx, E., 1990. *Church: The Human Story of God*, London, SCM Press.

Schleiermacher, F. D. E., 1928. *The Christian Faith*, Edinburgh, T&T Clark.

Schwöbel, C., and Gunton, C. E., eds, 1991. *Persons, Divine and Human*, Edinburgh, T&T Clark.

Sedgwick, P., 1999. *The Market Economy and Christian Ethics*, Cambridge, Cambridge University Press.

Sedgwick, P., ed., 1995. *God in the City: Essays and Reflections from the Archbishop's Urban Theology Group*, London, Mowbray.

Seigel, J. E., 1968. *Rhetoric and Philosophy in Renaissance Humanism ... Petrarch to Valla*, Princeton, Princeton University Press.

Selbourne, D., 1994. *The Principle of Duty*, London, Sinclair-Stevenson.

Seligman, A., 1992. *The Idea of Civil Society*, New York, Macmillan, Free Press.

Selznick, P., 1992. *The Moral Commonwealth: Social Theory and the Promise of Community*, Berkeley, University of California Press.

Sheldrake, P., 2001. *Spaces for the Sacred*, London, SCM Press.

Sheppard, D., 1974. *Built as a City*, London, Hodder.

—— 1983. *Bias to the Poor*, London, Hodder.

Shils, E., 1975. *Center and Periphery: Essays in Macrosociology*, Chicago and London, University of Chicago Press.

Skelton, R., ed., 1964. *Poetry of the Thirties*, Harmondsworth, Penguin.

Smart, N., 1971. *The Religious Experience of Mankind*, London, Fontana.

Smith, J. E., 1968. *Experience and God*, Oxford, Oxford University Press.

Southern, R. W., 1970. *Medieval Humanism*, Oxford, Oxford University Press.

Stoneall, L., 1983. *Country Life, City Life: Five Theories of Community*, New York, Praeger.

Storr, A., 1989. *Solitude*, London, Flamingo.

Sugden, C., ed., 1998. *Death of a Princess: Making Sense of a Nation's Grief*, London, Silver Fish.

Sykes, S. W., 1995. *Unashamed Anglicanism*, London, Darton, Longman & Todd.

Sykes, S. W., Booty, J., and Knight, J., eds, 1998. *The Study of Anglicanism*, London, SPCK; Philadelphia, Fortress Press.

Symington, N., 1986. *The Analytical Experience*, London.

Taylor, C., 1989. *Sources of the Self: The Making of Modern Identity*, Cambridge, Cambridge University Press.

Temple, W., 1963. *Christian Faith and Life*, London, SCM Press.

Tester, K., 1992. *Civil Society*, London, Routledge.

Thiselton, A., 1995. *Interpreting God and the Postmodern Self*, Edinburgh, T&T Clark/Scottish Journal of Theology.

Thomas, K., 1984. *Man and the Natural World: Changing Attitudes in England 1500–1800*, Harmondsworth, Penguin.

Tilby, A., 1999. 'Life-Shaping Media and Christian Truth', *Crucible* (October–December), pp. 311–30.

Todorov, T., 1990. *Genres in Discourse*, Cambridge, Cambridge University Press.

Tolstoy, L., 1978. *Anna Karenin*, trans. R. Edwards, Harmondsworth, Penguin.

Tönnies, F., 1955. *Community and Association (Gemeinschaft und Gesellschaft)*, London, Routledge & Kegan Paul.

Toulmin, S., 1990. *Cosmopolis: The Hidden Agenda of Modernity*, New York, Free Press.

Towler, R., 1974. *Homo Religiosus*, London, Constable.

Towler, R., *et al.*, 1982–. *Religious Research Project Papers*, Leeds, University of Leeds Department of Sociology.

Turner, B. S., ed., 1990. *Theories of Modernity and Postmodernity*, London, Sage.

Turner, F. M., 1993. *Contesting Cultural Authority: Essays in Victorian Intellectual Life*, Cambridge, Cambridge University Press.

Turner, V. W., 1968.'Myth and Symbol' in D. L. Sills, ed., *International Encyclopedia of Social Science*, New York, Macmillan and The Free Press.

—— 1969. *The Ritual Process*, London, Routledge & Kegan Paul; Chicago, Aldine Press.

Ullmann, W., 1967. *The Individual and Society in the Middle Ages*, London, Methuen.

—— 1977. *Medieval Foundations of Renaissance Humanism*, London, Elek.

Van Gennep, A., 1960. *The Rites of Passage*, London, Routledge & Kegan Paul.

Vanstone, W. H., 1982. *The Stature of Waiting*, London, Darton, Longman & Todd.

Vattimo, G., 1991. *The End of Modernity: Nihilism and Hermeneutics in Post-Modern Culture*, Cambridge, Polity Press.

Voltaire, 1947. *Candide*, trans J. Butt, Harmondsworth, Penguin.

216   *References*

Von Balthasar, H. U., 1982. *The Glory of the Lord: A Theological Aesthetics*, vol. 1: *Seeing the Form*, Edinburgh, T&T Clark.

Von Franz, M.-L., 1980. *Projection and Re-Collection in Jungian Psychology*, La Salle, Open Court.

Walter, T., ed., 1999. *The Mourning for Diana*, Oxford, New York, Berg.

Ward, G., 1997. *The Postmodern God*, Oxford, Blackwell.

—— 2000. *Cities of God*, London, Routledge.

Warnke, G., 1993. *Justice and Interpretation*, Cambridge, MA, MIT Press.

Weil, S., 1952. *The Need for Roots*, London, Routledge.

Whaling, F., 1986. *Christian Theology and World Religions*, Basingstoke, Marshall Pickering.

Wicker, B., 1975. *The Story-Shaped World: Fiction and Metaphysics*, London, Athlone Press.

Wilkinson, J., 1998. *The Bible and Healing: A Medical and Theological Commentary*, Edinburgh, Handsel Press; Grand Rapids, Eerdmans.

Williams, Raymond, 1973. *The Country and the City*, London, Chatto & Windus.

Williams, Rowan, 2000. *Lost Icons: Reflections on Cultural Bereavement*, Edinburgh, T&T Clark.

Wilson, B., 1969. *Religion in Secular Society: A Sociological Comment*, London, Pelican.

Wilson, B., ed., 1992. *Religion: Contemporary Issues: The All Souls Seminars in the Sociology of Religion*, London, Bellew Press.

Wingren, G., 1964. *Gospel and Church*, Edinburgh and London, Oliver & Boyd.

Winnicott, D. W., 1965. *The Maturation Process and the Facilitating Environment*, London, Hogarth Press.

—— 1971. *Playing and Reality*, New York and London, Tavistock Publications.

Wittgenstein, L., 1968. *Philosophical Investigations*, Oxford, Blackwell.

Woodhead, L., and Heelas, P., eds, 2000. *Religion in Modern Times: An Interpretative Anthology*, Oxford, Blackwell.

Young, F., ed., 1995. *Dare We Speak of God in Public?*, London, Mowbray.

Zizioulas, J. D., 1985. *Being as Communion*, New York, St Vladimir's Seminary Press.

Index of Subjects

Index of Names